THE COMPLETE AI ADVANTAGE COLLECTION

COLLECTION

THE 3 IN 1 COLLECTION TO HARNESS THE POWER OF ARTIFICIAL INTELLIGENCE, GAIN A COMPETITIVE EDGE, AND BOOST EFFICIENCY THROUGH AUTOMATION

SAMUEL THORPE

CONTENTS

THE ESSENTIAL BEGINNER'S GUIDE TO AI
A BREAKDOWN OF ARTIFICIAL INTELLIGENCE AND MACHINE LEARNING TO ELEVATE YOUR CAREER AND SIMPLIFY EVERYDAY LIFE
SAMUEL THORPE

THE AI IN BUSINESS ADVANTAGE
HARNESS THE POWER OF ARTIFICIAL INTELLIGENCE TO DRIVE GROWTH, CUT COSTS, AND GAIN A COMPETITIVE EDGE
SAMUEL THORPE

MASTER CHATGPT EFFORTLESSLY
THE SIMPLE WAY TO UNDERSTAND NATURAL LANGUAGE PROCESSING, BOOST EFFICIENCY THROUGH AUTOMATION, AND WRITE POWERFUL PROMPTS
SAMUEL THORPE

THE ESSENTIAL BEGINNER'S GUIDE TO AI

A BREAKDOWN OF ARTIFICIAL INTELLIGENCE AND MACHINE LEARNING TO ELEVATE YOUR CAREER AND SIMPLIFY EVERYDAY LIFE

SAMUEL THORPE

INTRODUCTION

In a world where Artificial Intelligence (AI) touches almost every aspect of our lives—from the smartphones in our hands to sophisticated diagnostic tools in hospitals and the emerging technologies that promise to reshape our work environments—it's essential to understand this transformative force. AI is everywhere, subtly integrated into our daily routines, enhancing experiences, and solving complex problems, yet its workings remain a mystery to many. You might not realize it, but AI is likely playing a role in how you came across this book.

As an author deeply fascinated by the potential of AI, I've dedicated myself to breaking down complex AI and Machine Learning (ML) concepts into understandable, engaging narratives. This book is crafted especially for you, a beginner with no prior exposure to technical jargon, ensuring that you feel welcomed into the world of AI. My goal is simple: to empower you to elevate your career and simplify your life by unlocking the potential of AI.

This book takes a unique, step-by-step approach to unravel AI and ML. We'll start from the very basics, gradually building up to more complex concepts, always linking back to real-world applications.

From navigating ethical waters to tackling hands-on projects, this guide ensures that you not only learn but also apply your knowledge. I promise to keep our journey conversational and instructive —think of me as a friend who's just as excited about AI as you will soon be.

We will explore a variety of themes: understanding the foundational elements of AI, how AI is enhancing various industries, the ethical considerations that come with technological advancements, and a glimpse into the future of AI. Each chapter is designed to build upon the last, ensuring you gain a holistic understanding of what AI can do and how it's done.

Let's also clear the air about some common AI myths. Despite dramatic portrayals in movies and books, AI is not about robots taking over the world. Nor is it a magical solution to all problems. This book will help you separate fact from fiction, providing a balanced view of AI's capabilities and limitations.

I invite you to dive into this book with an open mind and a curious heart. Engage with the content, reflect on the exercises, and don't hesitate to question and explore further. The path to AI literacy is not just about reading; it's about interacting, thinking critically, and creatively applying ideas to your life.

Together, let's demystify AI and discover how this powerful tool can enhance our creativity, solve daunting challenges, and significantly improve our everyday lives. Ready to get started? Let's begin this exciting journey into the world of Artificial Intelligence, a journey that promises not just to inform, but also to transform.

CHAPTER 1
UNDERSTANDING AI
BASICS

Have you ever asked your phone for the weather forecast or used a streaming service that suggests movies based on your previous watches? If so, you've interacted with artificial intelligence, probably without even thinking about it as AI. This chapter is your gateway to understanding what AI really is, how it has evolved over the years, and how it seamlessly integrates into our daily lives, often without a trace of visibility. Here, we begin by stripping down AI to its core, ensuring you grasp the fundamental concepts before we move on to its various applications and implications.

1.1 WHAT IS AI? - UNRAVELING THE BASICS FOR ABSOLUTE BEGINNERS

When we talk about artificial intelligence, we're referring to a broad area of computer science that is focused on building smart machines capable of performing tasks that typically require human intelligence. These tasks could range from recognizing speech, making data-based decisions, translating languages, and more. AI is essentially about creating algorithms—a set of rules or instructions given to a computer to help it learn on its own. This capability to mimic human intelligence and improve over time through learning and data correction is what makes AI both fascinating and incredibly powerful.

The journey of AI began much earlier than many people realize, with its roots dating back to the mid-20th century. One of the pivotal moments in the history of AI was the development of the Turing Test by Alan Turing in 1950. This test was designed to see if a machine's ability to exhibit intelligent behavior is indistinguishable from that of a human, setting a foundational definition of what it means for machines to 'think'. Another significant milestone was the advent of neural networks in the 1980s, which are systems modeled loosely on the human brain and are capable of learning from observational data. Understanding these milestones helps us appreciate how AI has evolved from a theoretical concept into a transformative technology that impacts various sectors of society today.

Despite its widespread use, AI is often misunderstood. Many people confuse AI with robotics, thinking of them as one and the same. While they can be interconnected—AI might power robots —they are distinct fields. Robotics is about building robots, which are hardware with the ability to perform tasks, whereas AI involves creating software that can perform tasks that require human intelligence. Clarifying these differences is crucial for anyone beginning their AI learning journey.

To see AI in action, look no further than your smartphone. Virtual assistants like Siri and Alexa are powered by AI and are designed to respond to your voice commands and help you manage your daily tasks. Another everyday example of AI is the recommendation algorithms used by services like Netflix and Amazon, which analyze your past behavior to suggest what you might like next. These examples illustrate not only the prevalence of AI in our daily lives but also its role in enhancing our experiences and interactions in ways that are both subtle and significant.

Interactive Element: Test your understanding of AI basics with this quick quiz. Answer the following questions to see how well you've grasped the concepts:

1. What is AI primarily concerned with creating?
2. Name the test developed by Alan Turing.
3. What is the difference between AI and robotics?
4. Can you name two everyday applications of AI?

This quiz will help reinforce your learning and ensure you have a solid grasp of AI fundamentals before moving on to more complex topics.

1.2 MACHINE LEARNING SIMPLIFIED: HOW COMPUTERS LEARN FROM DATA

Imagine if you could teach your computer to sort through your emails, categorizing them into 'urgent', 'important', and 'can wait'. Or better yet, envision a scenario where your computer learns your preferences over time and starts organizing your schedule, suggesting when you should take a break or tackle high-priority tasks. This is not just wishful thinking; it's a practical application of a subset of AI known as machine learning. Machine learning (ML) is based on the idea that systems can learn from data, identify patterns, and make decisions with minimal human intervention. It's like teaching your computer to think and make decisions based on past experiences, only that these 'experiences' are data it has analyzed over time.

Machine learning is often perceived as complex, but it boils down to three main types: supervised learning, unscheduled learning, and reinforcement learning. Each type has its unique approach and application, making ML a versatile tool across various sectors. In supervised learning, the machine learns from a dataset that has inputs paired with the correct outputs. It's similar to a teacher-student scenario where the teacher (you) provides the student (machine) with example questions and the correct answers so that the student can learn and later predict the answers on their own. For instance, email filtering where the system learns to flag emails as 'spam' or 'not spam' based on training with numerous labeled examples.

On the other hand, unsupervised learning involves data that has no historical labels. The system is not told the "right answer." The algorithm must figure out what is being shown. The goal is to explore the data and find some structure within it. It's like putting a child in a room full of toys sorted by color without them knowing the concept of color. They gradually learn to categorize toys by noticing differences and similarities, which is key in market segmentation, where businesses identify different customer segments for targeted marketing.

Reinforcement learning is a bit different. The algorithm learns to perform an action from experience by making certain decisions and receiving rewards in scenarios where clear feedback is given. Think of it as training a dog to fetch; the dog experiments with different behaviors and learns from the consequences, like getting a treat for a successful fetch.

The process of machine learning isn't just about feeding data into an algorithm. It starts with collecting relevant data, which is crucial as the quality and quantity of data directly influence how well a machine learning model can learn. Once data is collected, it's split into training and test datasets. The training data is used to teach the model, while the test data is used to evaluate its accuracy. The model learns by adjusting its parameters each time it makes a mistake, improving its predictions over time. After training, the model's performance is assessed, and if the results are satisfactory, it can be deployed in real-world applications, continuously learning and adapting from new data it encounters.

The impact of machine learning in various sectors is profound. In healthcare, ML models predict patient diagnoses based on symptoms and medical history, improving treatment accuracy and patient outcomes. In finance, it's used for credit scoring, assessing the risk of loan defaults based on past transaction data, which helps in making informed lending decisions. Each application of ML not only exemplifies its utility but also highlights how it's becoming an indispensable tool in modern-day problem-solving and decision-making processes.

As we explore more about machine learning, remember that at its core, ML is about empowering computers to make decisions and predictions, mimicking human-like intelligence but at a transformative scale and speed. Whether streamlining operations, personalizing experiences, or predicting future trends, machine learning stands as a pillar of modern AI applications, driving innovations that seemed like science fiction not too long ago.

1.3 DEEP LEARNING DEMYSTIFIED: UNDERSTANDING NEURAL NETWORKS

If you've ever marveled at how your smartphone can recognize your face or how virtual assistants seem to understand your requests, you've witnessed the power of deep learning in action. Deep learning, a subset of machine learning, employs algorithms inspired by the structure and function of the human brain, known as neural networks. These networks recognize patterns and make connections that escape even the most observant humans. Let's explain how these neural networks work and why they are so effective for tasks involving large amounts of complex data.

At its core, a neural network consists of layers of nodes, or "neurons," each designed to recognize different pieces of a complex puzzle. Picture it somewhat like how your brain works during a conversation. One part of your brain interprets the words, another part processes the tone of voice, and yet another part predicts the next words. Similarly, in a neural network, the first layer—the input layer—receives the raw data, which could be anything from pixels of an image to words in a sentence. This data then passes through one or more hidden layers, where the heavy lifting occurs. Each hidden layer's nodes focus on recognizing various aspects of the data, progressively refining the insights as data moves deeper into the network. Finally, the output layer delivers a coherent response or decision based on the analysis done by the hidden layers.

This architecture allows neural networks to handle and interpret vast and complex datasets much more efficiently than traditional machine learning models, which typically require manual feature selection and are limited to more straightforward tasks. Deep learning automates feature extraction, making it capable of handling unstructured data like images, sound, and text more effectively. This capability is why deep learning has become the backbone of many sophisticated AI applications, from automatic speech recognition systems that transcribe your voice messages to complex image recognition systems that power everything from medical diagnostics to autonomous vehicles.

The applications of deep learning are as impressive as they are varied. In the realm of healthcare, deep learning models process and analyze thousands of medical images to identify patterns that might elude human eyes, such as early signs of diseases like cancer. In the automotive industry, deep learning powers the advanced computer vision systems used in autonomous vehicles to interpret live footage from multiple cameras and sensors, allowing the car to make split-second decisions while navigating roads. Another everyday application is in the personalization algorithms used by services like YouTube or Spotify, which analyze your viewing or listening history to recommend new content tailored specifically to your tastes.

Each of these applications relies on deep learning's ability to sift through massive datasets to identify patterns and make informed predictions or decisions, showcasing its transformative power across various sectors. Whether it's enhancing the accuracy of predictive diagnostics in medicine, improving safety in autonomous transport, or simply making your playlist more enjoyable, deep learning continues to push the boundaries of what machines can learn and achieve. As we continue to generate more data and require more automation, the role of deep learning in our lives is set to grow, making it an exciting area of AI not just to learn about but to watch as it evolves and reshapes our world.

1.4 KEY DIFFERENCES BETWEEN AI, MACHINE LEARNING, AND DEEP LEARNING

Navigating the landscape of AI, machine learning (ML), and deep learning (DL) can initially seem like deciphering a complex family tree. Each of these technologies builds on the previous one, forming a hierarchy that is crucial to understanding their individual contributions to our digital world. At the broadest level, artificial intelligence encompasses any technique that enables machines to mimic human behavior. Machine learning, nested within AI, refers specifically to algorithms that allow software applications to become more accurate in predicting outcomes without being explicitly programmed. Deep learning, a further subset of machine learning, involves layers of neural networks that learn and make intelligent decisions on their own.

Let's visualize this relationship using a simple analogy. Think of AI as the entire tree, ML as one of its main branches, and DL as a branch sprouting from ML. This tree grows in a garden called technology, where each segment, from the root to the smallest leaf, plays a crucial role in the ecosystem. Just as a branch depends on the trunk and roots for nutrients, deep learning also relies more broadly on the frameworks and principles of machine learning and AI.

The capabilities of each technology vary significantly. AI can be programmed to perform a wide range of tasks, such as understanding human speech, competing in strategic games like chess, or autonomously operating cars. Machine learning narrows that focus to analyzing data and making predictions or decisions based on that data, like suggesting what movie you might enjoy next on Netflix or detecting fraudulent transactions. Deep learning dives even deeper, handling very specific tasks with greater complexity, such as translating languages in real time or identifying objects in a video.

When considering the development and deployment of these technologies, the complexity and requirements escalate from AI to deep learning. Implementing a basic AI algorithm might require less data and computational power than a machine learning system, which needs vast datasets to train on and more processing power to analyze this data and learn from it. Deep learning, by comparison, demands even more, often requiring high-end GPUs and significant amounts of labeled data to train effectively. For example, training a deep learning model to recognize and differentiate between various types of animals in photos involves feeding thousands, if not millions, of labeled images into the neural network, requiring extensive resources and time.

Looking into the future, the potential and trends of these technologies continue to evolve at an unprecedented pace. AI is set to become more ubiquitous, with an increasing number of automated and intelligent systems being integrated into both industrial and consumer applications. Machine learning models will become more efficient and accessible, potentially running on smaller devices like smartphones, making technology smarter and more interactive. Deep learning could revolutionize fields such as healthcare by providing more precise diagnostics and personalized treatment plans, thanks to its ability to analyze and learn from complex medical data.

As these technologies develop, they will not only become more integrated into our daily lives but will also create new paradigms for how we interact with the digital world. The growth of AI, machine learning, and deep learning represents not just a technological evolution but a significant shift in how we harness computational power to enhance human decision-making and creativity. This ongoing transformation promises to unlock new possibilities that are currently beyond our imagination, reshaping industries and perhaps even the very fabric of society in the decades to come.

1.5 EVERYDAY AI: RECOGNIZING AI IN DAILY LIFE

As you go about your day, from the moment you ask your smart speaker for the weather forecast to when you use your phone to navigate through traffic, artificial intelligence is subtly orchestrating many of your daily activities. It's fascinating how integrated AI has become, often functioning quietly in the background, enhancing our routines and decisions with a level of convenience and personalization that was once the stuff of science fiction. Let's explore how AI surrounds us in subtle yet significant ways and understand the mechanisms behind these interactions that make your life easier and more connected.

One of the most ubiquitous ways AI presents itself is through navigation apps like Google Maps or Waze. These apps use a complex form of AI to analyze vast amounts of data from various sources in real time to suggest the quickest routes to your destination. The AI considers current traffic conditions, road work, and even historical data on route speeds at different times of the day. When you input your destination, the AI quickly calculates the optimal path from point A to B, considering all these variables. It's a seamless process that many of us take for granted, yet it's a sophisticated AI application that significantly impacts our daily efficiency and schedule management. Similarly, social media platforms use AI to tailor your feed based on your interactions. The posts and ads you see are not random; they are carefully curated by algorithms that learn from your likes, shares, and the amount of time you spend on different posts. This personalization not only makes your social media experience more engaging but also helps platforms maximize your time on their app, showing how AI strategies can serve both user preferences and business goals.

The benefits of AI in everyday life extend beyond just convenience. Personalization is a significant advantage, as seen in how online shopping experiences are tailored to individual preferences. AI systems analyze your browsing and purchase history to recommend products that you're more likely to buy. In smart homes, AI optimizes energy use by learning your living patterns and adjusting lighting, heating, and cooling systems accordingly, improving comfort and reducing energy consumption and costs. These examples illustrate AI's role in enhancing the efficiency of our daily activities and personalizing experiences in ways that are both economically and environmentally beneficial.

However, the pervasive use of AI also brings forth ethical considerations that we must not overlook. As AI technologies collect and analyze vast amounts of personal data to make decisions, questions about privacy, consent, and data security come to the forefront. It's crucial to consider how this data is being used, who has access to it, and how decisions made by AI algorithms can affect individuals and communities. Although these topics will be explored in more depth in later chapters, it's important to start thinking about the ethical dimensions of everyday AI applications. For instance, when a navigation app suggests a route, it's based on aggregating data from countless users. While beneficial, this process raises questions about surveillance and data privacy that we, as a society, need to address.

As we continue to navigate through an increasingly AI-integrated world, recognizing and understanding these AI-driven interactions can empower us to make more informed decisions about the technologies we use daily. Whether it's choosing which app to download, setting privacy settings on social media, or even deciding how to engage with AI in our homes, having a foundational understanding of how AI works and its implications helps us maintain control in a digital age where AI is everywhere. This knowledge not only enhances our ability to leverage technology to improve our lives but also ensures we are aware of and can advocate for ethical practices in AI development and deployment. As AI continues to evolve and become even more intertwined with our daily routines, staying informed and engaged with how it works and impacts our lives is more important than ever.

1.6 AI TERMINOLOGY MADE EASY: A BEGINNER'S GLOSSARY

Navigating through the world of Artificial Intelligence (AI) can sometimes feel like learning a new language. To help you become fluent, let's break down some of the essential AI terminology that you'll come across throughout this book and in the broader AI community. Understanding these terms is not just about expanding your vocabulary; it's about building a solid foundation that will enable you to engage with AI concepts more confidently and communicate your ideas more effectively.

First up, let's talk about algorithms. An algorithm in AI is like a recipe in a cookbook. It's a set of instructions or rules designed to perform a specific task. When you hear about AI learning or making decisions, what's actually happening is that an algorithm is processing data and following predefined rules to perform that task. For example, an algorithm in your email service helps filter out spam by recognizing patterns in the messages that you mark as spam and applying these rules to incoming emails to predict whether they're spam or not.

Next, we encounter the term data set. This is simply a collection of data. In AI, data sets are used to train models. You can think of it as the raw material that you feed into your AI system; the quality and quantity of this data can significantly influence how well your AI system performs. For instance, a data set for a facial recognition system might consist of thousands of photos labeled with the names of the people in them. The AI uses this data to learn and make accurate identifications of individuals.

In the context of AI, a model is what an algorithm creates after learning from a data set. The model represents what the algorithm has learned, whether it's recognizing human faces, translating languages, or predicting weather patterns. Each model's effectiveness depends on the underlying data set and the specific algorithm it was trained with. For instance, a weather prediction model analyzes historical weather data and patterns to forecast future weather conditions.

Lastly, training is a crucial phase in the life of an AI model. This is where the model learns from the data set. Training involves feeding the algorithm large amounts of data so that it can adjust its actions based on the patterns and correlations it finds. The algorithm's performance improves over time as it learns from more data. For example, the more you use a voice-activated assistant like Siri or Alexa, the better it gets at understanding your speech patterns and preferences, thanks to continuous training from your interactions.

The importance of understanding these terms cannot be overstated. They are the building blocks of AI literacy, enabling you to grasp more complex concepts as you advance. They also equip you to share your ideas and contribute to conversations about AI, whether in casual discussions or professional settings. Knowing the correct terms can help demystify AI, making it more approachable and less intimidating.

If you're keen on deepening your understanding of AI terminology, there are plenty of resources available. Websites like Machine Learning Mastery and the AI section on Khan Academy offer detailed explanations and tutorials that can help you get a firmer grasp of key concepts. Books like "AI: A Very Short Introduction" by Margaret A. Boden provide a broader overview of AI and its language, offering context that can enrich your understanding. Additionally, online glossaries from reputable AI research organizations like DeepMind or OpenAI are valuable tools for quick reference and clarification of terms as you encounter them.

Engaging with these resources not only helps solidify your grasp of AI terminology but also enhances your ability to participate in the broader AI discourse. Whether you're reading AI research papers, collaborating on projects, or simply satisfying your curiosity, a strong command of AI language is invaluable. As you continue to explore AI, keep revisiting these terms and incorporating them into your vocabulary. The more familiar they become, the more confident you'll feel navigating the exciting field of Artificial Intelligence.

CHAPTER 2
PRACTICAL
APPLICATIONS OF AI

A rtificial Intelligence is not just a futuristic notion; it's here, revolutionizing industries and everyday life. In this chapter, we will explore how AI is making significant strides in various sectors, beginning with healthcare—a field where AI's impact is profoundly life-changing. From predictive analytics that forecast health trends to robotic surgeries that enhance precision and reduce recovery times, AI's role in healthcare is both transformative and inspiring. Let's dive into these advancements and understand how they are not only improving the quality of care but also reshaping the landscape of medical treatments and patient interaction.

2.1 AI IN HEALTHCARE: REVOLUTIONIZING PATIENT CARE

Predictive Analytics in Patient Monitoring

Imagine a world where doctors can predict potential health issues before they become serious problems. Thanks to AI, this is rapidly becoming a reality. Predictive analytics in healthcare uses algorithms and machine learning to analyze vast amounts of patient data from various sources—electronic health records, wearables, and genetic information—to forecast health trends. This method allows healthcare providers to identify at-risk patients and intervene earlier, potentially preventing conditions from worsening. For instance, by analyzing data from heart rate sensors, AI can predict cardiac events before they occur, enabling timely medical interventions that can save lives. This proactive approach personalizes patient care and significantly reduces the burden on healthcare systems by avoiding costly emergency treatments.

AI in Medical Imaging

Moving deeper into the medical field, AI's precision becomes crucial in diagnosing diseases from medical imaging. Techniques like MRI and CT scans are vital for early disease detection, but they rely heavily on the expertise of radiologists who interpret these images. AI enhances this process by providing tools that can analyze medical images with incredible accuracy and speed. For example, AI systems are trained to detect subtle patterns in imaging data that might be overlooked by human eyes, such as early signs of cancer or minute changes in brain scans that could indicate the onset of a neurological disorder. This capability not only speeds up the diagnostic process but also increases its accuracy, which is crucial for diseases where early detection can drastically improve the prognosis.

Robotic Surgery

In the operating room, AI is transforming surgeries through the use of robotic assistance. These robotic systems, guided by AI, help surgeons perform complex procedures with a level of precision and control that exceeds human capabilities. The da Vinci

Surgical System, for example, allows surgeons to operate through just a few small incisions with more precision, flexibility, and control than traditional techniques. This method significantly reduces recovery times and minimizes the risk of infection, making surgeries safer for patients and less taxing on surgeons. Real-world outcomes from hospitals using robotic surgery systems demonstrate reduced hospital stays and lower readmission rates, highlighting the tangible benefits of integrating AI into surgical practices.

Virtual Health Assistants

Lastly, AI-driven virtual health assistants are making healthcare more accessible. These systems use natural language processing to interact with patients, providing preliminary diagnostics based on symptoms described by the user. For instance, virtual health assistants can remind patients to take their medication, schedule appointments, and even provide basic healthcare advice, much like a triage nurse. This technology is especially beneficial in rural or underserved areas where medical professionals are scarce. By handling routine inquiries and monitoring patient health, these AI assistants free up human healthcare providers to focus on more complex cases, thereby enhancing overall patient care and engagement.

Interactive Element: Reflective Journaling Prompt

Take a moment to reflect on how AI in healthcare could personally impact your life or the lives of your loved ones. Consider scenarios such as managing chronic illnesses, undergoing surgeries, or even routine medical check-ups. How do you feel about relying on AI for these health-related aspects? Write down your thoughts and feelings. This reflection can help you appreciate the human aspect of technological advancements and consider the ethical dimensions of AI in healthcare.

As we continue to explore AI's practical applications, it becomes clear that its potential to improve and save lives is immense. The integration of AI into healthcare is just one example of how this technology is being used to tackle some of the most significant challenges facing various industries today.

2.2 HOW AI IS TRANSFORMING RETAIL AND E-COMMERCE

Imagine stepping into a store where the shelves rearrange themselves as you walk through, showcasing products that seem tailored just for you—items that match your style, fit your budget and even complement what you bought last week. This isn't a scene from a futuristic movie; it's the present reality in the e-commerce and retail industries, powered by artificial intelligence. AI is redefining how consumers shop and how retailers manage their operations, making the shopping experience more personalized and efficient than ever before.

Personalization of Customer Experience

In the realm of retail, the personal touch matters a lot, and AI is the maestro of personalization. By analyzing vast amounts of data —what you view, what you buy, how you navigate online stores— AI algorithms learn your preferences and shopping habits. They use this information to tailor your shopping experience, recommending products you're more likely to purchase. For instance, if you've been browsing for books within a specific genre, AI can highlight new arrivals, best-sellers, and even lesser-known books in that category. This kind of personalization makes your shopping experience more relevant and enjoyable, mimicking the helpful, personalized advice you would get from a favorite shopkeeper.

Inventory Management

Behind the scenes, AI plays a crucial role in inventory management, a critical yet challenging aspect of retail. Traditional methods often lead to either surplus stock or stockouts, both of which are costly for businesses. AI transforms this by predicting demand more accurately, ensuring that inventory levels are optimized. It analyzes patterns from historical sales data and considers factors like seasonality, market trends, and even social media sentiment to forecast product demand. This predictive capability allows retailers to stock just the right amount of each product, reducing waste and ensuring that popular items are not out of stock, which in turn enhances customer satisfaction.

AI in Logistics

The logistics of getting a product from the warehouse to your doorstep has also been revolutionized by AI. In warehouses, AI-driven robots efficiently pick and pack orders, speeding up processing times and reducing human error. But the real magic happens in delivery logistics. AI optimizes delivery routes in real time, considering factors like traffic conditions, weather, and the locations of all packages to be delivered that day. This not only speeds up delivery times but also reduces fuel consumption, making the process both faster and more environmentally friendly. The dynamic routing also adapts instantly to changes, such as a driver calling in sick or a vehicle breakdown, ensuring that such disruptions cause minimal impact on customer service.

Customer Service Automation

Finally, AI significantly enhances customer service through the use of chatbots and virtual assistants. These AI-powered tools provide 24/7 customer service, handling everything from tracking order status to managing returns and answering FAQs. What makes them particularly effective is their ability to learn from each interaction. Over time, they become better at understanding and responding to customer queries, providing responses that are increasingly accurate and contextually appropriate. This improves the efficiency of customer service departments and enhances the overall customer experience, providing quick and accurate answers to questions that might otherwise require a long wait for human assistance.

These AI-driven innovations are not just about making shopping more enjoyable or efficient—they're reshaping the very fabric of the retail industry. As AI technology continues to evolve, its impact on retail and e-commerce will likely grow, further personalizing shopping experiences, streamlining operations, and enhancing customer satisfaction. As we move forward, the integration of AI in retail promises to bring even more profound changes, making it an exciting time for both consumers and retailers.

2.3 AI IN PERSONAL FINANCE MANAGEMENT

In the intricate world of personal finance, managing your investments, guarding against fraud, optimizing spending, and assessing creditworthiness can feel overwhelming. Thankfully, Artificial Intelligence is stepping in to simplify and secure these aspects, making sophisticated financial management tools accessible to everyone, not just the financially savvy. Let's explore how AI is transforming personal finance management, bringing expert advice and robust security measures right to your fingertips.

Automated Financial Advising

Navigating the world of investments can be daunting. Where do you invest? How do you balance risk and return? AI-driven financial advising technologies are here to guide you through these decisions by providing personalized investment advice and portfolio management. These AI advisors, often referred to as robo-advisors, use algorithms to assess your financial goals, risk tolerance, and investment timeline to suggest the best investment strategies tailored just for you. For instance, if you're aiming for retirement savings, AI can help allocate your investments in a diversified portfolio that balances growth with risk over time. This not only democratizes financial advice—previously the domain of the wealthy—but also enhances it by removing human bias and emotional decision-making from the investment process. Whether you're a beginner looking to start your investment journey or an experienced investor seeking optimization, AI in financial advising makes the process more accessible and aligned with your personal financial goals.

Fraud Detection and Prevention

As our financial activities shift online, the risk of fraud and security breaches has surged. Here, AI proves to be a formidable ally. By continuously analyzing patterns of behavior in transaction data, AI systems can identify anomalies that may indicate fraudulent activities. These systems learn from vast datasets of historical transactions what normal and abnormal patterns look like. For example, suppose an unusually large transaction is made from a location or device that doesn't match your usual pattern. In that case, AI can flag this transaction in real time and alert you and the bank, potentially stopping fraud in its tracks. This immediate response is crucial in preventing the loss of funds and the associated stress and disruption that fraud can cause in our lives. By safeguarding your finances with AI, you gain peace of mind knowing that your money is being monitored around the clock by smart, adaptive technology.

Optimization of Spending

Beyond saving and investing, efficient management of day-to-day expenses plays a crucial role in financial health. AI steps in here by analyzing your spending habits, categorizing expenses, and identifying areas where you can save. Imagine an AI tool that integrates with your bank accounts and credit cards, giving you a comprehensive dashboard of your spending in real time. It could highlight recurring subscriptions you might have forgotten about or suggest budget adjustments if you're spending too much on dining out. By providing these actionable insights, AI helps you optimize your spending without the need to pore over bank statements or track expenses manually. This helps maintain financial discipline and empowers you to make informed decisions that enhance your financial freedom and stability.

Credit Scoring

Finally, when it comes to borrowing, whether it's for buying a home, a car, or managing credit, how financial institutions assess your creditworthiness is crucial. Traditional credit scoring methods can often leave out individuals with little to no credit history or those who don't use credit traditionally. AI changes this landscape by using alternative data—such as your rental payment history, utility bill payments, and even your shopping habits—to assess creditworthiness. This method provides a more holistic view of an individual's financial behavior, making credit more accessible to a broader group of people and potentially lowering interest rates due to better risk assessment. The inclusivity that AI brings to credit scoring not only opens up opportunities for many to access necessary funds but also propels a shift towards a more equitable financial system.

As AI continues to evolve, its integration into personal finance management transforms how we interact with our money. From making expert financial advice accessible to protecting our hard-earned money from fraudsters, AI in personal finance management is indeed a game-changer. The sophisticated analysis and real-time processing capabilities of AI provide a level of personalization and security that was once unimaginable, allowing you to manage your finances with confidence and ease. Whether you're planning for retirement, buying your first home, or simply trying to make better financial decisions, AI's role in personal finance is an invaluable ally in your financial journey.

2.4 THE ROLE OF AI IN MODERN AGRICULTURE

Agriculture, the backbone of human civilization, is undergoing a remarkable transformation powered by advancements in Artificial Intelligence. The fields that once solely depended on the intuition and experience of farmers are now benefiting from AI technologies that bring precision, efficiency, and sustainability to the forefront of farming practices. Let's delve into how AI is reshaping agriculture, enhancing everything from crop management to the entire supply chain.

Precision Farming

At the heart of modern agriculture's transformation is precision farming—an approach that uses AI and data analytics to make farming more controlled and accurate. AI systems in precision farming collect data from various sources, such as satellite images, weather forecasts, and field sensors monitoring soil and crop health. This data is then analyzed to make informed decisions about when to plant, water, and apply nutrients or pesticides. For instance, AI can analyze data from moisture sensors to determine the exact amount of water needed for different parts of a field, thereby optimizing water usage and reducing waste. This method not only conserves resources but also ensures that crops grow under ideally suited conditions, enhancing yield and quality. Moreover, AI-driven precision farming can adapt to changing environmental conditions, offering dynamic adjustments to farming practices that help mitigate the effects of climate variability on crop production.

Disease and Pest Prediction

Another significant advantage of integrating AI in agriculture is its capability to predict and manage crop diseases and pest infestations. AI models trained on historical data can identify patterns and predict outbreaks before they become widespread. These systems use images from drones or satellites to inspect crops and analyze signs of stress or disease. When a potential threat is detected, the AI system alerts farmers and recommends targeted treatments. This timely intervention is crucial in preventing the spread of diseases and pests, which can devastate crops and lead to significant economic losses. By addressing problems early and locally, farmers can avoid broad-spectrum pesticide use, which is better for the crop, the environment, and the ecosystem.

Agricultural Robots

Robots are also taking on more roles in agriculture, thanks to AI. These agricultural robots, or agribots, perform various tasks such as planting seeds, weeding, and harvesting crops. For example, robotic harvesters can be equipped with computer vision AI to recognize ripe fruits and vegetables, carefully picking them without damaging the plant or the produce. This not only speeds up the harvesting process but also reduces the physical strain on human workers. Similarly, weeding robots use AI to differentiate between crops and weeds, precisely removing unwanted plants without the use of herbicides. These robots are beneficial in large-scale farming operations where the efficiency and precision of robots can lead to substantial cost savings and higher production rates.

Supply Chain Optimization

AI's impact extends beyond the fields and into the agricultural supply chain. From the moment crops are harvested to when they reach the consumer, AI can optimize the journey, ensuring efficiency and minimizing losses. AI systems analyze data from the supply chain to predict and manage the storage and transportation of produce. This includes determining the optimal time to harvest crops for peak freshness, predicting the demand in markets, and planning the most efficient routes for transportation. By optimizing these elements, AI reduces spoilage and waste, ensuring that more produce reaches the consumer in the best possible condition. This not only improves profitability for farmers but also contributes to more sustainable food production and distribution practices.

As AI continues to evolve, its integration across various aspects of agriculture promises to revolutionize this sector further. These advancements not only enable farmers to meet the increasing food demands of a growing global population but also do so in a manner that is sustainable and mindful of future generations. The transformation brought by AI in agriculture is a testament to how technology can help humanity adapt and thrive, even in sectors as ancient and established as farming.

2.5 AI-POWERED HOME AUTOMATION: A CLOSER LOOK

Imagine walking into your home after a long day, and with just a simple voice command, the lights adjust to your preferred setting, the temperature is just right, and your favorite music starts to play softly in the background. This scenario isn't a peek into a distant future but a reality made possible today by AI-powered home automation. These smart home devices are redefining convenience and security in our living spaces, making homes smarter, safer, and more energy-efficient.

Smart home devices like thermostats, lighting systems, and security gadgets have become increasingly popular thanks to the convenience and control they offer. For instance, smart thermostats learn from your habits and adjust the heating and cooling systems in your home to optimize comfort and energy use. Over time, they recognize your schedule and temperature preferences, automatically adjusting to ensure maximum comfort when you are home and energy savings when you are away. Similarly, smart lighting systems can be programmed and controlled remotely. You can adjust the brightness, set schedules, and even change colors to create the perfect ambiance for any occasion, all from your smartphone. These systems not only add convenience to your daily routine but also help reduce unnecessary energy usage by ensuring lights are off when not needed.

The benefits of AI in home automation extend beyond just comfort and convenience; they also encompass significant enhancements in home security. Modern AI-powered security systems employ sophisticated technologies like facial recognition and motion detection to enhance the safety of your home. For example, security cameras equipped with AI can differentiate between known and unknown faces, alerting you only when an unrecognized individual is at your door. This reduces false alarms and ensures that you are only notified of potential threats. Similarly, AI-driven motion sensors are capable of distinguishing between different types of movement. They can tell if the movement is caused by a pet, a person, or just a blowing curtain, which helps minimize false alarms and enhance the overall security of your home.

Integration and management of these various devices are where AI really shines, bringing disparate elements together into a cohesive system. Through a centralized interface, often on a smartphone app, AI integrates the control of various devices, from thermostats and lights to security cameras and even kitchen appliances. This integration allows for scenarios where your security system can communicate with your lights and audio system to simulate occupancy when you're away on vacation, potentially deterring burglaries. The ease with which these systems can be managed and monitored not only simplifies your life but also gives you unparalleled control over your environment, no matter where you are. Whether you're at the office or on a beach halfway around the world, you can check in on your home, adjust settings, and ensure everything is just as it should be.

The impact of AI in home automation is profound, offering a combination of enhanced convenience, improved energy efficiency, and increased security. As these technologies continue to evolve, the way we interact with the spaces around us will become increasingly seamless and intuitive, making our homes not just places of comfort but also personal hubs of technology-driven, customized living environments.

2.6 AI IN EDUCATION: PERSONALIZED LEARNING EXPERIENCES

In the evolving landscape of education, AI's integration is proving to be a game-changer, particularly in personalizing learning experiences. This technology's ability to adapt educational content to fit the unique needs of each student is nothing short of revolutionary. AI-driven systems analyze individual learning patterns and progress, allowing them to tailor coursework in ways that optimize each student's learning potential. For instance, if a student excels in mathematics but struggles with reading, AI can adjust the curriculum to provide more advanced math problems while simultaneously offering additional reading support. This personalized approach helps maintain students' interest and keeps them challenged, significantly enhancing both engagement and learning outcomes.

Furthermore, AI's role in education extends to automated grading and feedback, which significantly lightens the workload for educators and provides students with immediate, actionable feedback. AI systems can quickly assess and grade a range of assignments, from simple quizzes to complex essays, highlighting areas that need improvement. This not only speeds up the process but also ensures consistency in grading, which can sometimes vary greatly between different teachers. More importantly, it allows educators to spend less time on administrative tasks and more on teaching and interacting directly with their students, fostering a better learning environment.

Engagement and interaction in learning are further enhanced by AI through the use of virtual tutors and interactive platforms. These AI tutors are available 24/7, providing students with on-demand assistance whenever they need it. Whether a student is struggling with a particular problem late at night or needs to review a concept before an exam, AI tutors can provide personalized guidance and explanations, making learning more accessible. Additionally, interactive AI platforms can transform traditional learning activities into more dynamic and engaging experiences. For example, they can simulate real-world scenarios for subjects like history or science, allowing students to explore ancient civilizations or conduct virtual experiments, which enhances both understanding and retention of knowledge.

Another significant advantage of AI in education is its ability to streamline administrative tasks. AI automates numerous behind-the-scenes operations, from scheduling classes and managing school databases to tracking attendance and student progress. This automation not only reduces the possibility of human error but also frees up administrative staff to focus on more strategic tasks that directly contribute to the quality of education. For educators, this means less time spent on paperwork and more on developing innovative teaching methods and engaging with students.

AI's transformative impact on education opens up exciting possibilities for enhancing learning experiences, making education more inclusive, efficient, and adapted to the needs of every student. It represents a shift towards a more student-centered approach where each learner can thrive at their own pace and style. As we look ahead, the integration of AI in education holds the promise of not just incremental changes but a fundamental shift in how we teach and learn.

As this chapter closes, we reflect on the profound influence AI has across various sectors. From healthcare and retail to personal finance and education, AI's capabilities are not only enhancing operational efficiency but also improving the quality of life. Each application, whether it's managing crops in agriculture or personalizing learning experiences in education, underscores AI's role as a pivotal element in modern society. Looking forward, the next chapter will delve into ethical considerations, exploring how we can navigate the challenges posed by AI to ensure it benefits society as a whole. This exploration is crucial as we strive to harness AI's potential responsibly and ethically, ensuring it serves as a force for good in the ever-evolving technological landscape.

CHAPTER 3
HANDS-ON WITH AI

I magine stepping into the shoes of an AI developer, crafting an intelligent system that not only understands but also responds intelligently to human language. This chapter is your workshop, a space where theory meets practice, and you can roll up your sleeves and start building. We begin with one of the most engaging AI projects you can undertake: creating your very own chatbot. Whether it's for fun, for a business, or just to impress your friends, building a chatbot is an excellent way to apply your newfound AI knowledge in a practical and enjoyable way.

3.1 BUILDING YOUR FIRST CHATBOT: A STEP-BY-STEP GUIDE

Choosing the Right Platform

The first step in your chatbot creation journey involves selecting the right platform. Think of this as choosing the right type of soil and tools for planting a garden. Each platform has its features, benefits, and limitations, so your choice depends on what you need your chatbot to do. Platforms like Dialogflow (by Google) and Microsoft Bot Framework are excellent for beginners and those looking to implement a chatbot quickly. Dialogflow offers an intuitive, user-friendly interface with powerful natural language understanding capabilities. It integrates smoothly with many apps and services, making it versatile for various applications. Microsoft Bot Framework, on the other hand, is robust, offering extensive customization options and seamless integration with Microsoft's suite of tools. Both platforms provide comprehensive documentation and strong community support, which are invaluable when you're just starting.

Designing Conversations

Once you've chosen your platform, the next exciting phase is designing conversation flows. This is where you script how your chatbot will interact with users. Effective chatbot conversations are engaging and provide a smooth and logical flow of information. Start by mapping out typical interactions, including greetings, responses to common queries, and what to do if the chatbot doesn't understand a request. A good practice is to keep the conversation natural and human-like. Use clear, concise language, and remember to infuse some personality—make your chatbot friendly or witty, depending on your target audience. Think about the paths your users might take during the interaction and design your chatbot to guide them through these paths effortlessly. Tools like flowcharts or mind maps can be incredibly helpful in visualizing and planning these interactions.

Integrating AI

Integrating AI into your chatbot involves setting up natural language processing (NLP) capabilities, which allow the chatbot to understand and process user input. Both Dialogflow and

Microsoft Bot Framework come with built-in NLP features. These platforms use machine learning models to analyze the text input from users, understand the context, and determine the appropriate response based on the conversation scripts you've designed. Setting this up involves training your chatbot with examples of possible user interactions, including questions or statements and how the chatbot should respond. The more examples you provide, the better your chatbot will become at understanding and responding to users. This process, known as training the model, is pivotal as it directly affects the effectiveness of your chatbot.

Testing and Iteration

The final step is testing and refining your chatbot. Release your chatbot in a controlled environment or initially to a limited audience to gather feedback. Observe how it interacts with users and note any issues or areas for improvement. Does it understand the user's requests? How does it handle unexpected queries? Use this feedback to refine the conversation flows and retrain your chatbot. Remember, building an effective chatbot is an iterative process. It involves continuously testing, gathering user feedback, and improving the model. The goal is to enhance the chatbot's ability to handle a wide range of interactions more accurately over time.

Interactive Element: Quiz

To test your understanding of the chatbot building process, try this quick quiz:

1. What are the two recommended platforms for building your first chatbot?

2. What is the purpose of designing conversation flows in chatbot development?

3. Explain the role of natural language processing in chatbots.

4. Why is it important to test and iterate when developing a chatbot?

Engaging in this hands-on project consolidates your learning and empowers you to venture into more complex AI applications. By building a chatbot, you're taking a significant step from being a passive learner to an active creator in the field of AI, moving closer to mastering the practical skills that will allow you to innovate and perhaps even transform the digital landscapes of tomorrow.

3.2 IMPLEMENTING BASIC AI IN WEB DESIGN

AI-Driven Layouts

When it comes to creating a website, the layout is like the foundation of a house—it sets the structure and tone for the entire user experience. Traditionally, web designers would manually adjust layouts based on content and user interaction, a process that could be both time-consuming and inflexible. Enter AI-driven web design tools, which revolutionize this process by automating layout creation and making adaptive design decisions in real-time. These tools use AI algorithms to analyze the content and context of a website, automatically generating layouts that are both aesthetically pleasing and functionally effective. For instance, if a website has a large amount of textual content mixed with multi-media elements, the AI can intelligently organize these elements for optimal user engagement and readability. Moreover, these layouts aren't static; they adapt based on user interaction. If the AI notices that certain types of content are engaging users more, it can adjust the layout dynamically to highlight these areas, ensuring the website remains effective and engaging over time. This not only streamlines the design process but also ensures that the website can evolve according to user needs and preferences without constant manual updates.

Enhancing User Experience

User experience on a website goes beyond just aesthetics—it's about how easily and pleasantly users can interact with the site. AI takes user experience to a new level by personalizing and optimizing the user journey on a website. One of the most impactful applications of AI in this area is through dynamic content display and predictive search functionalities. Dynamic content display powered by AI analyzes user behavior, such as the pages they linger on and the links they click, to tailor the content that is displayed. This means that if a user spends a lot of time in the blog section of a tech website, AI can prioritize showing more blog content on their homepage or suggest similar articles. Predictive search, on the other hand, enhances user experience by making search smarter. As users begin to type in the search bar, AI algorithms predict what they are looking for and provide real-time suggestions. This not only speeds up the user's search process but also makes it more intuitive, as the AI learns from each interaction to provide more accurate predictions over time.

Using AI for Accessibility

Web accessibility remains a crucial topic as the digital space strives to be inclusive for all users, including those with disabilities. AI is playing a pivotal role in enhancing website accessibility by automating and refining features that make content accessible to a broader range of people. For example, AI can automatically generate alt text for images, which is crucial for visually impaired users who rely on screen readers to access web content. Furthermore, AI can optimize website navigation for users with limited mobility by enabling voice navigation commands. This allows users to navigate, interact, and access content through voice commands, thereby reducing the reliance on traditional mouse or keyboard inputs. AI can also dynamically adjust text sizes and color contrasts based on a user's preferences or needs, enhancing readability for users with visual impairments. By integrating these AI-driven accessibility features, websites can cater to a broader audience, ensuring that everyone has equal access to digital content and services.

Analytics and Optimization

Lastly, AI's role in analyzing user data and optimizing website performance cannot be understated. Every interaction a user has with a website generates data—data that AI tools can analyze to glean insights into user behavior and website performance. These tools use machine learning algorithms to process large volumes of data, identifying patterns and trends that might not be immediately obvious. For instance, AI can track which pages have the highest drop-off rates, suggesting areas of the site that might be causing user frustration. It can also identify the most effective calls-to-action based on conversion rates, providing clear direction on what works best for engaging users. Furthermore, AI-driven A/B testing can automate the process of testing different versions of a web page to determine which one performs better in terms of user engagement and conversion rates. This not only helps in making informed design and content decisions but also continuously optimizes the website to meet user expectations and business goals effectively. By leveraging AI in analytics and optimization, web designers and developers can ensure that the site remains efficient, engaging, and aligned with user needs, ultimately leading to a superior online experience.

3.3 CREATING A SIMPLE AI MODEL TO PREDICT WEATHER PATTERNS

Data Collection

Embarking on the task of creating an AI model to predict weather patterns, the initial step involves gathering historical weather data. This data serves as the cornerstone of our predictive model, offering insights into past weather conditions that we can analyze and learn from. Public sources like the National Oceanic and Atmospheric Administration (NOAA) are invaluable for accurate and comprehensive data. The NOAA provides a wealth of information, including temperature, precipitation, wind speeds, and more, collected over decades across various geographic locations. Accessing this data involves navigating the NOAA's website and exploring their Climate Data Online portal. Here, you can specify the type of data, the geographic region, and the time frame you're interested in. It's essential to download a substantial amount of data to cover different seasons and weather conditions to ensure your model can learn to predict weather patterns under various scenarios. Once collected, organize the data in a manageable format, such as a CSV file, which can easily be imported into most data analysis tools. This organized data will form the training set that teaches your AI model about the complexities of weather patterns.

Model Selection

With your data ready, the next crucial phase is selecting the appropriate machine learning model for weather prediction. For beginners, regression models are a suitable choice due to their effectiveness in predicting numerical values, such as temperature or rainfall, based on historical data. Regression models work by establishing a relationship between input features (like humidity, pressure, and wind speed) and the target variable (such as temperature). This relationship is then used to make predictions about future weather conditions. Among the various types of regression models, the Linear Regression model is particularly user-friendly for those new to AI, providing a good balance between simplicity and predictive power. However, if your data includes time-series elements, which is typical for weather data, considering a more sophisticated approach like Time Series Forecasting or even LSTM (Long Short-Term Memory) networks, a type of deep learning for sequential data, might yield more accurate predictions. Tools like Python's sci-kit-learn library offer implementations of these models, which you can experiment with to see which best fits your data's characteristics.

Training the Model

Training your chosen model is where the magic happens. This process involves feeding your model the historical weather data so it can learn and identify patterns. Begin by dividing your data into two sets: a training set and a test set. The training set is what you'll use to teach your model, while the test set will help evaluate how well your model has learned. Using Python and libraries like TensorFlow or sci-kit-learn, load your data and initiate your model. During training, adjust the model parameters, such as the learning rate or the number of epochs, which can significantly impact the model's performance. Tuning these parameters might require some trial and error, but it's a crucial step in optimizing your model's ability to predict accurately. As your model trains, it adjusts its internal parameters to minimize the difference between its predictions and the actual observed values in the training data. This iterative refinement is crucial for developing a model that not only understands the historical data but can also make reliable predictions about future weather conditions.

Interpreting Results

After training, it's time to interpret your model's predictions. Use your test set to evaluate the model's performance. This involves comparing the model's weather predictions against the actual observed weather conditions in the test data. Tools like Python's matplotlib library can help you visualize this comparison, allowing you to see where the model performs well and where it doesn't. Understanding the accuracy of your predictions is crucial, especially if you're planning to use this model in practical scenarios, such as planning outdoor events or agricultural activities. If the predictions are sufficiently accurate, you could apply this model to generate weather forecasts based on current weather data. For instance, by feeding the model real-time data from weather sensors, you can predict upcoming weather conditions, helping farmers decide the best time to plant or harvest crops. This practical application demonstrates AI's power in interacting with the natural world and highlights how such technologies can be leveraged to make informed, data-driven decisions that can impact economics, safety, and efficiency in various sectors.

3.4 AI IN PHOTOGRAPHY: ENHANCING IMAGES AUTOMATICALLY

The magic of photography captures moments, tells stories, and even bridges gaps across time and space. Yet, even the most skilled photographers can face challenges like poor lighting or a less-than-perfect composition. This is where Artificial Intelligence (AI) steps in, transforming good photos into great ones without extensive manual effort. Let's delve into how AI is revolutionizing the art of photography, enhancing images through automated processes and creative innovation.

Understanding Image Processing AI

In the realm of photography, AI is like a highly skilled assistant that refines photos quickly and efficiently. At the core of AI-driven image enhancement are techniques such as exposure correction and color adjustment. Exposure correction is vital because it ensures that your images are neither too dark (underexposed) nor too bright (overexposed), which can obscure details. AI analyzes the image to identify areas that need adjustment and modifies the exposure to bring out the best in every pixel. Similarly, color adjustment is crucial for making images pop. AI assesses the colors in an image, enhancing them to appear more vibrant and true to life without the colors becoming unnatural. These adjustments are based on complex algorithms that replicate an experienced human editor's decision-making process, ensuring that the photos you take tell the intended story with visual clarity and impact.

Using AI Tools

For those eager to harness these AI capabilities, several tools and software packages make these sophisticated technologies accessible to photographers at all skill levels. Adobe Photoshop, for instance, offers AI features through Adobe Sensei, which includes auto-correction capabilities that adjust contrast, exposure, and color balance with a single click. Another powerful tool is Luminar AI, designed specifically to leverage artificial intelligence in enhancing photos. It goes beyond basic corrections by offering features such as sky replacement, where AI detects the sky in any photo and replaces it with a more dynamic or appropriately lit version, and portrait enhancer, which can subtly refine facial features and lighting to improve portrait photos. These tools are designed with user-friendliness in mind, meaning you don't need deep knowledge of photo editing software to achieve professional-quality results.

Practical Editing Tasks

Beyond basic enhancements, AI in photography excels at more complex editing tasks that traditionally require detailed manual intervention. Consider the common issue of unwanted objects in your photos, such as power lines or an unintended person in the background. AI tools can automatically identify and remove these objects, cleaning up the scene without a trace. Imagine you're photographing a serene landscape, but a trash can is spoiling the view. With AI, removing that trash can be as simple as a few clicks, and the area is seamlessly filled in to match the surrounding environment. Another frequent challenge is poor lighting conditions. AI can intelligently brighten images, adjust shadows and highlights, and even simulate the effect of golden hour light, all while maintaining the natural look of the photo. This capability is particularly useful in scenarios like wedding photography, where you might not have control over lighting and need to ensure that every photo looks its best.

Creative Uses of AI in Photography

The creative applications of AI in photography are pushing the boundaries of what's possible. Style transfer is an exciting area where AI applies the style of one image, such as a famous painting, to another, transforming ordinary photos into intriguing art pieces. This technology analyzes the artistic elements of the style reference, such as brush strokes and color palettes, and intelligently applies them to your photo, all while preserving the original content and context. Another innovative use of AI is automated composition suggestions. Here, AI analyzes the elements of a photo and suggests cropping or adjustments that could enhance the visual impact based on the rules of composition, such as the rule of thirds. This tool is incredibly helpful for amateur photographers looking to learn about composition, as it provides real-time suggestions and explanations for the recommended adjustments. These creative tools are not just about enhancing photos; they are about reimagining what your photography can convey, enabling you to explore new artistic avenues with the support of advanced AI technology.

As you can see, AI's role in photography is transforming not only how we enhance images but also how we conceive of and create visual art. With these AI tools at your disposal, the potential to elevate your photography and explore new creative possibilities is immense. Whether you're correcting simple flaws or experimenting with complex artistic effects, AI in photography empowers you to achieve your vision with greater ease and sophistication.

3.5 SETTING UP VOICE-CONTROLLED DEVICES USING AI

Voice-controlled devices have transformed the way we interact with our homes, offering a blend of convenience and futuristic charm that seemed out of reach just a few years ago. Among the array of options available, the Amazon Echo and Google Home stand out due to their advanced AI capabilities, wide range of functions, and ease of integration with various smart home systems. These devices act as central hubs for voice-activated control in your home, allowing you to manage everything from your music playlist to your thermostat with just a few spoken commands.

Choosing the right voice-controlled device often boils down to your specific needs and which ecosystem you're already invested in. If you're a user of Amazon's services and products, an Amazon Echo might be more beneficial, as it seamlessly integrates with Amazon Music, Audible, and other Amazon services. On the other hand, Google Home is ideal for those who are deep into the Google ecosystem, utilizing services like Google Calendar, Google Maps, and Google Play Music. Both devices have iterations that include screens, offering visual interactions with features like video playback or video calling, enhancing functionality beyond mere voice commands.

Once you've selected your device, the setup process is designed to be user-friendly to ensure a smooth start. First, placement is crucial for optimal performance. Position your device centrally in the room you frequent most, away from walls and obstructions for better sound recognition. Both Amazon Echo and Google Home require a stable Wi-Fi connection, so ensuring your home network is reliable and robust is essential. Download the respective app—Alexa for Amazon Echo and Google Home for Google Home—on your smartphone, which will guide you through the process of connecting your device to the internet. Follow the in-app instructions to link your device to your Wi-Fi network, and sign in with your Amazon or Google account to personalize your experience. This initial setup is crucial as it ensures your device is ready to respond accurately to your commands and can integrate smoothly with other smart devices in your home.

Customizing AI features in your voice-controlled device can significantly enhance its utility. Both platforms allow you to set up routines, which are essentially automated actions triggered by specific commands or at certain times. For example, you could create a morning routine that, upon a single voice command, turns on your lights, reads out the day's weather forecast, and starts brewing your coffee. Furthermore, integrating other smart devices like thermostats, smart lights, and security cameras allows for a fully interconnected home. The customization process involves exploring the smart home section in your device's app, where you can add and manage connections to other smart devices. Configuring these can be as simple as enabling skills in the Alexa app or linking devices in the Google Home app, which allows you to control these devices through voice commands seamlessly.

Security considerations are paramount when integrating AI-powered voice-controlled devices into your home. Since these devices are always listening for their wake word, there's a natural concern about privacy and data security. It's essential to regularly review and manage your voice recording history through the respective apps, where you can listen to and delete recordings. Both Amazon and Google provide options to turn off the microphone on their devices manually, which can be used during private moments. Additionally, ensure your home Wi-Fi network is secure by using strong, unique passwords and enabling network encryption, which adds an extra layer of security against external breaches. Regularly updating your device software and associated apps is also crucial, as these updates often include security enhancements that protect your personal information.

As you delve into the world of AI-powered voice control, embracing these devices' capabilities can significantly enhance your daily routines, offering convenience and a touch of magic to your regular interactions with technology at home. By understanding the setup process, customizing features to suit your lifestyle, and implementing security best practices, you can fully leverage the benefits of your voice-controlled devices while ensuring your data remains protected.

3.6 DIY AI PROJECTS FOR HOME AUTOMATION

Bringing artificial intelligence into your living space doesn't have to be daunting or overly technical. In fact, with today's accessible technologies, creating a DIY home automation project can be an exciting and rewarding adventure. Let's explore some simple projects incorporating AI into your home, making it smarter and more responsive to your needs.

Project Ideas

A great starting point for integrating AI into your home is through projects like a smart thermostat or AI-powered security cameras. A smart thermostat can learn from your habits and adjust the heating and cooling of your home for optimal comfort and efficiency. For instance, it could lower the heat automatically when you leave for work and bring it back up just before you return. Similarly, AI-powered security cameras can enhance your home's security by distinguishing between known family members and strangers, sending alerts only when unusual activity is detected. These projects not only introduce you to the practical benefits of home automation but also give you a glimpse into the potential of AI to adapt and respond to the unique patterns of your household.

Tools and Resources

To get started on these projects, you will need some basic tools and resources. The heart of many DIY AI projects is a microcontroller like Raspberry Pi or Arduino, which serves as the brain of your automation system. These microcontrollers are powerful, cost-effective, and supported by a large community of enthusiasts and experts whose insights and code samples can be incredibly helpful. Alongside the microcontroller, you'll need various sensors depending on your project—temperature sensors for a smart thermostat, or motion sensors for security cameras. Additionally, you'll require basic electronics components such as resistors, wires, and breadboards, which are available in starter kits from electronics suppliers. For software, platforms like Python, along with libraries such as TensorFlow or OpenCV, are excellent for integrating AI capabilities. These tools provide the necessary framework to program your devices and incorporate machine learning models that enable your projects to learn and adapt over time.

Step-by-Step Instructions

Let's walk through setting up a simple AI-powered thermostat. First, assemble your Raspberry Pi, connecting it to a power source and a display. Install the Raspbian operating system and ensure it's connected to the internet. Next, connect a temperature sensor to the GPIO (General Purpose Input Output) pins on the Raspberry Pi. You can find tutorials online for the specifics of wiring. Once your hardware is set up, write a Python script that reads the temperature from the sensor and decides whether to turn the heating on or off. To add AI, you could use a machine learning algorithm that predicts the optimal temperature settings based on time of day, historical preferences, and even external weather conditions. Train your model with data you collect over time or simulate data to begin with. Finally, implement this model in your Python script so that your thermostat can automatically adjust its settings in the most efficient and comfortable way.

Troubleshooting Common Issues

When venturing into DIY projects, you might encounter a few bumps along the way. Common issues include incorrect wiring, software bugs, or data inaccuracies. If your smart thermostat isn't responding as expected, double-check your connections and ensure your sensors are working correctly. In your software, debug by checking the logs for any error messages that can give you clues on what might be wrong. If the issue lies with the AI model, ensure your training data is accurate and representative of the conditions under which the model will operate. Online forums and communities for Raspberry Pi, Python, and machine learning are invaluable resources, offering advice and solutions from people who have likely faced similar challenges.

Embarking on DIY AI projects not only enhances your living space but also deepens your understanding of how AI technologies work in a practical, hands-on context. These projects bridge the gap between theoretical knowledge and real-world application, showing you firsthand how AI can be customized and integrated into everyday life. By taking the initiative to build and troubleshoot your own AI systems, you develop technical skills and a problem-solving mindset crucial in the technology age.

As we close this chapter on hands-on AI projects, remember that the journey of learning and building with AI is iterative and dynamic. Each project enhances your understanding and skills, preparing you for more complex challenges. Next, we will explore the ethical considerations in AI, ensuring that as we become more proficient in implementing AI solutions, we also remain vigilant and thoughtful about their implications on privacy, security, and society.

CHAPTER 4
ETHICAL CONSIDERATIONS IN AI

A s we venture deeper into artificial intelligence, it becomes increasingly important to address the ethical dimensions accompanying technological advances. AI is not just about algorithms and data; it's about real-world implications that affect real people. This chapter delves into the critical topic of data privacy in AI applications—a subject that resonates deeply with anyone who uses technology today. Here, we'll explore what data privacy means in the context of AI, the risks involved, the technologies designed to enhance privacy, and some real-world case studies that highlight the challenges and solutions in this area.

4.1 UNDERSTANDING DATA PRIVACY IN AI APPLICATIONS

Defining Data Privacy

Data privacy in AI refers to the right of individuals to control their personal information and how AI systems use it. It's about ensuring that personal data, from your shopping preferences to your medical records, is used in a manner that respects your privacy and autonomy. In an AI context, data privacy is not just about keeping data secure from unauthorized access; it's also about how data is collected, analyzed, and used to make decisions. This is critical because AI can process vast amounts of data at an unprecedented scale and speed, making it a powerful tool that, if not appropriately governed, could infringe on individual privacy rights.

Risks Associated with AI

The integration of AI into everyday applications brings several privacy risks. One of the main concerns is data breaches, where sensitive information could be exposed due to security vulnerabilities. Another risk is unauthorized data sharing, where AI systems might share data with third parties without user consent. Additionally, there's the risk of surveillance, where AI could be used to monitor individuals without their knowledge or consent. These risks are not just hypothetical; they have real consequences, affecting everything from personal security to public trust in AI technologies.

Privacy-Enhancing Technologies

To combat these risks, several privacy-enhancing technologies have been developed. Differential privacy, for instance, adds randomness to the data being processed by AI systems, making it difficult to identify individual data points without affecting the overall analytical insights. This means an AI system can learn about general patterns without accessing specific individual data. Another method is federated learning, where AI models are trained across multiple decentralized devices or servers without exchanging the data itself. This technique allows AI to learn from a vast pool of data while keeping that data stored locally on users' devices, enhancing privacy.

Case Studies

Consider the case of a popular fitness tracking app that used AI to provide personalized health insights. The app collected data on users' locations, health metrics, and daily activities. However, a flaw in the app's privacy settings allowed third parties to access sensitive health data without user consent. This incident could have been mitigated by implementing stronger data encryption and more transparent user consent mechanisms. By analyzing such cases, we learn the importance of robust privacy protections and the need for ongoing vigilance to adapt to new threats.

Interactive Element: Reflection Section

Reflect on your experiences with AI and data privacy. Have you ever felt uncomfortable about the information an app or a device was collecting about you? Write down your thoughts and consider what privacy protections you would like to see in place to feel more secure using AI technologies.

As we navigate the complexities of AI and data privacy, it's clear that ensuring the ethical use of AI is not just about protecting data but about maintaining trust and integrity in the technologies that are becoming integral to our daily lives. This exploration into data privacy sets the stage for a broader discussion on the ethical challenges we face in the age of AI, reminding us that behind every dataset and algorithm are individuals whose rights and dignity must be upheld.

4.2 THE BIAS PROBLEM IN AI: CAUSES AND SOLUTIONS

When we talk about bias in artificial intelligence, we are referring to systematic and unfair discrimination that can be perpetuated by AI systems. This might seem surprising because many think of technology as objective or neutral. However, AI systems learn from large datasets that they are trained on, and these datasets can contain biases that reflect historical, social, or cultural inequalities. Sometimes, the very algorithms that process and learn from this data can amplify these biases, rather than mitigate them. Moreover, the teams that design, develop, and deploy AI systems can also introduce bias, often unintentionally, by influencing which data to use and how algorithms are structured.

The origins of bias in AI are multifaceted. At the data level, bias can arise during the dataset collection process where the data may not represent all groups. For instance, if an AI system is trained primarily on data from male users, it may not perform as well for female users. This type of bias is known as sample bias. Another common source is label bias, which occurs during the data labeling process when the labels assigned to data reflect subjective or erroneous beliefs. Algorithmic bias occurs when the algorithms used to process data and make decisions create biases due to their underlying mechanics or the way they are programmed. Finally, developer bias includes the preconceptions and assumptions made by those who create AI systems, which can influence how problems are framed and which solutions are pursued.

These biases can lead to unfair outcomes and discrimination, particularly in sensitive areas such as hiring practices and law enforcement. In hiring, AI tools can screen resumes and predict candidate suitability. However, if the AI has learned from historical hiring data that reflects gender or ethnic biases, it may perpetuate these biases by favoring candidates from certain groups over others. In law enforcement, predictive policing tools can suggest where crimes are likely to occur based on past crime data. However, if the underlying data is biased—reflecting higher arrest rates in certain communities due to over-policing—these tools can lead to unfair targeting of these communities, exacerbating social inequalities.

Several strategies can be employed to mitigate bias in AI. One effective approach is to ensure diversity in the team that designs and develops AI systems. A diverse team can provide a range of perspectives that can help identify and reduce biases that might not be apparent to a more homogeneous group. Conducting regular bias audits is another crucial strategy. These audits involve systematically reviewing AI systems to detect and address biases in datasets, algorithms, and outcomes. Moreover, adopting inclusive data practices—such as ensuring that data is representative and labels are accurate—can help prevent biases from entering AI systems at the data level.

Regulatory and ethical frameworks also play a critical role in managing AI bias. Many governments and international bodies are now developing guidelines and regulations that require transparency and fairness in AI applications. These regulations often mandate regular bias assessments and dictate that individuals affected by AI decisions have a right to explanation. For instance, the European Union's General Data Protection Regulation (GDPR) includes provisions that aim to protect individuals from unfair automated decisions. Such frameworks not only help prevent bias but also build public trust in AI technologies by ensuring they are used responsibly.

In tackling the bias problem in AI, it's important to recognize that technology reflects the values of the society it is developed in. As such, the challenge of bias in AI is not only about improving algorithms but also about addressing the broader societal inequalities that they mirror. By understanding the origins and manifestations of AI bias and implementing comprehensive strategies to combat it, we can harness the benefits of AI while ensuring it serves the needs of all members of society fairly.

4.3 ETHICAL AI: BALANCING INNOVATION WITH RESPONSIBILITY

When we talk about ethical AI, we refer to the development and application of AI technologies in a manner that considers moral principles and values. Key principles like transparency, account-ability, and harm prevention underpin ethical AI. Transparency in AI ensures that the operations and decisions made by AI systems can be understood by humans, allowing us to trace and under-stand how conclusions are reached. Accountability refers to the responsibility of creators and operators of AI systems to ensure they operate fairly and are answerable for any failures. Lastly, harm prevention involves measures to ensure that AI systems do not cause unintended harm to individuals or society. These princi-ples are essential to build trust in AI systems and ensure they contribute positively to society.

However, the path to truly ethical AI is fraught with challenges, particularly due to the rapid pace of AI innovation. Technological advancements often need to improve the ability of regulations and ethical guidelines to keep pace, creating gaps that can lead to ethical dilemmas. For instance, the competitive pressures in the tech industry can lead companies to prioritize speed to market over thorough ethical reviews, potentially overlooking how AI applications affect user privacy or fairness. Market demands, such as the push for more personalized services, can also encourage the use of AI systems in ways that might compromise ethical stan-dards, unless carefully managed.

Promoting ethical practices in AI development and deployment is crucial and requires concerted efforts from all stakeholders involved. One effective approach is implementing ethical audits, where AI systems are regularly examined to ensure they adhere to ethical standards and regulations. These audits help identify potential ethical issues early on, allowing developers to address them before the systems are deployed. Engaging with stakeholders, including AI developers, users, and those potentially affected by AI systems, is another key strategy. This engagement can be facilitated through public consultations and forums that allow for a diverse range of views and concerns to be raised and addressed, ensuring that AI systems are developed with a broad range of human values in mind.

The global perspectives on ethical AI highlight the diversity in how different cultures and countries address AI ethics. For instance, the European Union has taken a proactive approach by establishing clear guidelines that prioritize user privacy and data protection. In contrast, other regions might emphasize innovation and the economic benefits of AI, potentially leading to different ethical priorities and standards. This variation poses a challenge for global cooperation on AI ethics, as multinational companies may have to navigate a complex landscape of regulations and ethical expectations. However, it also presents an opportunity for learning and harmonization of ethical standards that reflect a wide range of cultural values and societal needs.

Understanding and integrating these diverse perspectives is essential for the development of AI systems that are not only technologically advanced but also socially responsible. As AI continues to evolve and permeate various aspects of our lives, balancing innovation with ethical responsibility is more crucial than ever. It ensures that AI technologies enhance societal well-being while respecting human dignity and rights, paving the way for a future where AI and humanity can coexist in harmony and mutual benefit.

4.4 AI AND EMPLOYMENT: ADDRESSING THE FEARS OF JOB DISPLACEMENT

The rise of artificial intelligence has sparked intense debates around its impact on employment, often casting a shadow of fear over potential job displacement. While it's true that AI can automate tasks, it's equally important to understand that this technology isn't just about replacing jobs but transforming them. In sectors like manufacturing, retail, and even professional services such as law and accounting, AI is reshaping job roles rather than simply eradicating them. In manufacturing, for instance, AI-driven robots handle repetitive tasks, allowing human workers to focus on more complex and creative problem-solving tasks. This shift not only enhances productivity but also elevates the nature of work, requiring a new set of skills.

The transformation in job roles underscores the importance of upskilling and reskilling the workforce to thrive in an AI-enhanced job market. Upskilling refers to the process of individuals learning new skills to excel in their current roles, while reskilling is about training employees in entirely new skill sets for different roles. Effective upskilling and reskilling initiatives are crucial in ensuring that the workforce can meet the demands of an evolving job landscape shaped by AI. For example, AT&T's ambitious retraining program, "Future Ready," is designed to equip its employees with the skills needed in a digital economy, offering courses in data science, cybersecurity, and more. Similarly, Amazon's "Upskilling 2025" program pledges to invest significant resources in training its workers in areas like software engineering and machine learning. These programs prepare employees for future demands and demonstrate a commitment to their workforce's longevity and success.

AI also creates new job categories and economic opportunities that did not exist before. The emergence of roles such as AI ethics officers, who ensure AI technologies are used responsibly, and data annotation specialists, who prepare data for AI training, reflect the new types of employment generated by AI advancements. These roles are crucial in the ecosystem of AI development and deployment, underscoring the technology's capacity to create employment opportunities rather than merely diminish them. Furthermore, the need for human-AI collaboration specialists is becoming apparent as businesses seek to optimize the interaction between human workers and AI systems. This role involves designing workflows and interfaces that help humans and AI work effectively together, ensuring that AI tools enhance productivity and job satisfaction.

Amid these shifts, it's essential to consider social policies that can mitigate the negative impacts of AI on employment. Policies such as universal basic income (UBI) propose providing all citizens with a regular, unconditional sum of money, irrespective of other income. This type of policy could help cushion the economic impact on those whose jobs are displaced by AI, providing them with financial stability as they transition to new roles or seek retraining. Similarly, job guarantee programs could offer a safety net by ensuring that everyone who wants to work has access to a job that pays a living wage, potentially funded or subsidized by government initiatives. These policies not only provide immediate financial relief but also help maintain social stability and stimulate economic growth by boosting consumer spending.

As AI continues to evolve and integrate into various sectors, the narrative around AI and employment needs to shift from one of fear to one of opportunity. By focusing on the transformation and creation of job roles, actively investing in upskilling and reskilling initiatives, and implementing supportive social policies, society can harness the benefits of AI while ensuring that the workforce adapts and thrives in this new technological era. This proactive approach will not only alleviate fears of job displacement but also open up a spectrum of opportunities that could redefine professional landscapes and economic structures for the better.

4.5 THE ROLE OF AI IN SURVEILLANCE: A DOUBLE-EDGED SWORD

In today's interconnected and digitally driven world, artificial intelligence has become a pivotal ally in enhancing surveillance and security systems. AI's ability to process and analyze vast amounts of data in real time has significantly improved public safety and crime prevention. Consider the sophisticated security cameras equipped with AI technologies that can detect unusual activities or recognize faces in a crowd. These systems operate continuously, scanning for potential threats and alerting authorities to suspicious behaviors that might indicate criminal activities. Such capabilities enable quicker responses to incidents, potentially stopping crimes before they happen or swiftly mitigating their consequences. For instance, in cities where these systems are implemented, there has been a noticeable decrease in street crimes, as potential offenders are aware of the high likelihood of being caught.

However, the power of AI in surveillance also raises substantial privacy concerns. The very technologies that help secure spaces can also intrude on the privacy of individuals. Surveillance systems, particularly those with facial recognition capabilities, can track individuals without their consent, collecting data on their movements and activities. This kind of surveillance can lead to a significant erosion of personal privacy and civil liberties, creating a society where everyone might feel watched, potentially stifling freedom of expression and behavior. It's a classic scenario of a double-edged sword, where the benefits of enhanced security are counterbalanced by the risks of increased surveillance and potential overreach.

Navigating this landscape requires stringent regulations to balance these benefits and risks effectively. Governments and regulatory bodies need to establish clear guidelines on how AI surveillance systems can be used, ensuring they enhance security without infringing on individual rights. This includes setting boundaries on what kinds of data can be collected, how long it can be stored, and who can access it. Additionally, there should be transparency about the deployment of surveillance technologies, giving the public insight into when and how these tools are used, which helps in maintaining public trust. Moreover, individuals should have the right to access the data collected about them and request corrections or deletions if that data is inaccurate or improperly collected.

Let's consider a case study that underscores the need for balanced regulatory measures. In a well-known retail chain, AI-powered cameras were used to prevent shoplifting by analyzing customers' behaviors for suspicious activities. While the technology effectively reduced theft, it also mistakenly flagged innocent behaviors as suspicious, leading to unwarranted confrontations and a public outcry over privacy violations. This situation could have been mitigated by implementing stricter guidelines on what behaviors are monitored and ensuring a human supervisor reviewed AI assessments before any action was taken. This case highlights the delicate balance between utilizing AI for security and maintaining ethical standards that protect individual privacy.

Navigating the complexities of AI in surveillance is a delicate task. While AI offers transformative potentials for enhancing security, the implications for privacy and civil liberties are significant. Establishing robust regulatory frameworks and maintaining an open dialogue about the ethical use of surveillance technologies are crucial steps in leveraging the benefits of AI while safeguarding the foundational values of privacy and freedom. As we continue to explore and implement AI in various aspects of life, understanding and addressing these dual aspects of AI surveillance will be essential for building a society that respects both security and individual rights.

4.6 ENSURING TRANSPARENCY IN AI ALGORITHMS

Transparency in AI algorithms isn't just a nicety—it's a necessity for fostering trust and accountability in the systems that increasingly influence our daily lives. When AI decisions impact everything from individual credit scores to healthcare treatment plans, understanding how these decisions are made becomes crucial. Transparent AI systems allow users and regulators to verify that these systems operate fairly and without bias, ensuring that the AI's actions can be justified and, if necessary, corrected. This level of openness is essential not only for building trust but also for facilitating broader adoption of AI technologies across sensitive sectors.

Achieving transparency in AI involves several methodologies that make the inner workings of AI systems more understandable and accessible. Open-source models are a significant step towards this goal. By making the code and algorithms of AI systems publicly available, open-source initiatives encourage a collaborative approach to development, where a diverse community of developers, ethicists, and users can review, modify, and improve the AI systems. This openness not only democratizes AI development but also accelerates innovation and helps quickly identify and rectify potential flaws or biases in the systems.

Moreover, clear documentation plays a critical role in enhancing transparency. Detailed documentation that explains how AI models are built, trained, and deployed helps users understand the decisions made by AI. This should include information on the data used for training the models, the decision-making processes, and the rationale behind these processes. For instance, healthcare providers using AI systems for patient diagnosis can benefit greatly from clear documentation that explains how the AI reaches its conclusions, which in turn can help in explaining these decisions to patients.

Explainable AI (XAI) is another burgeoning field that focuses on creating AI models that not only make decisions but also provide explanations that are understandable to humans. Techniques in XAI, such as feature importance, which highlights what inputs most significantly impact the output of an AI model, help demystify the decision-making processes of AI systems. This is particularly useful in sectors like finance, where understanding the factors that influence things like loan approval can help ensure fairness and eliminate hidden biases.

However, implementing transparency in AI is not without its challenges. Technically, creating models that are both accurate and interpretable can often be a complex task. The most powerful AI models, like those involving deep learning, are notoriously difficult to interpret because of their complex and layered structures. Balancing model performance with interpretability often requires innovative approaches and can sometimes lead to trade-offs. From a business perspective, companies might resist transparency due to fears of revealing proprietary information or competitive insights.

Overcoming these hurdles requires a cultural shift towards valuing ethical practices and transparency within organizations, alongside regulatory incentives that promote open and explainable AI.

The impact of increased transparency in AI is profound, particularly in sectors like healthcare and finance where decisions can have significant consequences. In healthcare, transparent AI systems allow for better patient outcomes by providing clear rationales for AI-generated diagnoses, which doctors can use to make informed treatment decisions. In finance, transparency helps in building trust with customers who might be wary of AI systems determining their creditworthiness or managing their investments. By understanding how these decisions are made, customers are more likely to trust and accept the AI's role in managing their finances.

In essence, transparency is the cornerstone of ethical AI. It ensures that AI systems are not only effective and efficient but also fair, understandable, and accountable. As we continue to integrate AI into various facets of our lives, striving for transparency in AI algorithms will be crucial for ensuring these technologies work for and not against us. This commitment to transparency not only enhances the functionality and acceptance of AI but also aligns its development with the core values of society, paving the way for a future where AI and humans collaborate with trust and confidence.

As this chapter on ethical considerations in AI concludes, we reflect on the imperative of integrating strong ethical practices in developing and deploying AI technologies. From ensuring data privacy and reducing bias to enhancing transparency and addressing employment impacts, the ethical dimensions of AI are broad and complex. Yet, they are also critically important for ensuring that AI technologies enhance societal well-being while respecting human dignity and rights. Looking ahead, the next chapter will explore the exciting possibilities of AI in transforming industries, where these ethical considerations will continue to play a crucial role in shaping the development of AI for the betterment of society.

CHAPTER 5
AI FOR PERSONAL AND PROFESSIONAL GROWTH

5.1 AI SKILLS FOR THE WORKPLACE: WHAT EMPLOYERS LOOK FOR

In today's rapidly evolving job market, understanding and leveraging AI technologies are becoming increasingly crucial, not just for tech professionals but across various sectors. Whether you're in healthcare, finance, or the arts, the infusion of AI into everyday business processes is reshaping career landscapes and creating new opportunities for those who are adept at these skills. Let's explore the essential AI skills that are gaining traction in the workplace and how you can integrate these competencies into your current role to stay ahead in your career.

Essential AI Skills

Machine learning, natural language processing (NLP), and robotics represent just the tip of the iceberg when it comes to AI skills that employers are eagerly seeking. Machine learning expertise, for instance, is highly valued as businesses rely more on data-driven decision-making. Understanding how to create, train, and implement models that can predict consumer behavior, optimize operations, and even drive strategic growth can make you an invaluable asset to any team. Similarly, NLP skills are crucial as businesses look to enhance customer interactions through chatbots and AI-driven communication tools. Mastery in NLP can enable you to improve these interactions, making digital communication more human-like and intuitive. Robotics skills are also in high demand, especially in industries like manufacturing, logistics, and healthcare, where automation is becoming increasingly prevalent.

Integrating these AI skills into your current job doesn't mean starting from scratch or stepping out of your role. Instead, it involves recognizing how AI can enhance your effectiveness and value within your existing position. For instance, if you're in marketing, understanding machine learning could allow you to analyze customer data better and personalize marketing campaigns. If you're in finance, skills in predictive analytics could help you forecast market trends more accurately. The key is to identify the touchpoints where AI intersects with your role and to seek out training and development opportunities in those areas.

Case Studies of AI Adoption in Workplaces

Consider the case of a retail company that integrated AI to personalize shopping experiences. By employing machine learning specialists, the company was able to analyze customer data and provide personalized recommendations, significantly boosting sales and customer satisfaction. Another example is a logistics company that used robotics to automate its warehouse operations. By training its existing workforce in robotics management and maintenance, the company not only increased efficiency but also enhanced the skill set of its employees, preparing them for more advanced roles in the industry.

Resources for AI Skill Development

For those looking to develop AI skills, numerous resources are available that cater to various learning styles and professional needs. Online platforms like Coursera and Udacity offer courses in machine learning, NLP, and robotics, often developed in partnership with leading universities and companies. These courses range from beginner to advanced levels, providing certifications that can add significant value to your resume. Additionally, attending AI workshops and seminars can provide practical, hands-on experience and networking opportunities with other AI professionals. For a more immersive learning experience, consider AI bootcamps, which are intensive training programs designed to build your skills in a short, focused period.

Interactive Element: AI Skills Checklist

To help you identify and develop the AI skills most relevant to your career, here's a checklist you can use:

- Identify the AI skills most relevant to your industry: Research and list the AI technologies impacting your sector.
- Assess your current skill level: Honestly evaluate your current AI knowledge and identify areas for improvement.
- Set learning goals: Based on your assessment, set specific, measurable learning goals.
- Choose the right resources: Select courses, workshops, or books that best suit your learning style and professional needs.
- Apply your skills: Look for opportunities within your current role where you can apply your AI skills. This could

be a project at work or even a personal project that allows you to practice your skills.

- Review and reflect: Regularly review your progress towards your learning goals and adjust your learning plan as needed.

This checklist not only guides you through the process of developing AI skills but also ensures that your learning is aligned with your career objectives, maximizing the impact of your efforts.

By embracing AI and integrating these skills into your professional toolkit, you are not just preparing for future opportunities but also positioning yourself as a key player in your industry's evolution. The work landscape is changing, and AI is a significant driver of this change. Equip yourself with the knowledge and skills to navigate this new terrain, and watch as doors to new and exciting career paths open up before you.

5.2 USING AI TO ENHANCE PERSONAL PRODUCTIVITY

In a world where time often feels like it's slipping through our fingers, AI-powered tools have emerged as a beacon of efficiency, helping us harness our days with greater precision and effectiveness. Picture this: your day is organized flawlessly by an intelligent system that understands your priorities and habits, nudging you towards completing your tasks and doing so with time to spare for yourself. AI in personal productivity isn't just about doing more— it's about enhancing the quality of your time.

AI Tools for Time Management

Let's start with how AI simplifies managing schedules—an aspect of daily life that many of us struggle with. Automated calendar schedulers and task managers powered by AI can transform how you plan your day. These aren't your ordinary scheduling tools; they learn from your interaction patterns and can suggest optimal times for meetings, remind you of deadlines, and even reschedule appointments when conflicts arise. For instance, imagine a scenario where your AI scheduler notices you often have an energy dip in the afternoon. It could suggest scheduling your critical tasks in the morning and lighter, more administrative tasks for when your energy wanes. This kind of smart scheduling not only helps in better time management but also aligns your work tasks with your natural productivity peaks, which can make a huge difference in how much you accomplish in a day.

Enhancing Focus and Efficiency

Distractions are the arch-nemesis of productivity, and here, too, AI comes to the rescue. Focus-enhancing apps use AI to help minimize distractions by understanding your work habits and creating an environment conducive to focus. These apps can mute notifications when you need to concentrate, block distracting websites, and even play background sounds that boost concentration. More sophisticated systems can analyze your work patterns over time and identify the times of day when you're most focused, suggesting you tackle your most challenging tasks during these windows. By adapting to your behavioral patterns, AI creates personalized strategies to help you maintain focus, transforming potential distractions into mere background noise.

Personalized Learning Experiences

AI's impact extends into personal development through customized learning platforms that adapt to your unique learning pace and style. These platforms use AI to create a personalized curriculum that adjusts in real time based on your progress and areas of strength or struggle. For example, suppose you're learning a new language, and you excel at grammar but struggle with vocabulary. In that case, the AI system will adjust your coursework to provide more vocabulary exercises and fewer grammar ones. It ensures that you spend time improving where you need it most, making your learning experience as efficient as it is effective. This adaptive learning approach not only keeps you engaged but also ensures that you are always challenged, accelerating your learning process and helping you achieve your personal development goals faster.

AI in Daily Decision Making

In the realm of decision-making, AI-driven analytics tools are like having a personal consultant who guides you through making smarter, data-driven decisions. These tools can analyze vast amounts of data to provide insights that might not be visible at first glance. Whether it's deciding the best financial investment based on market trends or choosing the right project management strategies based on past outcomes, AI helps by providing a clear analysis of the options. For professionals, this means less time spent on data crunching and more on strategic thinking and execution. For personal decisions, it can mean better choices that align closely with your long-term goals and values.

As AI continues to evolve, its integration into personal produc-tivity tools makes it increasingly possible to lead a more organized, focused, and efficient life. By leveraging AI, you can transform not only how you work but also how you learn, plan, and make decisions, leading to a more productive and fulfilling personal and professional life.

5.3 AI FOR ENTREPRENEURS: AUTOMATING AND SCALING YOUR BUSINESS

For entrepreneurs, the allure of Artificial Intelligence (AI) goes beyond its technological novelty; it's about its transformative potential in automating and scaling business operations. Imagine having a virtual team that works tirelessly, with impeccable accuracy and efficiency, taking on routine tasks like managing inventory, handling customer inquiries, and keeping the books in order. This isn't just a productivity booster; it's a game changer that allows you, the entrepreneur, to focus on strategic growth and innovation.

AI for Business Automation

AI's capability to automate business operations spans several key areas. In inventory management, AI systems can predict stock levels effectively, manage orders, and even suggest inventory adjustments based on real-time sales data and market trends. This kind of automation reduces the likelihood of overstocking or stockouts, ensuring that capital isn't tied up unnecessarily and that sales opportunities aren't missed. In customer service, AI chatbots provide 24/7 interaction with customers, handling inquiries, solving common issues, and forwarding more complex issues to human operatives. This ensures that customer interactions are managed efficiently, improving satisfaction while freeing human agents to handle tasks requiring more nuanced engagement. Financial bookkeeping, too, benefits from AI. With AI-driven systems, financial entries are recorded in real-time, budgets are analyzed, and financial health indicators are reported with recommendations for cost-saving or investment opportunities. This automation not only ensures accuracy in financial management but also provides timely insights that can aid strategic financial planning.

Scaling with AI

As your business grows, scalability becomes a critical challenge. AI can play a pivotal role here, especially through predictive analytics and marketing strategies tailored by AI algorithms. Predictive analytics can forecast market trends, consumer behavior, and potential revenue streams, allowing businesses to make informed decisions about where to allocate resources, when to expand into new markets, and how to price products. AI-driven marketing, on the other hand, personalizes customer interactions based on individual preferences and behaviors, enhancing engagement and loyalty. AI can precisely segment audiences, tailor marketing messages, and optimize marketing campaigns in real-time to ensure the highest possible conversion rates. This targeted approach not only maximizes marketing budgets but also drives growth by ensuring that marketing efforts are focused on the most promising prospects.

Real-Life Success Stories

Consider the story of a small online apparel store that integrated AI to optimize its inventory and customer service. By using AI to analyze sales data and customer feedback, the store was able to predict which styles were likely to be popular in the upcoming season and adjust their inventory accordingly. This led to a 20% increase in sales and a reduction in unsold stock. Another example is a tech startup that used AI to automate its customer support, reducing response times from several hours to minutes and dramatically increasing customer satisfaction. These success stories highlight not just the potential of AI in automating and scaling operations and its impact on overall business success.

Challenges and Solutions

While the benefits are significant, integrating AI into business operations comes with challenges. One common hurdle is the initial cost and complexity of implementing AI solutions. For many small businesses, this can be daunting. However, the advent of AI-as-a-service platforms has made AI more accessible to small and medium-sized enterprises by reducing the need for upfront investment in AI infrastructure and expertise. Another challenge is the resistance to change within organizations. This can be mitigated by gradual implementation and by focusing on education and training for employees to ensure they understand the benefits of AI and how to use new systems effectively.

For entrepreneurs looking to thrive in a competitive market, AI presents opportunities that are too valuable to ignore. AI can transform a small business into a dynamic, efficient, and competitive enterprise by automating routine tasks, optimizing operations, and enabling scalable growth. As AI technology continues to evolve, its accessibility and applications will only expand, making now an opportune time for entrepreneurs to explore how AI can be integrated into their business strategies.

5.4 HOW TO STAY UPDATED ON AI TRENDS AND TECHNOLOGIES

Staying informed about the latest developments in Artificial Intelligence (AI) can seem like a daunting task given the rapid pace at which the field evolves. However, keeping abreast of these changes is crucial not only for those directly working with AI but also for anyone interested in the potential impacts of these technologies on their industries and daily lives. Here are practical ways to ensure you remain knowledgeable about the cutting-edge advancements in AI without feeling overwhelmed.

Following AI Trends

The first step to staying updated is knowing where to look. Numerous websites, journals, and influencers can serve as your go-to resources for the latest in AI. Websites like TechCrunch, Wired, and The Verge regularly feature articles on the latest developments in AI technology and industry applications. For those looking for more scholarly material, journals such as 'Journal of Artificial Intelligence Research' and 'AI Magazine' offer in-depth research papers and reviews written by experts in the field. Following influencers and thought leaders on platforms like Twitter and LinkedIn can also provide you with insights and commentary that can help demystify complex topics. Influencers like Fei-Fei Li, Andrew Ng, and Lex Fridman share valuable content that spans from introductory material to advanced research discussions. By curating your information sources and regularly dedicating time to explore these materials, you can build a robust understanding of current trends and methodologies in AI.

Participating in AI Conferences and Workshops

There is no substitute for learning directly from experts and networking with peers; AI conferences and workshops offer just that. Events such as the Neural Information Processing Systems (NeurIPS) conference, the International Conference on Machine Learning (ICML), and the AI Summit series provide platforms for learning about the latest research, practical applications, and ethical considerations in AI. These gatherings are ideal for first-hand experiences, offering workshops where you can gain practical skills and listen to presentations from leaders in the field. Additionally, these events often provide opportunities to ask questions and engage in discussions, allowing for deeper understanding and clarification of complex concepts. If attending in person is challenging, many conferences now offer virtual attendance options, making them more accessible to a global audience.

Utilizing Continuous Learning Platforms

For those who prefer structured learning, continuous learning platforms offer courses that are regularly updated to reflect the latest advancements in AI. Platforms like Coursera, edX, and Udemy feature courses created by universities and industry leaders, covering a wide range of topics from basic AI principles to advanced applications. These platforms often provide interactive elements such as peer discussions and projects, which can enhance understanding and retention of information. Additionally, many courses offer certificates upon completion, which can be an excellent addition to your professional profile, showcasing your commitment to staying current in your field.

The Role of Networking in Staying Informed

Building a professional network in the AI community can significantly enhance your learning experience. Networking isn't just about career opportunities; it's a gateway to exchange ideas, solve problems collaboratively, and get insights into how various industries implement AI. Participating in online forums and local meetups can connect you with like-minded individuals and experts who can share their experiences and advice. Platforms like Meetup.com often list AI groups by region, providing opportunities to connect with professionals in your area. Additionally, LinkedIn groups dedicated to AI topics are excellent for virtual networking, allowing you to participate in discussions and connect with global AI professionals.

By actively engaging in these activities, you create a personalized and effective ecosystem for staying updated on AI advancements. Whether through academic journals, interactive courses, professional networks, or industry conferences, the resources available to deepen your understanding of AI are vast and varied. Engaging with these opportunities not only enhances your professional capabilities but also enriches your perspective on how AI continues to shape our world.

5.5 NETWORKING IN THE AI COMMUNITY: TIPS AND PLATFORMS

Networking within the AI community is more than just exchanging business cards or a quick handshake at professional gatherings. It's about building meaningful relationships and connecting with others who share your passion for artificial intelligence. Whether you're a seasoned AI professional or just starting, networking can provide a plethora of benefits, from enhancing your knowledge to opening doors to new career opportunities. Let's dive into effective strategies for building your network, key platforms where AI enthusiasts gather, and the tangible benefits of these professional relationships.

Building Professional Networks

Crafting a robust professional network in the AI field involves more than just attending AI events; it requires a strategy and a genuine interest in the people you meet. Start by setting clear networking goals: Are you looking to learn new skills, find a mentor, or perhaps identify job opportunities? Understanding your goals will guide your networking efforts and help you seek out the most relevant events and platforms. When attending conferences or workshops, plan which sessions to attend and research the speakers and attendees beforehand. This preparation allows you to engage in meaningful conversations and make connections that align with your professional interests.

One effective networking strategy is to volunteer at AI conferences or seminars. This role can provide a behind-the-scenes look at the event and offer opportunities to meet speakers and attendees in a more relaxed setting. Additionally, consider joining AI-related groups on professional networks like LinkedIn or specialized forums such as GitHub or Stack Overflow. Participate actively in discussions, share your insights, and ask thoughtful questions. This visibility can help establish your reputation as a knowledgeable and engaged member of the AI community. Remember, the key to effective networking is reciprocity; always think about how you can add value to your connections, whether by sharing relevant articles, offering your expertise, or providing support on projects.

Key AI Networking Platforms

The digital age has made it easier than ever to connect with AI professionals, regardless of geographical boundaries. LinkedIn remains a primary professional network where many AI experts share their insights, discuss new trends, and post job opportunities. Joining AI-focused LinkedIn groups can provide access to a wealth of information and connect you with like-minded professionals. For real-time interactions, Twitter is invaluable. Many AI thought leaders, such as Andrew Ng and Yann LeCun, regularly tweet about AI advancements, share educational resources, and engage with the community.

Offline, community meetups like those found on Meetup.com offer a chance to engage with local AI enthusiasts. These gatherings range from informal meetups discussing AI trends to more structured workshops where you can hone your skills. Such face-to-face interactions can strengthen your connections and provide a deeper understanding of the practical applications of AI in various industries. Additionally, annual AI

CHAPTER 6
OVERCOMING AI
CHALLENGES

S tepping into the world of Artificial Intelligence (AI) can feel like you're entering a labyrinth of complex theories and intricate algorithms. But what if you had a map that not only guided you through this maze but also made the journey enjoyable and enlightening? That's exactly what we aim to provide in this chapter. We'll equip you with tools and techniques that simplify AI, making it more approachable and less daunting, even if you're just starting out. Our focus here is to transform what might seem like arcane knowledge into something you can grasp, use, and even enjoy learning about.

6.1 SIMPLIFYING AI: TOOLS AND TECHNIQUES TO LEARN EFFECTIVELY

The beauty of learning AI today is that you can access many tools designed to make complex concepts more tangible and understandable. Let's start with visualization tools. These are incredibly powerful in breaking down AI's complexities into something you can see and interact with. For instance, platforms like TensorFlow Playground allow you to tweak neural network parameters and instantly see how these changes affect the network's performance.

It visually demonstrates what happens when you adjust the learning rate or alter the number of layers in a neural network. This immediate feedback helps demystify the inner workings of neural networks, making the abstract concepts of AI concrete and manipulatable right before your eyes.

Moving on to interactive learning platforms, these are your gyms for mental workouts in AI. Websites like Codecademy or Khan Academy offer courses where you can write actual code, see it run, and watch how it performs tasks in real time. These platforms provide a hands-on experience that textbooks alone cannot offer. They allow you to experiment, make mistakes, and learn in a controlled environment where you can immediately see your actions' consequences. This trial-and-error process is crucial in learning, especially in a field like AI, where understanding your code's and algorithms' impact shapes your grasp of how AI works.

Now, not everyone who wants to learn AI comes from a computing background, and that's perfectly okay. There are numerous resources out there designed specifically for non-experts. Take, for example, the book "AI for Everyone" by Andrew Ng. It's written expressly for those without a technical back-ground, breaking down AI concepts into digestible, understand-able parts. Books like these focus on conveying the intuition behind AI rather than the heavy mathematical underpinnings. They provide a gateway to understanding AI from a high-level perspective, making the technology accessible to a broader audience.

Lastly, the power of analogies and real-life examples in learning cannot be overstated. By relating AI concepts to everyday experiences, these tools bring a level of relatability to the subject matter. For instance, explaining a neural network in AI can be quite abstract, but if you compare it to how our human brain works—

taking inputs, processing information through layers of neurons, and producing outputs—the concept becomes less intimidating and more graspable. These analogies aid in understanding and make the learning process engaging and relevant to your everyday life.

Interactive Element: Try It Yourself

To solidify your understanding, let's engage in a small exercise. Visit TensorFlow Playground and experiment with changing different parameters of a neural network. Try increasing the learning rate and observe how quickly the model learns. What happens when you add more layers? Reflect on these changes and jot down your observations. This exercise will help you see first-hand the impact of these parameters on the learning process.

By leveraging these tools and approaches, AI becomes less of a daunting subject and more of an exciting field ripe with possibilities. Whether you're a visual learner who benefits from seeing concepts in action, a hands-on experimenter who learns by doing, or someone who finds understanding through storytelling and analogies, there are resources available to cater to your learning style. With these tools at your disposal, diving into AI can be an enlightening and enriching experience, opening up a world where technology meets creativity and innovation.

6.2 OVERCOMING THE INTIMIDATION OF AI COMPLEXITY

Embarking on learning AI can sometimes feel like standing at the base of a towering mountain—daunting, if not outright intimidating. But what if you could transform that mountain into a series of small, climbable hills? It starts with a shift in mindset. Embracing a growth mindset that views challenges as stepping stones rather than stumbling blocks is crucial. This perspective encourages you to see each obstacle in your AI learning process as an opportunity to grow, expand your understanding, and develop resilience. Remember, every expert was once a beginner, and they reached proficiency not through inherent talent but through persistent effort and a willingness to learn from mistakes.

The key to making AI less overwhelming is to break it down into small, manageable goals. Instead of aiming to master AI overnight, set realistic, achievable milestones. For instance, start with understanding basic AI concepts before moving on to more complex algorithms. Each small goal you achieve acts as a stepping stone towards greater confidence and competence. This approach keeps you motivated and structures your learning journey into a series of attainable steps, making the process more digestible and less intimidating.

Now, let's talk about the power of community in learning AI. Peer learning, or learning alongside others, can significantly demystify the complexities of AI. Joining study groups or online communities offers multiple benefits. It provides a support system where you can share experiences, ask questions, and find solutions together. Learning in a group setting can also expose you to diverse perspectives and techniques, enriching your understanding of AI. Furthermore, explaining concepts to peers is a fantastic way to reinforce your own knowledge. In environments like GitHub or local meetups, you can connect with others navigating the AI landscape. These communities often foster a collaborative spirit that makes tackling difficult concepts more approachable and less daunting.

Celebrating small successes is another essential element in your AI learning path. Each time you understand a new concept, debug a piece of code successfully, or simply make progress in your learning, take a moment to acknowledge and celebrate your achievement. These celebrations act as positive reinforcements that boost your motivation and remind you of the progress you're making, no matter how small. They help build a positive feedback loop in your learning process, making the journey enjoyable and rewarding. Whether it's mastering a tricky algorithm or successfully implementing your first AI model, recognizing these victories can significantly enhance your learning experience and encourage you to keep pushing forward.

By adjusting your mindset, setting manageable goals, engaging in peer learning, and celebrating your successes, you can effectively reduce the intimidation factor associated with AI. These strategies not only make learning AI more accessible but also more enjoyable. As you continue to explore AI, remember that every challenge is an opportunity to grow, and every small victory is a step towards mastering this transformative technology.

6.3 CHOOSING THE RIGHT AI LEARNING RESOURCES

Diving into the vast ocean of Artificial Intelligence (AI) learning resources can be both exhilarating and overwhelming. Whether you're a visual learner who thrives on diagrams and flowcharts, a reader who absorbs information best through detailed texts, or a hands-on experimenter eager to code, understanding your learning style is your first step toward choosing the right AI resources. Let's explore how you can identify and match your learning preferences with the most effective learning tools.

Start by reflecting on how you've successfully learned other subjects in the past. Do videos and live demonstrations help you grasp concepts quickly? Or do you find that reading provides the most thorough understanding? Perhaps interactive quizzes and exercises give you the clarity you need. Once you identify your preference, you can align it with AI learning resources tailored to your style. For visual learners, infographics and video tutorials that illustrate AI concepts like neural networks or machine learning processes can demystify complex information, making it more digestible. If you're a reader, delve into foundational books and articles that provide comprehensive insights into AI theories and applications. Meanwhile, if you learn by doing, seek out interactive coding platforms where you can write, test, and refine AI algorithms in real time.

Now, let's navigate through the myriad of AI resources available. For a well-rounded understanding, it's beneficial to explore a variety of materials. Here's a curated list of resources that have been vetted for their accessibility and suitability for beginners:

1. Books: "Artificial Intelligence: A Guide for Thinking Humans" by Melanie Mitchell provides an insightful overview of AI, suitable for those who appreciate deep dives into how AI is transforming various aspects of society.
2. Online Courses: For interactive learners, platforms like Coursera offer courses like "AI For Everyone" by Andrew Ng. This course is designed for non-technical people and introduces AI concepts without the complicated math.
3. Workshops: Local workshops or online webinars can offer real-time interaction with AI experts, providing clarity and immediate feedback that can enhance your understanding and confidence.

Deciding between free and paid resources often involves weighing your current needs against your educational goals. Free resources are a great way to start; they often provide substantial foundational knowledge. Websites like MIT OpenCourseWare offer free course materials that can introduce you to basic and advanced AI concepts without any financial commitment. However, paid courses often have additional benefits such as structured learning paths, professional mentorship, certification, and more intensive projects that can provide deeper insights and hands-on experience. If you're considering a career in AI or looking to master specific skills, investing in a comprehensive paid course or bootcamp might be worthwhile.

Keeping your AI knowledge current is crucial given the rapid pace of technological advancements in the field. Subscribe to AI newsletters from reliable sources like the Artificial Intelligence section on ArXiv.org or follow AI research labs and thought leaders on social media platforms to stay updated on the latest research breakthroughs and industry trends. Regularly updating your learning resources can also involve revisiting foundational concepts through updated versions of textbooks or newer editions of online courses that reflect the latest technological advancements and ethical discussions in AI.

By carefully selecting your AI learning resources according to your personal learning style, and staying committed to continuously updating your knowledge base, you can effectively navigate the complexities of AI education. This approach enhances your learning experience and ensures that you remain at the forefront of AI advancements, ready to apply your knowledge to real-world problems and innovations.

6.4 PRACTICAL TIPS FOR APPLYING AI KNOWLEDGE

In the vast and evolving field of Artificial Intelligence, understanding the theory is just one part of the equation; applying this knowledge in practical scenarios can vastly enhance your grasp and appreciation of what AI can truly accomplish. Whether it's through developing projects that solve real-world problems, competing in AI challenges, or gaining hands-on experience through internships, the real test of your AI skills comes through application. This hands-on approach not only solidifies your understanding but also prepares you for professional challenges, making your learning journey both comprehensive and fulfilling.

Real-World Projects

Imagine applying your AI knowledge to create a solution that predicts the most efficient routes for delivery trucks in your city, or perhaps developing a system that can help small farmers predict crop yields more accurately. Engaging in real-world projects allows you to apply your acquired theoretical knowledge to solve practical problems. It's about moving beyond the classroom into the real world where the complexities and unpredictabilities of life make learning dynamic and impactful. When you begin working on a project, start small. Identify a problem that's manageable yet challenging, and gradually scale up as your skills improve. This approach not only keeps you motivated but also ensures that you are continuously learning and adapting. Moreover, these projects can serve as powerful portfolio pieces that showcase your skills to potential employers or educational institutions. They become proof of your ability to not only understand AI but also apply it effectively in real-world scenarios.

Participation in Competitions

Participating in AI competitions can be particularly rewarding for those who thrive on challenge and competition. Platforms like Kaggle offer many challenges ranging from beginner-friendly to expert-level. These competitions task you with solving real problems companies face, from automating vehicle identification to enhancing agricultural productivity through drone imagery analysis. What makes these competitions invaluable is the exposure to a community of AI practitioners and industry experts. You gain insights into how others approach problem-solving in AI, learn new techniques, and compare your solutions with peers. This competitive yet collaborative environment pushes you to refine your skills and innovate, often leading to breakthroughs in your understanding and capabilities. Moreover, success in these competitions can attract attention from potential employers who value such practical demonstration of AI skills.

Internships and Volunteering

If you're looking to deepen your practical knowledge of AI, consider pursuing internships or volunteer positions in companies or organizations that utilize AI technologies. These opportunities provide you with a firsthand look at how AI is applied in professional settings. You get to work on real projects, learn from experienced professionals, and understand the day-to-day challenges and workings of AI in business or social contexts. Internships can be particularly transformative, as they provide not only practical experience but also professional mentorship, which is crucial in navigating your career path in AI. Volunteering, on the other hand, could involve contributing to social projects that leverage AI for good, such as developing AI tools to aid in disaster response or healthcare. Such experiences not only enhance your resume but also give you the satisfaction of contributing to meaningful causes and applying your AI skills to make a tangible difference in the world.

Building a Portfolio

As you progress in your AI learning journey, compiling a portfolio of your projects and accomplishments becomes crucial. Think of your portfolio as a living document that showcases your growth and expertise in AI. Include a variety of projects that demonstrate your range of skills, from data analysis and model building to AI application development. Make sure to detail the problem, your approach, the AI techniques used, and the outcome of each project. A well-maintained portfolio not only helps potential employers understand your capabilities but also serves as a reflection of your learning journey, highlighting your growth, versatility, and commitment to applying AI in diverse scenarios. Additionally, maintaining a blog or a GitHub repository where you regularly update projects and share insights can enhance your visibility in the AI community, opening up further opportunities for collaboration and innovation.

By engaging in real-world projects, participating in competitions, gaining hands-on experience through internships, and meticulously building a portfolio, you effectively bridge the gap between theoretical knowledge and practical application. This not only enhances your understanding and skills in AI but also prepares you for the challenges and opportunities that lie ahead in your AI career or academic pursuits. As you continue to apply your knowledge, remember that each project, each competition, and each internship is a step towards mastering AI, equipped not just to understand but to innovate and lead in the field.

6.5 DEALING WITH RAPID CHANGES IN AI TECHNOLOGIES

The realm of Artificial Intelligence is as dynamic as it is intriguing, continually evolving at a pace that can sometimes feel overwhelming. Staying updated with the latest advancements and shifts in the AI landscape is not just about keeping your knowledge fresh; it's about actively participating in the ongoing dialogue of technological progress. One effective strategy to remain informed is by following leading AI researchers and institutions on platforms like Twitter and LinkedIn or through their personal blogs and websites. These thought leaders often share insights into cutting-edge research, developments, and trends that can give you a clearer understanding of where the field is heading. Additionally, subscribing to AI-focused newsletters from reputable sources such as the MIT Technology Review or the Artificial Intelligence section in ArXiv can provide you with a curated flow of information and articles, ensuring you're always in the loop with minimal effort.

Adopting an adaptive learning approach is essential in a field that changes as quickly as AI. This means being open to continuously updating your skills and knowledge base. It's about embracing the mindset that learning is a never-ending process. This approach involves not just passively consuming information but actively seeking new methods, tools, and technologies. Online platforms like edX or Coursera frequently update their courses to reflect new developments and provide advanced topics that can help you stay ahead. Engaging with these learning modules allows you to adapt your skills to current demands, ensuring you remain relevant in the job market or in your field of research. For instance, if a new programming library or tool becomes standard in the industry, taking a short course or a workshop can get you up to speed quickly, rather than being left behind.

Building a solid foundation in the fundamental concepts of AI is crucial amid these rapid changes. While new algorithms and technologies are constantly being developed, the core principles of machine learning, neural networks, and data processing remain relatively constant. Understanding these foundational elements means you can more easily adapt to new tools and technologies as they emerge. For this purpose, revisiting classic texts in AI and machine learning or enrolling in courses that focus on these fundamentals can be incredibly beneficial. These resources ground your knowledge and provide a framework that you can build upon, no matter how much the specifics might evolve.

Networking with other AI professionals offers another layer of engagement with the evolving world of AI. Platforms like LinkedIn and specialized online communities such as Stack Exchange or GitHub provide spaces where you can connect with peers, share knowledge, and get insights on emerging trends. As previously mentioned, attending AI conferences, webinars, and meetups, even virtually, can expand your professional network and expose you to new ideas and applications in AI. Through these interactions, you gain access to a community of learners and professionals who are also navigating the changes in the field. This network can be a vital resource for exchanging tips on handling new AI technologies, discussing theoretical implications, or even collaborating on projects that can further your understanding and exposure to practical AI applications.

In sum, dealing with the rapid changes in AI technology requires a proactive approach: staying informed through continuous learning, grounding yourself in fundamental concepts, and engaging with a community of like-minded professionals. These strategies prepare you to adapt to new developments and empower you to contribute to the evolution of AI technology. As you integrate these practices into your learning routine, you'll find that keeping pace with AI advancements becomes a more manageable and rewarding part of your professional journey or academic pursuits.

6.6 HOW TO ASK EFFECTIVE QUESTIONS IN AI FORUMS

Venturing into the world of Artificial Intelligence (AI) can sometimes leave you with more questions than answers. And what better place to seek clarity than in AI forums and communities where experts and enthusiasts converge? Engaging effectively in these spaces not only helps you gain insights but also connects you with a global community that can propel your learning journey. Let's explore how you can maximize your interactions in these forums, starting with identifying the right places to ask your questions.

Popular AI forums such as Stack Overflow are treasure troves of information where you can ask technical questions and receive answers from professionals. Similarly, Reddit's r/MachineLearning community offers a more casual environment, perfect for broader discussions and advice. For a more professional setting, LinkedIn groups dedicated to AI and machine learning provide a platform to connect with industry experts. Each of these forums has its own culture and norms, so it's wise to spend some time lurking—reading and observing—before jumping into conversations. This helps you understand the kind of questions that are welcomed and how they are typically structured.

Formulating your questions clearly and concisely is crucial in these forums. Start by being specific about your problem. Include details about the AI techniques or tools you are using, any code snippets (properly formatted), and a clear description of the issue you're facing. Vague questions often get vague answers or, worse, no response at all. To avoid this, frame your question in a way that invites detailed responses. For example, instead of asking, "Why doesn't my algorithm work?" a better question would be, "Why does my neural network model trained on XYZ data not converge? Here are the parameters and the error logs I've used." This not only makes it easier for others to provide specific advice but also demonstrates your effort in solving the problem before seeking help.

Before you post your question, doing some preliminary research is essential. Try to find the answer on your own by searching the forum's archives or using search engines. This effort not only enriches your understanding but also respects the community's time. It often leads to discovering previous discussions that can offer new insights or solutions. This research might also guide you in refining your question further, ensuring it is unique and has not been answered extensively before. Documenting your research in your question post also shows your initiative and often makes others more willing to help.

Engaging constructively with responses is the final step in maximizing your forum experience. When you receive answers, engage actively by asking follow-up questions if something isn't clear. Thank contributors for their time and input, and provide feedback on the solutions offered. This polite acknowledgment not only fosters a positive community atmosphere but also encourages others to assist you in the future. If a particular answer solved your problem, marking it as the accepted solution helps future readers with similar issues. This act of engagement turns a simple Q&A into a dynamic learning experience, enriching the knowledge base of the entire community.

By identifying the right forums, formulating clear questions, doing preliminary research, and engaging constructively with responses, you enhance your learning experience and contribute to the broader AI community. These practices ensure that AI forums are invaluable resources in your learning journey, helping you navigate challenges and broaden your understanding of this dynamic field.

As we close this chapter on overcoming AI challenges, we've armed ourselves with strategies to simplify AI, embrace its complexities, select the best resources, apply our knowledge practically, and keep pace with its rapid advancements. Each section has built upon the last, equipping you with the tools to not only learn AI but to thrive in its ever-evolving landscape. As we turn the page, we'll explore the exciting realm of AI technologies and their future, ready to understand and engage with the next wave of innovations that continue to reshape our world.

CHAPTER 7
AI TECHNOLOGIES AND THEIR FUTURE

7.1 THE RISE OF GENERATIVE AI: CAPABILITIES AND CASE STUDIES

Understanding Generative AI

Imagine being able to create something entirely new from something that already exists—whether it's a piece of music, a work of art, or a written article—just by instructing a computer. This isn't a futuristic fantasy; it's the reality of what we call generative AI. Generative AI stands out in the AI landscape for its ability to generate new content based on patterns and data it has learned from existing materials. It utilizes advanced machine learning techniques, particularly deep learning models like Generative Adversarial Networks (GANs), to produce outputs that can sometimes be indistinguishable from content created by humans.

For instance, consider a generative AI model trained on thousands of paintings from the Renaissance period. This model can generate new images that carry the stylistic signatures of that era, yet are completely original creations. Similarly, in the realm of text, generative AI can craft stories, code, or even poetry by learning from vast corpora of written works. This technology pushes the boundaries of creativity and automation, offering tools that augment human capabilities and open up new possibilities for personal and commercial use.

Applications in Various Fields

The applications of generative AI are as diverse as they are fascinating. In the art world, artists collaborate with AI to push the limits of creativity. These collaborations often result in stunning pieces that are a blend of human imagination and algorithmic computation, bringing new perspectives and aesthetics to the forefront. In journalism, generative AI is being utilized to automate the creation of news reports on straightforward topics like sports results and financial updates, freeing human journalists to tackle more complex stories that require emotional depth and analytical thought.

Entertainment, too, is seeing the integration of generative AI, particularly in music and scriptwriting. AI algorithms can analyze existing music tracks to understand patterns in melody, rhythm, and harmony and then use this knowledge to compose new compositions. Scriptwriting AI tools can generate dialogues and narrative arcs by learning from a database of successful movies and shows, providing a creative springboard for human writers to refine and enhance.

Ethical Considerations

However, with great power comes great responsibility, and generative AI is no exception. One of the most pressing concerns is the creation of deepfakes—highly realistic and potentially deceptive digital manipulations of audio or video. Deepfakes pose significant challenges to privacy, security, and trust, potentially being used to create misleading content that could influence public opinion or personal reputations. Additionally, there are intellectual property concerns as generative AI blurs the lines of authorship and originality. Who owns the rights to a piece of music or art created by an AI that was trained on publicly available data?

Future Potential

Looking ahead, generative AI has immense potential to revolutionize industries and enhance human creativity. As technology advances, we can expect generative AI to become more sophisticated, with enhanced abilities to collaborate with humans and create works that are increasingly complex and nuanced. This evolution will likely spur new industries and transform existing ones, offering exciting opportunities for innovation and growth.

Generative AI not only exemplifies the remarkable capabilities of modern AI technologies but also highlights the complex ethical landscapes we must navigate. As we continue to explore and expand these technologies, our focus must remain on harnessing their potential responsibly, ensuring they contribute positively to society, and fostering an environment where creativity and innovation can flourish alongside ethical and legal considerations.

7.2 AI IN AUTONOMOUS VEHICLES: CURRENT STATE AND FUTURE PROSPECTS

Current Technologies

Let's shift gears and explore the realm of autonomous vehicles (AVs), where AI not only drives but navigates the complexities of the roads with a precision that aims to match and eventually exceed human capabilities. At the heart of autonomous vehicles are sophisticated AI technologies that integrate sensors, machine learning models, and advanced navigation systems to create a seamless and safe driving experience. The vehicles are equipped with a suite of sensors, including LiDAR (Light Detection and Ranging), cameras, ultrasonic, and radar, all working in concert to provide a 360-degree view of the environment. These sensors collect data in real-time about everything from the speed of nearby vehicles to the distance to the next stop sign.

Machine learning models play a pivotal role in processing this vast amount of sensor data. They predict the actions of other road users and make split-second decisions that are crucial for safe driving. For instance, if a pedestrian suddenly steps onto the road, the vehicle's AI system quickly evaluates the situation and decides whether to stop, slow down, or swerve, based on the vehicle's speed, the pedestrian's movement, and the proximity of other objects. This decision-making process is continually refined as the AI systems learn from vast amounts of driving data, enhancing their predictive capabilities over time.

The navigation systems in autonomous vehicles are also powered by AI, which uses detailed maps and real-time data to plot the most efficient routes. These systems are continuously updated with information about road conditions, traffic congestion, and even weather changes, ensuring that the vehicle can adapt its route on the fly to optimize travel time and safety.

Safety and Efficiency

Integrating AI in autonomous vehicles brings significant improvements in safety and efficiency, which are paramount in the evolution of transportation. Studies and trials have shown that AI-driven vehicles can reduce traffic accidents, most of which are caused by human error. Autonomous vehicles don't get distracted, tired, or impaired, which significantly lowers the chances of accidents. For example, in cities where autonomous vehicles have been tested, results have indicated a decrease in rear-end collisions and traffic infractions, underscoring the potential for these technologies to improve road safety.

Efficiency is another critical benefit. Autonomous vehicles can optimize driving patterns to reduce fuel consumption and emissions. By communicating with each other and with traffic management systems, these vehicles can synchronize their speeds and routes, smoothing traffic flows and reducing stop-and-go traffic, which not only saves time but also decreases the carbon footprint of driving.

Regulatory and Infrastructure Challenges

However, the road to widespread adoption of autonomous vehicles has its bumps. Regulatory and infrastructure challenges are significant hurdles. Currently, there is a patchwork of regulations governing autonomous vehicles, varying widely from one jurisdiction to another. This inconsistency can hinder the deployment of AVs as manufacturers must navigate a complex array of laws that may not only differ by country but even by state or region within a country.

Moreover, existing road infrastructures are not fully equipped to support the unique needs of autonomous vehicles. Most roads are designed with human drivers in mind, and significant investment is needed to upgrade infrastructure to better accommodate AVs. This includes everything from updating road signs and signals to be machine-readable, to installing sensors in roads for better vehicle communication.

Vision for the Future

Looking forward, the future of transportation with AI-powered autonomous vehicles is poised to be transformative. Urban planning and logistics will likely undergo significant changes as cities adapt to accommodate AVs. We can envision urban environments with fewer parking lots, as self-driving cars can drop passengers off and either park themselves efficiently or serve other passengers. This change could free up valuable urban space for green areas, pedestrian paths, or additional housing.

In logistics, autonomous vehicles could revolutionize supply chains by optimizing delivery routes and times, reducing costs, and improving service reliability. Integrating AVs could lead to faster, more efficient delivery services that are available 24/7, regardless of human work schedules.

As we steer into the future, the integration of AI in autonomous vehicles promises not only to reshape our roads and cities but also to redefine our very concept of mobility. Embracing these changes requires a thoughtful approach, balancing innovation with safety, efficiency, and inclusivity to ensure that the benefits of autonomous vehicles are realized across society.

7.3 THE IMPACT OF AI ON TRADITIONAL INDUSTRIES

Revolutionizing Manufacturing

In the bustling world of manufacturing, the advent of AI has ushered in not just incremental improvements but transformative changes that redefine how products are made. It's like having a highly skilled assistant who never tires, continually learns, and always seeks the most efficient way to accomplish tasks. In particular, the implementation of AI in automating manufacturing processes is a game-changer. Imagine robots on an assembly line equipped with AI capabilities that allow them to adapt to new tasks through machine learning. These robots can perform complex assembly tasks, reduce errors, and increase production speed, significantly enhancing productivity and reducing costs.

Predictive maintenance is another critical area where AI is making a substantial impact. By analyzing data from machine sensors, AI can predict when a machine is likely to fail or need maintenance. This foresight allows for repairs to be scheduled during non-production periods, minimizing downtime and maintaining steady production flows. For example, an AI system might analyze vibration data from a motor and predict that it's likely to fail within the next month, prompting preemptive maintenance that prevents unexpected breakdowns and costly disruptions.

Moreover, AI significantly optimizes the supply chain in manufacturing. By using algorithms to predict market demands and streamline logistics, AI systems can ensure that materials are supplied and products are distributed efficiently. This optimization reduces waste, cuts costs, and improves delivery times, making the entire manufacturing process more responsive to market conditions and customer needs.

Transforming Agriculture

Shifting our focus to the fields of agriculture, AI is seeding innovations that promise to feed a growing global population sustainably. One of the most notable applications is in crop monitoring. AI-driven systems equipped with drones or satellite imagery can analyze crop health across vast areas, detecting issues such as pest infestations or nutrient deficiencies. This technology enables farmers to address problems quickly and accurately, leading to healthier crops and improved yields.

Automated harvesting systems are another revolutionary AI application in agriculture. These systems use AI to determine the optimal time to harvest crops, considering factors like crop maturity and weather conditions. Once the time is right, AI-powered machines perform the harvesting, maximizing efficiency and reducing the need for manual labor. This automation not only speeds up the harvesting process but also helps mitigate the challenges of labor shortages in agriculture, ensuring that crops are harvested at their peak and post-harvest losses are minimized.

These AI-driven advancements in agriculture highlight a shift towards more sustainable farming practices. By enabling more precise agriculture, AI helps in using resources like water, fertilizers, and pesticides more efficiently, which is crucial for sustainable farming. Moreover, the increased productivity and reduced waste contribute to greater food security, an essential aspect as the global population continues to grow.

Innovation in Financial Services

Turning to the financial sector, AI is proving to be a powerful ally in reshaping services from trading floors to personal banking. Algorithmic trading, where AI algorithms buy and sell stocks at high speeds, is a prime example. These algorithms can analyze large datasets quickly, execute trades at the best possible prices, and adjust trading strategies in real time. This capability enhances market liquidity and stabilizes stock prices, benefiting all market participants.

In personal banking, AI is personalizing the customer experience like never before. Banks use AI to analyze individual spending habits and offer personalized financial advice or product recommendations. For instance, if an AI system notices that a customer frequently incurs overdraft fees, it might suggest a banking product that offers overdraft protection or better management tools. This personalization not only improves customer satisfaction but also helps customers manage their finances more effectively.

Fraud detection is another area where AI is making significant contributions. By constantly learning from transactions, AI can identify patterns indicative of fraudulent activity. When it detects a potential fraud, such as an unusual transaction pattern, it alerts the bank and the customer, helping to prevent losses before they occur. This proactive approach to fraud detection is becoming essential as financial transactions increasingly move online, where the anonymity and volume of transactions can otherwise make fraud detection challenging.

Challenges and Opportunities

Despite these exciting advancements, the integration of AI into traditional industries is not without its challenges. Workforce displacement is a significant concern, as AI and automation could replace jobs, especially in sectors like manufacturing and agriculture. However, this challenge also presents opportunities for growth and efficiency. Industries can harness AI to create new job roles that focus on managing AI operations and improving human-machine collaboration, leading to a more skilled workforce.

Moreover, the need for new skill sets creates opportunities for education and training sectors to innovate and expand, providing learning platforms that can equip workers with the skills needed to thrive in an AI-driven future. As industries continue to integrate AI, the focus should be on leveraging AI not just for automation but also for augmenting human capabilities, ensuring that AI acts as a partner in progress rather than a replacement.

As we explore AI's profound impact across various sectors, it becomes clear that while the challenges are significant, the opportunities for innovation, efficiency, and sustainability are immense. By navigating these challenges thoughtfully, industries can harness AI to enhance their operations and drive forward a more productive and sustainable future.

7.4 AI IN SPACE EXPLORATION: OPPORTUNITIES AND CHALLENGES

AI-driven Missions

Imagine the vastness of space, a frontier that remains largely a mystery despite our best efforts due to its sheer magnitude and complexity. Here, Artificial Intelligence (AI) is not just a helpful tool; it's a critical mission partner. AI's role in space exploration is pivotal, handling tasks ranging from analyzing astronomical data to operating rovers on distant planets. For instance, AI algorithms process data from telescopes like the Hubble Space Telescope, identifying and categorizing celestial bodies, and even detecting phenomena such as exoplanets that might be obscured or too subtle for human eyes. The volume and complexity of this data make AI an indispensable tool for astronomers who rely on its processing power to uncover new insights about our universe.

Beyond observation, AI plays a hands-on role in interplanetary exploration. Mars rovers, for example, are equipped with AI-driven systems that allow them to navigate the Martian terrain autonomously. These systems analyze the terrain to avoid obstacles, select paths, and even conduct scientific experiments without direct human intervention. This autonomy is crucial, given the significant communication delay between Earth and Mars, which can be up to 20 minutes one way. This delay makes real-time control impossible, so the rovers must think for themselves, making on-the-spot decisions about their movements and tasks. Similarly, AI is integral to satellite communications, managing complex networks of satellites that must adjust their operations in response to shifting conditions and commands. These satellites handle everything from GPS navigation to weather forecasting, and AI helps optimize their routes and data management tasks to ensure efficiency and accuracy.

Enhancing Research and Discovery

The processing of vast amounts of space data by AI opens doors to discoveries that were previously beyond human reach. The sheer volume of data generated by space exploration missions is staggering. For example, a single pass by a space telescope can generate terabytes of data, capturing information that could hold the keys to understanding the origins of the universe or identifying potentially habitable planets. AI excels in sifting through this data, identifying patterns, anomalies, and correlations that might elude even the most trained astronomers.

Moreover, AI's capability to simulate complex space phenomena through models and simulations allows researchers to hypothesize and test theories at speeds and accuracies that manual calculations could never achieve. These simulations can mimic everything from the formation of galaxies to the behavior of black holes, providing invaluable insights that guide further research and exploration strategies. The ability to quickly iterate and refine these models based on new data and discoveries accelerates the pace of space science, pushing the boundaries of what we know about the cosmos.

Navigational Autonomy

Navigating space is a challenge of precision and reliability, where even a minor error can lead to mission failure. AI systems onboard spacecraft provide critical navigational guidance, allowing these vessels to travel vast distances with remarkable accuracy. These systems process inputs from various sources, including star trackers and sensors, to determine the spacecraft's position and trajectory accurately. This data is crucial not only for maintaining the course but also for maneuvering through potentially hazardous environments, such as asteroid belts or the complex gravitational fields of planetary systems.

Autonomous navigation becomes even more critical as we aim for distant targets like asteroids or the outer planets. In these missions, AI's ability to make quick decisions about trajectory adjustments or emergency maneuvers can make the difference between success and failure. This autonomy ensures that spacecraft can respond to unexpected situations in real time, a capability that's essential when human intervention may be too slow or impossible due to the distances involved.

Addressing Challenges

Despite its vast potential, the use of AI in space exploration has its challenges. The extreme conditions of space, including high radiation levels, vast temperature extremes, and the vacuum of space, pose unique challenges to AI hardware and software. Radiation can corrupt data and damage electronic circuits, while temperature extremes can cause hardware to fail. Developing AI systems that can withstand these conditions requires robust engineering and constant innovation.

Additionally, the limited ability to transmit data across the vast distances of space presents another significant challenge. Bandwidth is limited, and transmission times can be lengthy, making it impractical to send large volumes of raw data back to Earth for processing. AI systems must, therefore, have the capability to process and prioritize data locally, sending back only the most relevant information. This need for high-level autonomy and decision-making capability places additional demands on AI systems, pushing the development of more advanced and reliable AI technologies.

Navigating these challenges requires a concerted effort and collaboration between technologists, engineers, and scientists. As we continue to push the boundaries of space exploration, AI will undoubtedly play a central role, not just as a tool, but as a cornerstone of mission design and execution, shaping the future of how we explore and understand our universe.

7.5 THE EVOLUTION OF AI IN GAMING

In the ever-evolving landscape of video games, artificial intelligence has moved from a backstage tool to a core component of game development and player interaction. AI in gaming goes beyond just enhancing graphics or optimizing performance; it fundamentally changes how games are designed and played. Game developers now use AI to create more dynamic and responsive environments, as well as to simulate realistic character behaviors, making gaming experiences more immersive and engaging than ever before.

When you play a modern video game, the environments you explore and the characters you interact with are often powered by sophisticated AI systems. These systems make in-game environments respond to your actions in real time, creating a world that feels alive and interactive. For instance, in open-world games, AI can control the weather systems, day-night cycles, and even the behavior of crowds, all of which react to and evolve based on your gameplay decisions. This responsiveness makes the game environment feel more like the real world, where actions have consequences, and the setting changes over time.

Character behavior simulation is another area where AI shines in game development. Non-player characters (NPCs) you encounter aren't just scripted entities; they're powered by AI that allows them to react intelligently to your actions and the game's evolving storyline. This AI-driven behavior includes everything from combat tactics employed by enemies to the social interactions you have with other characters in the game. For example, enemy characters might learn from your previous combat moves and adapt their strategy to counter yours, adding a layer of challenge and unpredictability that keeps the gameplay engaging.

The impact of AI on player experience extends to personalization and adaptability, transforming how games cater to different types of players. AI algorithms analyze your play style, performance, and preferences to adjust game difficulty levels automatically. This adaptive difficulty helps maintain a challenging yet achievable gameplay experience, ensuring that both novices and experienced players find the game engaging. Furthermore, AI enhances interactive storytelling, where the narrative changes based on your decisions. This personalization makes your gaming experience unique, as the story unfolds differently for each player based on the choices they make, leading to multiple possible endings and story arcs.

AI also steps into the role of a player within games, providing new challenges and interactions that enrich the gaming experience. In strategic games like chess or more complex eSports, AI players can perform at high levels, challenging even the best human players. These AI opponents learn from each game they play, continuously improving and adapting their strategies. This ability not only makes AI players formidable opponents but also provides human players with opportunities to learn and improve their skills by analyzing AI gameplay strategies.

Looking into the future, AI in gaming is set to revolutionize the field with fully interactive and immersive virtual reality (VR) experiences. Imagine stepping into a game where every element, from the environment to the characters, is controlled by AI, creating a completely immersive experience that adapts and evolves in real time. In these settings, AI could control the narrative flow, adapt the environment to your actions, and even alter the storyline based on your emotional responses, detected through biometric feedback. This level of interactivity could transform gaming into an experience that blurs the lines between virtual and reality, providing a platform for truly personalized and dynamic storytelling.

As AI continues to advance, its integration into gaming promises to deliver experiences that are increasingly immersive, personalized, and challenging. The use of AI not only enhances the enjoyment and engagement of games but also pushes the boundaries of what games can achieve, pioneering new ways of interacting with digital worlds. As we look forward to these developments, it's clear that AI will continue to play a pivotal role in shaping the future of gaming, driving innovations that will redefine the boundaries of this vibrant and creative industry.

7.6 PREDICTIVE ANALYTICS IN BUSINESS: HOW AI FORESEES MARKET TRENDS

Basics of Predictive Analytics

Diving into the world of business, let's unfold how AI doesn't just participate but actively predicts and molds future market trends. Predictive analytics, a significant branch of data science that involves statistical algorithms and machine learning techniques, is all about understanding the past to foresee the future. This sophisticated analysis allows businesses to view patterns within vast amounts of data, helping them predict future outcomes based on historical trends. Imagine it as a high-powered forecast that not only predicts whether it might rain but also anticipates the probable time and intensity of the rain based on historical weather patterns. In business terms, this might relate to predicting consumer behavior, stock levels, or potential sales spikes, allowing companies to make informed decisions that align closely with future market demands.

The role of predictive analytics in today's business environment is transformative. It empowers businesses to move from a reactive to a proactive stance. No longer are businesses merely reacting to trends and patterns; they are anticipating them and adapting strategies in real time. This shift not only enhances efficiency but also provides a significant competitive edge in rapidly changing markets. By understanding potential future scenarios, companies can craft strategies that cater to upcoming changes, ensuring they're always one step ahead.

Applications in Retail and E-commerce

In retail and e-commerce, predictive analytics is like having a crystal ball that reveals what customers might want even before they know it themselves. For example, by analyzing previous purchase data alongside browsing habits and customer demographics, AI can forecast future buying trends. This foresight allows retailers to stock products more accurately, manage inventory levels, and even adjust pricing dynamically to meet anticipated demand without overstocking or understocking.

Personalized marketing, another critical application, uses AI to tailor advertisements and promotions to individual consumers. Imagine receiving a coupon for your favorite snack just as you start craving it, or an offer on a pair of shoes you've glanced at a few times online. This level of personalization not only enhances the shopping experience for the consumer but also increases the effectiveness of marketing campaigns for businesses.

Moreover, AI-driven predictive analytics plays a crucial role in inventory management, a perennial challenge in the retail sector. By predicting the most popular products for the next season, AI helps retailers optimize their stock levels, ensuring they have enough supply to meet demand without excessive surplus. This optimization is crucial for maintaining cash flow and reducing holding costs, thereby boosting overall business efficiency.

Improving Decision Making

AI-driven insights are increasingly supporting the strategic decisions that steer companies toward success. Predictive analytics provides a foundation for making smarter, data-driven decisions. In strategic meetings, where once gut feelings and experience might have dominated, now informed predictions and data-backed forecasts lead the way. This evolution in decision-making processes helps businesses minimize risks and seize opportunities more confidently.

For instance, predictive analytics can help a company decide whether to expand into a new market, launch a new product line, or adjust marketing strategies. By analyzing data on consumer behaviors, economic conditions, and competitive landscapes, AI can provide scenarios that forecast the potential success of each decision. This capability allows companies to strategize with a clear understanding of potential outcomes, significantly reducing uncertainty and enabling more effective planning.

Challenges and Limitations

Despite its vast potential, predictive analytics has its challenges. Data quality is a primary concern; the old adage "garbage in, garbage out" holds particularly true in predictive analytics. Poor quality, inaccurate, or biased data can lead to predictions that are off the mark, potentially leading businesses astray. Additionally, the complexity of modeling can be a significant hurdle. The behavior of markets and consumers is not always predictable, and unexpected variables can lead to incorrect forecasts. The human element—irrationality, emotion, and unpredictability—adds another layer of complexity that can confound even the most sophisticated models.

Moreover, ethical considerations around privacy and consent are increasingly at the forefront as businesses navigate the use of personal data in predictive analytics. Balancing the benefits of predictive insights with the need to respect consumer privacy and trust is a delicate act that businesses must manage with care.

In conclusion, predictive analytics stands as a beacon of how AI is reshaping the business landscape, offering tools that anticipate the future and shape it. As businesses continue to navigate and leverage these technologies, the way forward involves not only embracing the power of predictive analytics but also addressing its challenges with innovation, responsibility, and an unwavering commitment to ethical practices. Moving forward into the next chapter, we will explore how this powerful tool is being integrated into more complex systems and environments, pushing the boundaries of what businesses thought was possible.

CHAPTER 8
ENGAGING WITH AI CULTURALLY AND SOCIALLY

As we delve into the expansive role of Artificial Intelligence in shaping our culture and society, it becomes evident that AI is not just a technological tool but a significant cultural force. This chapter invites you to explore the intriguing intersection of AI and creativity, particularly in the realm of art. Art, a reflection of human experiences and emotions, might seem like an unlikely field for AI integration. However, the collaboration between artists and AI reveals a fascinating blend of human ingenuity and algorithmic precision, opening new avenues for creative expression.

8.1 AI AND ART: EXPLORING THE INTERSECTION OF TECHNOLOGY AND CREATIVITY

Collaborative Creations

Imagine a scenario where an artist sketches the outlines of a landscape, and an AI system completes the painting, infusing it with colors and textures that the artist might not have envisioned. This is not a peek into a distant future but a reality today, where artists and AI collaborate to push the boundaries of traditional art forms. In these collaborations, AI does not replace the artist but rather works as a co-creator, offering new tools and possibilities that enhance the creative process. For instance, AI algorithms analyze vast datasets of styles and techniques, enabling them to suggest or even generate novel features in artworks that can inspire artists. Such partnerships might lead to creations that neither humans nor machines could have achieved alone, highlighting the complementary nature of human and machine collaboration.

AI as a Tool and Artist

While AI's role as a tool in enhancing artistic creativity is widely accepted, its position as an autonomous creator sparks debates on authorship and the essence of creativity. Can a machine be truly creative, or is it merely mimicking patterns it has learned from analyzing existing artworks? When AI creates art, it often does so based on parameters set by human programmers and learns from a corpus of human-created pieces. However, when AI produces something unexpected or novel, some argue that it is displaying genuine creative prowess. This raises intriguing questions about the nature of art and creativity, challenging the traditional view that associates creativity solely with human consciousness.

Impact on the Art Market

The emergence of AI in art is also reshaping the art market, influencing both the valuation and perception of artworks. AI-generated art has started to find its place in galleries and auctions, sometimes fetching high prices that rival those of established human artists. This shift is not without controversy, as it challenges traditional notions of value and originality in art. Critics argue that art created by AI might lack the depth and context that human artists bring to their work, while proponents believe that AI introduces a new aesthetic that can coexist with human-made art. As AI continues to make inroads into the art world, it is likely to provoke further discussions on what constitutes value and originality in art.

Ethical and Cultural Considerations

The integration of AI into art also brings up ethical and cultural considerations. One concern is cultural appropriation, where AI, trained on a global dataset, might create artworks that use elements from cultures without understanding or respecting their significance. Additionally, there are concerns about the authenticity of AI-generated art. Does an artwork lose its authenticity if the creator is not human? These questions are not just philosophical but have practical implications for copyright laws and the rights of artists. As AI becomes more prevalent in creative fields, it is crucial to navigate these ethical waters carefully to ensure that AI enhances rather than diminishes cultural diversity and artistic integrity.

Interactive Element: Reflective Journaling Prompt

Consider the role of AI in your own experiences with art. Can you recall an instance where you interacted with AI-generated content, perhaps in music, visual arts, or writing? Reflect on how that experience made you feel about the blend of technology and creativity. Was it different from experiencing human-made art? This reflection can help you better understand your personal stance on the evolving landscape of AI in art.

8.2 HOW AI IS SHAPING MODERN COMMUNICATION

In our interconnected world, communication is a vital bridge between cultures, communities, and individuals. Artificial Intelligence is playing an increasingly significant role in enhancing and transforming how we connect and communicate. Let's delve into how AI is breaking down language barriers, personalizing our media consumption, revolutionizing customer service, and navigating the challenges it brings along.

Language and Translation

One of the most profound impacts of AI in communication is its ability to break down language barriers that have historically hindered global interaction. Advanced translation services powered by AI are not just about converting text from one language to another; they're about creating opportunities for deeper understanding and connection. These AI systems, utilizing complex algorithms like neural machine translation, learn from vast amounts of text data to provide translations that are not only accurate but also contextually appropriate. For instance, platforms like Google Translate help users navigate websites, documents, and even real-time conversations in languages they do not speak. This capability is not just convenient; it's a bridge fostering international business, educational opportunities, and cultural exchange, making the world a smaller, more accessible place.

Personalization of Content

As you scroll through your social media feeds or watch videos on streaming platforms, AI is quietly working in the background, personalizing your content. This customization is made possible through AI algorithms that analyze your interaction patterns—

what you like, share, or spend time watching—and adjust the content you see accordingly. This AI-driven personalization shapes not only what information you consume but also how you perceive the world. While this can enhance your experience by keeping you engaged with content that interests you, it also raises concerns about creating echo chambers where diverse viewpoints are filtered out. Therefore, AI's role in media consumption is a double-edged sword that offers tailored experiences while potentially narrowing our worldviews.

AI in Customer Service

Customer service is another area where AI is making a significant impact. AI-powered chatbots and virtual assistants are now common on websites and in customer service operations, providing quick responses to customer inquiries and support issues. These AI systems are trained on data from thousands of customer interactions, enabling them to handle a wide range of queries with increasing sophistication. For example, if you've ever interacted with a virtual assistant to book a flight or get product recommendations, you've experienced AI in action. These systems can operate around the clock, providing a level of service consistency and availability that is challenging for human-only teams to achieve. However, while they offer efficiency, there are nuances in human communication that AI has yet to fully grasp, sometimes leading to responses that lack the empathy or understanding a human agent would provide.

Challenges in AI-mediated Communication

Despite the benefits, the integration of AI into communication channels is challenging. Privacy concerns are at the forefront, as these AI systems often require access to personal data to function effectively. There is an ongoing debate about the trade-offs between personalized experiences and privacy, with growing calls for regulations to protect user data. Additionally, the reliance on AI for communication can lead to a loss of personal touch—a critical element in human interaction. In customer service, for example, while AI can handle routine queries efficiently, complex or sensitive issues often require the empathy and understanding of a human agent. Balancing the efficiency of AI with the irreplaceable qualities of human interaction is a challenge that continues to shape the future of AI in communication.

In navigating these complexities, it's clear that AI is reshaping the landscape of communication in profound ways. From breaking down language barriers to personalizing digital experiences and transforming customer service, AI's role in communication is multifaceted and powerful. Yet, as much as AI enhances our ability to connect and interact, it also challenges us to rethink the ethics and impacts of mediated communication. As we continue to integrate AI into our communication systems, maintaining a balance between leveraging technology and preserving the human elements of connection will be crucial.

8.3 AI'S ROLE IN BUILDING SUSTAINABLE ENVIRONMENTS

When we talk about sustainability, it's often in the context of conserving natural resources and reducing our ecological footprint. Artificial Intelligence is playing a crucial role in this arena, not only by optimizing the use of resources but also by monitoring environmental changes that could have long-term impacts on our planet. AI's ability to process vast amounts of data quickly and accurately is a game-changer in environmental conservation and management.

AI's application in environmental monitoring is a prime example of technology as a force for good. Sensors equipped with AI are deployed across various ecosystems to collect data on everything from temperature and humidity to pollution levels and wildlife activity. This data is then analyzed to track environmental changes and trends. For instance, AI algorithms can predict changes in water quality or air pollution levels by analyzing historical data patterns and current measurements. This kind of monitoring allows for quicker responses to environmental threats, such as notifying cities about poor air quality days or adjusting water treatment protocols in real time to ensure safety standards are met. By providing a more comprehensive understanding of environmental dynamics, AI enables more effective management of natural resources, ensuring they are used efficiently and sustainably.

The concept of smart cities, where every device, home, and vehicle is interconnected and intelligently optimized for energy efficiency, is another area where AI is making a significant impact. In smart cities, AI is used to analyze traffic patterns to optimize signal timings and reduce congestion, which in turn can decrease vehicle emissions. Energy usage is another major focus; AI systems manage the distribution of electricity based on real-time demand and supply data, reducing waste and increasing efficiency. For example, street lights in an AI-driven smart city can adjust their brightness based on the presence of pedestrians, saving energy when full brightness isn't necessary. These applications of AI not only improve the quality of urban living but also contribute to the broader goals of reducing energy consumption and minimizing environmental impact.

Moving to renewable energy, AI's role becomes even more critical. The variability of renewable sources like solar and wind power has always been a challenge for energy grids. AI helps mitigate this by optimizing energy production and distribution based on predictive models considering weather forecasts, current energy production, and consumption patterns. In solar energy systems, AI can predict the optimal angle for solar panels throughout the day to maximize energy capture. For wind energy, AI algorithms analyze wind forecasts to predict power output, allowing for better integration into the power grid. These optimizations ensure that renewable energy sources are not just viable but are used in the most efficient manner possible.

However, the integration of AI into environmental strategies does not come without ethical considerations. One of the primary concerns is the potential for bias in decision-making processes. AI systems are only as good as the data they are trained on, and if this data is biased, the decisions made by AI could favor certain groups or regions over others. This is particularly problematic in environmental contexts, where unfair resource distribution can have dire consequences. Additionally, using AI to monitor and manage natural resources raises significant privacy concerns. The data collected can be highly sensitive, and there needs to be stringent measures in place to protect this information and ensure it is used ethically.

As we continue to explore AI's capabilities in fostering sustainable environments, it becomes clear that while AI offers powerful tools for environmental preservation and resource management, it also necessitates careful consideration of ethical implications. Balancing these factors is essential as we harness AI's potential to help us achieve a more sustainable future.

8.4 UNDERSTANDING AI'S INFLUENCE ON MEDIA AND INFORMATION

In the constantly evolving landscape of media and information, Artificial Intelligence plays a pivotal role, particularly in the way news is produced and consumed. AI's integration into newsrooms is transforming the journalism industry, automating tasks that once required extensive human effort and subtly influencing the fabric of media integrity and objectivity. Let's explore how AI is reshaping news production, the complexities of bias and manipulation in AI-curated content, the role of AI in combating misinformation, and the potential future shifts in media consumption.

AI in news production is not just about efficiency; it's about redefining what's possible in content creation. Automated journalism, where AI systems generate news articles from data, is becoming increasingly prevalent. These systems can quickly turn sports data into game reports or financial data into earnings updates, tasks that would take much longer if done by humans. For example, AI-driven platforms like Wordsmith by Automated Insights are used by major media outlets to produce content at a scale and speed impossible for human journalists alone. This capability allows news outlets to cover more topics and events, potentially increasing the diversity of news. However, the reliance on AI for content generation raises questions about the depth and nuance of reporting. While AI is excellent at working with structured data, it lacks the human journalist's ability to perceive context or engage in deep investigative reporting. As such, while AI can augment the capabilities of newsrooms, it is not a replacement for the critical thinking and ethical judgment that human journalists bring to the table.

The conversation about AI in media inevitably leads to the issue of bias and manipulation. AI systems are only as unbiased as the data they are trained on and the algorithms that drive them. If an AI system is fed biased news content, its outputs will likely perpetuate those biases. This can profoundly impact public opinion and democracy, as skewed AI-generated content might influence political views or manipulate public sentiment. Moreover, the algorithms curating personalized news feeds on social platforms can create echo chambers, reinforcing users' existing beliefs and potentially polarizing society further. The challenge here is to develop AI systems that can detect and mitigate bias, ensuring that the news they produce and curate promotes a balanced view and supports informed public discourse.

In the fight against misinformation, AI tools offer a beacon of hope. Fact-checking, a critical yet resource-intensive task, is being revolutionized by AI. Automated fact-checking systems can quickly verify claims by cross-referencing them against credible sources and databases, providing real-time assistance to journalists and the public. For instance, tools like Full Fact in the UK use AI to monitor live TV and online news streams to check statements against previously verified facts. This not only speeds up the fact-checking process but also enhances its reach, potentially curbing the spread of false information. However, as AI systems become more adept at identifying falsehoods, the techniques used to create sophisticated misinformation, such as deepfakes, are also advancing. This ongoing battle between misinformation and fact-checking technologies underscores the need for continuous improvements in AI capabilities to safeguard truth in media.

Looking to the future, the role of AI in media consumption is set to expand even further. As AI technologies become more sophisticated, they will increasingly shape how information is produced, distributed, and consumed. We can anticipate more personalized and interactive media experiences, where AI not only curates content to match our preferences but also interacts with us in more engaging and immersive ways. Virtual reality news, AI-generated interactive reports, and real-time news updates tailored to individual contexts could become the norm. These advancements could transform passive media consumption into an active, personalized experience, changing how we understand and interact with the world around us. As we stand on the brink of these transformative changes, it is crucial to navigate the advancements in AI with a critical eye toward maintaining ethical standards and ensuring that the proliferation of AI technologies enhances, rather than undermines, the foundational principles of journalism and public discourse.

8.5 AI IN GOVERNANCE: ENHANCING PUBLIC SERVICES AND POLICY

Imagine a city where traffic jams are rare, public health services are proactive, and policy decisions are made on solid, data-driven foundations. This is not a utopian dream but a practical reality shaped by integrating Artificial Intelligence into governance. AI's potential to enhance the efficiency and accessibility of public services is monumental. Through predictive analytics, AI is transforming healthcare by identifying potential health crises before they become epidemics. In public transportation, AI optimizes traffic flow, reducing congestion and improving commuter experience. For instance, AI systems analyze vast amounts of data from traffic sensors and public transit systems to predict and manage traffic patterns. By doing so, they help city planners implement dynamic traffic routing strategies that keep vehicles moving smoothly, saving commuters time and reducing the environmental impact of idling engines.

AI's role extends beyond logistical optimizations; it is becoming a pivotal tool in policy-making. Governments and public agencies are increasingly turning to AI to help sift through complex data and extract actionable insights. This process, known as data-driven decision-making, allows for policies that are not only responsive but also anticipatory. AI algorithms can simulate the potential impacts of policy decisions, helping policymakers see the effects of their actions before they are implemented. For example, AI models could simulate the economic impact of a proposed tax change, helping to identify potential benefits and pitfalls. This capability makes policy-making more strategic and less prone to unintended consequences, leading to more stable and effective governance.

However, the use of AI in governance also necessitates a strong framework for transparency and accountability. The decision-making processes influenced by AI must be transparent to maintain public trust. Citizens need to understand how decisions that affect their lives are made, and AI's role in this process should be clear. This is crucial because, without transparency, the risk of mistrust in AI-driven decisions increases. Accountability is equally important; there must be mechanisms in place to ensure that decisions made with the aid of AI are fair, ethical, and in the public interest. This includes establishing clear guidelines on the ethical use of AI and having robust auditing systems to monitor AI activities within public agencies. By addressing these needs, governments can harness the benefits of AI while maintaining the confidence and trust of the public.

To illustrate the successful implementation of AI in government operations, consider the case studies of Singapore and Estonia. Singapore, known for its efficiency, has integrated AI into several facets of public service, from predictive healthcare to environmental monitoring. AI-powered systems in Singapore analyze health data from the population to predict outbreaks of diseases like dengue fever, enabling preemptive action. In Estonia, AI is used to streamline government services through the e-Estonia initiative, where AI assists in processing public service requests, from tax filings to voting, making public services more accessible to all citizens. These examples not only highlight the successes but also the lessons learned, such as the importance of public engagement and the continuous evaluation of AI systems to ensure they remain aligned with public needs and values.

In the realm of governance, AI presents a powerful tool to enhance public service delivery, inform policy-making, ensure transparency and accountability, and ultimately improve the quality of life for citizens. As governments around the world continue to explore the potential of AI, the experiences of pioneers in AI governance provide valuable insights and guidance. By learning from these examples, other nations can implement AI strategies that not only optimize public services but also foster a more informed, engaged, and satisfied citizenry.

8.6 THE SOCIAL NETWORK OF AI: BUILDING COMMUNITIES AND SHARING KNOWLEDGE

In a world where Artificial Intelligence (AI) continually reshapes landscapes across various sectors, its influence on community building and education marks a significant stride towards a more connected and informed society. As AI permeates deeper into our lives, it fosters the creation of vibrant communities both online and offline. These communities range from online forums and social media groups to professional networks and special interest groups, each serving as a hub where ideas, resources, and experiences are shared among AI enthusiasts and professionals. Imagine a digital town square where beginners can learn from experts, and innovators can find collaborators to bring visionary AI projects to life.

These AI communities play a crucial role in collaborative learning. In these dynamic environments, members share their latest findings, discuss emerging AI technologies, and tackle complex problems together. This collaborative approach not only accelerates individual learning but also propels the collective advancement of AI knowledge. For example, platforms like GitHub and Kaggle offer spaces where individuals can contribute to open-source AI projects or participate in AI competitions. These activities aren't just about solving problems but about learning from each other's approaches and solutions, which can be more enlightening than working in isolation. Additionally, AI meetups and conferences, such as NeurIPS and AI Expo, provide physical venues for sharing insights and fostering collaborations, enhancing the community's collective expertise.

AI's impact extends significantly into the realm of education, transforming traditional learning paradigms through personalized learning platforms and AI-driven educational tools. These platforms utilize AI to adapt to individual learning styles and paces, providing personalized educational experiences that maximize student engagement and learning outcomes. For instance, AI-powered educational platforms like Coursera or Khan Academy use algorithms to suggest courses, adjust content difficulty, and provide customized feedback based on individual performance. This personalization makes learning more accessible and effective, catering to diverse educational needs and backgrounds and enabling a more inclusive educational environment.

Moreover, the importance of building inclusive AI networks cannot be overstated. Inclusivity in AI communities ensures a diversity of perspectives, which is critical in developing and applying AI technologies. Diverse teams are more likely to identify and address potential biases in AI algorithms, leading to more equitable and effective AI solutions. Initiatives like AI4ALL and Women in Machine Learning are exemplary, focusing on increasing diversity in AI by providing education and mentorship to underrepresented groups. These efforts help democratize AI, ensuring that its benefits are widely distributed and that its development reflects a broad spectrum of human experiences and needs.

In conclusion, as AI continues to evolve and integrate into various aspects of our lives, the role of AI communities in fostering collaborative learning, enhancing education, and promoting inclusiveness becomes increasingly significant. By participating in these communities, individuals not only contribute to the advancement of AI but also gain invaluable knowledge and connections that can propel their personal and professional growth. As we turn the page, we will explore the ethical dimensions and societal implications of AI, understanding how to navigate the challenges and opportunities it presents. This ongoing conversation will equip us with the insights needed to harness AI responsibly and innovatively, ensuring it serves the common good.

KEEPING THE GAME ALIVE

Now you have everything you need to understand and use AI to make your life easier, it's time to pass on your newfound knowledge and show other readers where they can find the same help.

Simply by leaving your honest opinion of this book on Amazon, you'll show other learners where they can find the information they're looking for, and pass their passion for AI and machine learning forward.

Thank you for your help. The understanding of AI is kept alive when we pass on our knowledge – and you're helping me to do just that.

CONCLUSION

As we reach the final pages of our exploration into the expansive world of Artificial Intelligence, it's essential to reflect on the transformative journey we've embarked upon together. From healthcare improving patient outcomes through predictive analytics to retail enhancing customer experiences with personalized shopping, AI's role across various sectors like finance, agriculture, home automation, and education has been nothing short of revolutionary. In the creative arts, AI has opened new avenues for expression and innovation, underscoring its dual nature as both a tool for human enhancement and a transformative force reshaping industries.

Our journey began with unraveling the basic concepts of AI and machine learning, laying a solid foundation that allowed us to appreciate AI's remarkable capabilities and its practical applications. As we ventured deeper, we explored the technological advancements and the ethical considerations crucial to responsible AI deployment. Issues such as data privacy, algorithmic bias, and the societal impacts of automation have highlighted the collective responsibility we share—developers, users, and policymakers alike—to navigate these challenges with fore-sight and integrity.

The field of AI is ever-evolving, and the importance of continuous learning cannot be overstated. I encourage you, the reader, to remain curious and proactive in engaging with AI. Whether it's by staying updated with the latest research, participating in online forums, or enrolling in courses, every step you take builds upon your understanding and skills in this dynamic field.

Now, I invite you to not just be a bystander but an active partici-pant in the AI revolution. Explore how AI technologies can enhance your career, enrich your hobbies, and simplify your daily routines. Start with small projects, perhaps building a simple chatbot or experimenting with AI in photography, and gradually expand your horizons as you gain confidence and expertise.

Moreover, as we harness the power of AI for personal advance-ment, let us also consider our broader societal responsibilities. The potential for AI to address pressing global challenges like climate change, healthcare disparities, and educational needs is immense. By contributing to the development of ethical, inclusive, and socially beneficial AI, we can help steer the future towards a more equitable and sustainable path.

Looking ahead, the future of AI offers a vista of opportunities where human intelligence is augmented by artificial counterparts, leading to unprecedented levels of innovation and problem-solving capabilities. This future is not solely about the technolog-ical feats AI can achieve but also about the choices we make as a society to use this technology wisely and compassionately.

I encourage you to share your AI journey with others. Whether it's a project you've completed, an insight you've gained, or simply how AI has touched your life, your stories can inspire and educate, fostering a community of learners who grow together.

As we close, remember that the story of AI is still being written, and each one of us has a role to play in its narrative. The future is not just something we enter; it's something we create. Let's build it with vision, creativity, and care, ensuring AI enhances not just our capabilities but our humanity.

Thank you for joining me on this enlightening journey through the world of Artificial Intelligence. Let's continue to explore, learn, and shape a future where AI and humans evolve together, creating a synergy that propels us toward a brighter, more inclusive tomorrow.

REFERENCES

What Is AI Technology? https://www.dummies.com/article/technology/information-technology/ai/general-ai/4-ways-define-artificial-intelligence-ai-254174/

The History of Artificial Intelligence: Complete AI Timeline https://www.techtarget.com/searchenterpriseai/tip/The-history-of-artificial-intelligence-Complete-AI-timeline

Five machine learning types to know https://www.ibm.com/blog/machine-learning-types/

20 Deep Learning Applications in 2024 Across Industries https://www.mygreatlearning.com/blog/deep-learning-applications/

AI in Healthcare, Where It's Going in 2023: ML, NLP & More https://healthtechmagazine.net/article/2022/12/ai-healthcare-2023-ml-nlp-more-perfcon

The Impact of AI Technologies in Retail - V-Count https://v-count.com/the-impact-of-ai-technologies-on-retail-examining-benefits-and-transformations-in-shopping/

AI in Personal Finance Management: A New Era of Smart Planning https://www.fanews.co.za/article/technology/41/general/1204/ai-in-personal-finance-management-a-new-era-of-smart-planning/38751

How AI in smart home tech can automate your life https://www.zdnet.com/article/how-ai-in-smart-home-tech-can-automate-your-life/

Dialogflow Tutorial for Beginners (2024) https://chatimize.com/dialogflow-tutorial/

The rise of machine learning in weather forecasting https://www.ecmwf.int/en/about/media-centre/science-blog/2023/rise-machine-learning-weather-forecasting

The top 8 AI tools for UX design (and how to use them) https://www.uxdesigninstitute.com/blog/the-top-8-ai-tools-for-ux/

6 Amazing Raspberry Pi AI Projects https://www.makeuseof.com/raspberry-pi-artificial-intelligence-projects/

A Practical Guide to Building Ethical AI https://hbr.org/2020/10/a-practical-guide-to-building-ethical-ai

Recent Growing Conflict Between AI and Data Privacy https://www.haynesboone.com/news/publications/recent-cases-highlight-growing-conflict-between-ai-and-data-privacy

How to Reduce Bias in Machine Learning - TechTarget https://www.techtarget. com/searchenterpriseai/feature/6-ways-to-reduce-different-types-of-bias-in-machine-learning

AI Will Transform the Global Economy. Let's Make Sure It Benefits Humanity https://www.imf.org/en/Blogs/Articles/2024/01/14/ai-will-transform-the-global-economy-lets-make-sure-it-benefits-humanity

Top 27 AI Skills to Have for Landing a Job in 2024 https://www.analyticsvidhya. com/blog/2023/08/ai-skills/

The best AI productivity tools in 2024 https://zapier.com/blog/best-ai-productiv ity-tools/

Empowering Small Businesses: The Impact of AI on Leveling the Playing Field https://www.orionpolicy.org/orionforum/256/empowering-small-businesses-the-impact-of-ai-on-leveling-the-playing-field#:

AI Community Conference - NYC 2024 https://www.communitydays.org/event/ 2024-06-21/ai-community-conference-nyc-2024

Top 10 AI-based BI and Data Visualization tools https://redresscompliance.com/ top-10-ai-based-bi-and-data-visualization-tools/

Is "Generative AI for Everyone" on Coursera Worth it? Review ... https://medium. com/javarevisited/is-generative-ai-for-everyone-on-coursera-worth-it-review-dbc72b9926d0

AI in Peer Learning and Mentorship - Hyperspace https://hyperspace.mv/ai-peer-learning/

7 Highly-Informative Websites to Stay Up-to-Date with the Latest AI News and Trends https://www.jeffbullas.com/ai-news/

The state of AI in 2023: Generative AI's breakout year https://www.mckinsey.com/ capabilities/quantumblack/our-insights/the-state-of-ai-in-2023-generative-ais-breakout-year

Autonomous Vehicles: Evolution of Artificial Intelligence and ... https://www. mdpi.com/2504-2289/8/4/42#:

AI in precision agriculture is expected to increase crop yields by 30% while reducing water usage by 25%, significantly impacting the agricultural economy. The global market for AI in Agriculture is expected to reach $4 billion by 2026, reflecting the growing economic impact of AI in this sector. https://camoinasso ciates.com/resources/ai-in-action-part-1/

AI and the Future of Space Exploration https://hackernoon.com/ai-and-the-future-of-space-exploration

Embracing Creativity: How AI Can Enhance the Creative Process https://www.sps. nyu.edu/homepage/emerging-technologies-collaborative/blog/2023/embrac ing-creativity-how-ai-can-enhance-the-creative-process.html

The Role of AI in Overcoming Cross-Cultural Communication Barriers in Global

Business   https://klizosolutions.medium.com/the-role-of-ai-in-overcoming-cross-cultural-communication-barriers-in-global-business-adbde45d3ac0

The Rise of AI-Powered Smart Cities | S&P Global https://www.spglobal.com/en/research-insights/special-reports/ai-smart-cities

Ethics of Artificial Intelligence https://www.unesco.org/en/artificial-intelligence/recommendation-ethics

THE AI IN BUSINESS ADVANTAGE

ADVANTAGE

HARNESS THE POWER OF ARTIFICIAL INTELLIGENCE TO DRIVE GROWTH, CUT COSTS, AND GAIN A COMPETITIVE EDGE

SAMUEL THORPE

INTRODUCTION

Consider this: A small retail company on the brink of closure due to fierce competition and rising costs found new life by adopting AI. By implementing AI-driven analytics, they unraveled customer preferences hidden in vast amounts of data. The result? Personalized marketing campaigns that doubled their customer retention rates and slashed operational costs by 30%. This is not a futuristic tale; it's happening today. AI is not just reshaping businesses but redefining them in ways unimaginable a few years ago.

The purpose of this book is clear. It's a practical guide crafted for entrepreneurs, visionaries, business leaders, and managers eager to integrate AI into their operations. In these pages, you'll find the tools to turn AI from a buzzword into a catalyst for growth and efficiency. My vision is to make AI accessible, showing you how to utilize its power to drive transformation in your business.

AI's impact on business today is monumental. According to recent studies, over 60% of companies have already integrated some form of AI into their operations. The global AI market is projected to exceed $500 billion by 2025. Industries like healthcare, finance, and retail already see significant returns on their AI investments.

These numbers are not just figures; they are a testament to AI's growing influence.

Central to this book is a practical AI implementation framework. This framework guides you step-by-step, from grasping AI basics to integrating sophisticated AI solutions into your business. Each step is designed to deliver clear takeaways and actionable insights. Whether you're taking your first steps with AI or looking to deepen your understanding, this framework will serve as your roadmap.

The book emphasizes business transformation. AI is more than a tool; it's a driver of change. It can streamline processes, enhance decision-making, and open new revenue streams. Companies that effectively use AI gain a competitive edge, positioning themselves as industry leaders.

To make the concepts relatable, the book employs scenario-based learning. Hypothetical scenarios illustrate AI applications in real-world settings. These scenarios are crafted to be actionable, ensuring you can relate them to your own business challenges.

Aligning AI initiatives with business goals is crucial. AI projects should not exist in isolation. This book provides strategies to ensure AI efforts align strategically with your business objectives. By aligning AI with your goals, you maximize its potential to drive growth and efficiency.

The book is structured into key chapters, each offering practical insights. We start with the basics of AI, then move on to its application across various industries. We delve into the framework for AI implementation and discuss business transformation strategies. Finally, we explore future trends and how to stay ahead in the AI race.

By the end of this book, you'll have a comprehensive under-standing of AI. You'll possess practical strategies for its implemen-tation and the insights needed to drive business transformation and innovation. You'll be equipped to turn AI into a powerful tool for growth.

As the author, I am deeply passionate about helping business leaders navigate AI's complexities. I am committed to providing accurate, actionable information you can implement immediately. This book is my way of sharing what I've learned, helping you achieve transformative growth in your business.

Join me on this journey as we explore the power of AI. Together, we will unlock its potential to drive change and innovation in your business. The opportunity for transformation is here, and it starts with understanding and applying AI to its fullest potential.

CHAPTER 1
UNDERSTANDING AI FUNDAMENTALS FOR BUSINESS

Have you ever wondered how some companies seem to anticipate customer needs with uncanny precision? A leading fashion retailer managed to increase its sales by 50% using AI. They utilized AI algorithms to analyze shopping patterns, predicting trends before they hit the mainstream. By stocking the right products at the right time, they maximized their revenue and customer satisfaction. This is just one example of AI's transformative power in business. As a business leader, understanding these fundamentals is not just beneficial—it's essential.

1.1 DEMYSTIFYING AI: A BUSINESS LEADER'S GUIDE

Artificial Intelligence, often abbreviated as AI, is essentially about creating machines that can simulate human intelligence. At its core, AI involves designing systems that can solve problems, learn from data, and make decisions. It's like giving a computer the ability to think and act like a human but with far greater speed and accuracy. The journey of AI began decades ago, with milestones such as the creation of the first neural network and the development of machine learning algorithms. Today, AI is not just a theory; it's a practical tool used across industries to drive efficiency and innovation.

AI's relevance in business cannot be overstated. Take marketing, for instance. AI enables businesses to deliver personalized customer experiences by analyzing vast amounts of customer data to predict preferences and behaviors. This means tailored marketing strategies that resonate with individual customers, increasing engagement and conversion rates. In operations, AI optimizes processes by identifying inefficiencies and suggesting improvements. Whether it's streamlining supply chains or managing inventory, AI helps businesses operate smoother and smarter, ultimately saving time and money.

Understanding AI's components is crucial for anyone looking to leverage its capabilities. At the heart of AI systems are machine learning algorithms, which allow computers to learn from data without explicit programming. These algorithms process data inputs and produce outputs ranging from simple predictions to complex decisions. The data itself is a critical component; it fuels these algorithms, allowing them to improve over time. Knowing how data is collected, cleaned, and utilized is vital for successful AI implementation.

While AI holds immense potential, it also has its limitations. On the positive side, AI offers predictive analytics, helping businesses forecast trends and make informed decisions. It automates routine tasks, freeing up human resources for more strategic work. However, AI's effectiveness is heavily dependent on data quality. Poor data can lead to inaccurate predictions, which can be costly. Additionally, ethical concerns, such as data privacy and algorithmic bias, must be addressed to ensure AI is used responsibly.

AI is not a magic bullet; it's a powerful tool that can significantly enhance business operations when understood and applied correctly. As you explore AI's fundamentals, keep in mind its potential to transform your business and the importance of a strategic approach to its implementation.

1.2 KEY AI TECHNOLOGIES: MACHINE LEARNING, NEURAL NETWORKS, AND MORE

Machine learning is often heralded as the engine driving the AI revolution. It is a subset of AI characterized by its ability to learn from data, adapt, and improve without explicit programming. Imagine a system that can classify customer feedback into positive or negative categories or predict future sales based on past data. These tasks are possible through two primary forms of machine learning: supervised and unsupervised learning. Supervised learning involves training a model on a labeled dataset, where the outcome is known, to predict future outcomes. This encompasses techniques like classification, where the goal is to categorize input data, and regression, which involves predicting continuous outcomes, such as stock prices. Unsupervised learning, on the other hand, deals with unlabeled data and seeks to uncover hidden patterns through clustering and association. For instance, a retailer could use clustering to group customers with similar buying habits, enabling targeted marketing campaigns. Machine learning's importance in business lies in its ability to provide insights, enhance efficiency, and ultimately drive decision-making grounded in data.

Neural networks, often synonymous with deep learning, are inspired by the human brain's architecture, consisting of interconnected nodes or neurons arranged in layers. These networks excel at capturing complex patterns in data, making them invaluable for tasks like image recognition and natural language processing. Consider a neural network that powers an image recognition system for a security firm, identifying potential threats in real time. Structurally, these networks operate through layers—input, hidden, and output—each performing distinct functions. The input layer receives data, hidden layers process this data through weighted connections, and the output layer delivers the result. These networks can learn intricate patterns, making them ideal for applications requiring a high degree of precision. For instance, in natural language processing, neural networks can power chatbots that understand and respond to customer queries with human-like fluency, enhancing customer service automation. The versatility of neural networks makes them a critical component in the AI tool-kit, enabling businesses to automate complex tasks and improve service delivery.

Beyond machine learning and neural networks, other AI technolo-gies are reshaping business landscapes. Natural language processing (NLP), for example, focuses on the interaction between computers and humans through language, enabling machines to understand, interpret, and respond to human language. Businesses use NLP in chatbots and customer service automation, providing efficient and personalized customer interactions. Another pivotal technology is computer vision, which interprets and processes visual data from the world. In manufacturing, computer vision systems inspect products for quality control, ensuring that only items meeting stringent standards reach consumers. These tech-nologies demonstrate AI's expansive reach and capacity to trans-form different business functions.

When comparing these technologies, it's important to recognize their unique strengths and applications. Machine learning's strength lies in its adaptability and ability to make data-driven predictions, while neural networks are unparalleled in processing complex data patterns. NLP shines in understanding and gener-ating human language, making it indispensable for customer-facing applications. Computer vision excels in tasks requiring visual data analysis, crucial for industries reliant on image and video data. Despite their differences, these technologies often overlap and complement each other. For example, a retailer might use machine learning for demand forecasting, neural networks for visual merchandising, NLP for customer inquiries, and computer vision for in-store analytics. Understanding these distinctions allows business leaders to choose the right technology for their specific needs, maximizing AI's potential to drive innovation and efficiency.

1.3 AI VS. TRADITIONAL ANALYTICS: UNDERSTANDING THE DIFFERENCE

Traditional analytics has long been a cornerstone in business decision-making, serving as a reliable method for analyzing past data to inform future strategies. It operates primarily through two main approaches: descriptive and diagnostic analytics. Descriptive analytics summarizes historical data, providing insights into what has happened in a business. For instance, a retail store might use descriptive analytics to track sales trends over the past year, helping them understand peak seasons or popular products. Diagnostic analytics, however, delves deeper by examining the causes of past outcomes. It attempts to answer the "why" behind specific trends, such as why sales dipped during a particular quarter. These traditional methods offer a retrospective view, guiding businesses by analyzing past performance. However, they often require considerable manual effort and time to sift through data and draw actionable insights.

The landscape of analytics has evolved with the advent of AI, bringing about significant advancements that enhance or even replace traditional methods. AI introduces predictive and prescriptive analytics, which revolutionizes how businesses forecast and respond to future trends. Predictive analytics uses AI algorithms to analyze current and historical data, enabling businesses to anticipate future events. For example, a logistics company can predict potential supply chain disruptions and take preventive measures. Prescriptive analytics takes this a step further by recommending specific actions based on predictions. It tells you not only what's likely to happen but also suggests the best course of action. This capability empowers organizations to make proactive decisions, optimize outcomes, and reduce risks. The speed and accuracy of AI-driven analytics provide businesses the agility to adapt quickly in dynamic markets, starkly contrasting to the slower, more manual processes of traditional analytics.

The differences between AI and traditional analytics become clearer when comparing key metrics such as accuracy, speed, and scalability. AI analytics excels in providing high accuracy due to its ability to process vast amounts of data and learn from it continuously. This results in more precise predictions and insights. Regarding speed, AI outpaces traditional analytics by automating data processing and analysis, delivering insights in real time rather than over days or weeks. When it comes to scalability, AI's capability to handle large datasets without a significant increase in processing time makes it far superior. Traditional analytics, while valuable, often struggle with scalability as data volumes grow, leading to slower processing and outdated insights. These differences can be visually represented in comparative tables that highlight AI's advantages in these areas, providing a clear picture of how businesses can benefit from embracing AI.

The practical implications of integrating AI analytics into business operations are profound. Real-time decision-making, enabled by AI, enhances both agility and responsiveness. Companies can respond swiftly to market changes, customer preferences, or operational challenges, making data-driven decisions on the fly. This capability is invaluable in today's fast-paced business environment, where delays can mean missed opportunities. AI's predictive power allows businesses to anticipate customer needs, optimize inventory levels, and improve service delivery, all contributing to a competitive edge. In contrast, limited by its retrospective nature, traditional analytics often leaves businesses playing catch-up. The shift from traditional to AI analytics is not just a technological upgrade; it represents a fundamental change in how businesses operate and compete.

Side-by-Side Comparison: AI vs. Traditional Analytics

- Accuracy: AI offers high precision through continuous learning, whereas traditional analytics relies on static models.
- Speed: AI delivers insights in real-time, while traditional methods can be time-consuming.
- Scalability: AI handles large data volumes efficiently; traditional analytics struggles with scalability.

This shift towards AI-driven analytics signifies a transformative change in business operations. As AI continues to evolve, its integration into analytics will likely deepen, offering businesses even greater insights and capabilities. The potential for innovation in this space is vast, opening new avenues for growth and efficiency.

1.4 AI TERMINOLOGY FOR EXECUTIVES: A GLOSSARY OF ESSENTIAL TERMS

Navigating the world of Artificial Intelligence requires familiarity with its language. Understanding key terms is crucial for leveraging AI effectively in business. Let's start with "Algorithm." An algorithm is a set of instructions or rules designed to perform a task or solve a problem. In AI, algorithms process data to identify patterns and make decisions. Consider how algorithms are used in e-commerce to recommend products. They analyze browsing history, previous purchases, and even social media activity to suggest items a customer might buy next. This ability to predict preferences enhances customer experiences and drives sales.

Another fundamental term is the "Artificial Neural Network." These are computer systems inspired by the human brain's structure and function. They consist of interconnected nodes, or neurons, that process information similarly to how our brains do. Neural networks are pivotal in tasks like fraud detection in finance. They scan vast amounts of transaction data to identify suspicious activity, minimizing financial risks. Such systems learn from each transaction, improving their accuracy over time. This continuous learning makes neural networks indispensable in sectors where quick, precise decision-making is crucial.

"Big Data" is a term frequently encountered in discussions about AI. It refers to the massive volumes of data generated every second from sources like social media, sensors, and transactions. This data is the lifeblood of AI, providing the raw material for analysis and insight. In healthcare, for example, big data enables predictive diagnostics. By analyzing medical records, genetic information, and lifestyle data, AI systems can predict disease risks and recommend preventative measures, ultimately improving patient outcomes.

Machine learning, another critical term, refers to the ability of machines to learn from data and improve over time without being explicitly programmed. In business, machine learning automates customer segmentation processes. It analyzes customer data to create segments based on behaviors, preferences, and demographics. This allows businesses to tailor their marketing strategies, ensuring they reach the right audience with the right message. Machine learning turns data into actionable insights, driving efficiency and effectiveness.

"Predictive Analytics" is a term often associated with AI's potential. It involves using historical data to forecast future outcomes. Retailers, for instance, use predictive analytics for inventory optimization. AI systems can predict inventory needs by analyzing past sales data, customer demand, and seasonal trends, reducing overstock and understock situations. This cuts costs and ensures customer satisfaction by having the right products available at the right time.

In healthcare, terminology like "Predictive Diagnostics" is becoming commonplace. AI systems analyze patient data to identify potential health risks before symptoms appear. This proactive approach enables early intervention, improving patient care and reducing healthcare costs. Similarly, in finance, "Algorithmic Trading" refers to using AI-driven algorithms to execute trades at optimal times, maximizing returns and minimizing risks.

To illustrate these terms in action, consider the case of a global bank using neural networks to enhance its fraud detection system. The network identifies anomalies that could indicate fraudulent activity by analyzing transaction patterns. This has significantly reduced fraudulent transactions, saving the bank millions. Meanwhile, a leading retailer employs machine learning algorithms to optimize its supply chain. These algorithms predict demand fluctuations, ensuring inventory levels align with customer needs, thereby reducing costs and improving service delivery.

Understanding these terms is more than just an academic exercise. It's about equipping yourself with the knowledge to make informed decisions about AI investments and strategies. As AI continues to evolve and permeate every aspect of business, fluency in its language will become an invaluable asset. Whether you're discussing data strategies with technologists or evaluating AI solutions, this glossary of terms will serve as your guide.

1.5 THE AI LANDSCAPE: CURRENT TRENDS AND FUTURE DIRECTIONS

In today's rapidly shifting business environment, artificial intelligence is no longer a distant prospect but a present reality, reshaping industries globally. One of the most significant trends is democratizing AI through cloud platforms. Businesses of all sizes now have access to powerful AI tools that were once the domain of tech giants. This shift has leveled the playing field, enabling small and medium-sized enterprises (SMEs) to compete more effectively by leveraging AI for insights and automation. Cloud-based AI solutions reduce the need for heavy infrastructure investments, allowing businesses to scale their AI capabilities with ease and flexibility. According to a survey, workers using AI tools save over 30 minutes daily, underscoring AI's role in enhancing productivity (GFT, n.d). This accessibility is crucial, as more SMEs are adopting AI to innovate and streamline operations, transforming sectors like retail and manufacturing. The increasing adoption in these businesses is not just a trend; it's a movement toward a future where AI is integral to business strategy.

Looking ahead, AI technology is poised to evolve in ways that will further entwine human and machine capabilities. Enhanced AI-human collaboration will define the next wave of AI innovation. Businesses will increasingly rely on AI to augment human decision-making rather than replace it. This symbiosis will manifest in AI systems that support employees by providing data-driven insights, allowing them to focus on creative and strategic tasks. Another future direction is AI-driven innovation in product development. AI will accelerate the design process and enable the creation of products tailored to specific consumer needs through advanced data analysis and predictive modeling. This trend will empower companies to deliver more personalized offerings, strengthening customer loyalty and opening new revenue streams.

These trends and future developments will have profound impacts across various sectors. In finance, AI's ability to conduct real-time risk assessments will transform how financial institutions manage and mitigate risks. AI will analyze market conditions and financial data with unprecedented speed and accuracy, enabling quicker, more informed decisions. This capability will be crucial in a sector where timing and precision often dictate success. In the supply chain sector, AI-driven autonomous logistics will revolutionize how goods are managed and transported. AI systems will optimize routes, predict maintenance needs, and automate various logistics functions, reducing costs and increasing efficiency. Companies that adopt these AI innovations will find themselves at the forefront of their industries, equipped to respond swiftly to market demands and disruptions.

To prepare for these transformative trends, business leaders must take proactive steps. Investing in AI talent is paramount. Companies should focus on hiring skilled professionals and upskilling existing employees to ensure they have the expertise needed to implement and manage AI systems effectively. Upgrading IT infrastructure to support AI applications is another critical step. Businesses should explore scalable, cloud-based platforms that facilitate seamless AI integration and ensure data security and compliance. Also, fostering an innovation culture will help organizations remain agile and receptive to new AI advancements. By encouraging experimentation and collaboration, companies can cultivate an environment where AI-driven solutions thrive, positioning themselves for long-term success in a technology-driven world.

1.6 AI MYTHS DEBUNKED: WHAT EVERY BUSINESS LEADER SHOULD KNOW

In business, myths about AI abound, often clouding judgment and hindering progress. One prevalent myth is the fear that AI will replace all human jobs, creating an economy devoid of human labor. This notion, while widespread, oversimplifies AI's role and impact. AI is designed to augment human capability, not supplant it. It takes over repetitive, mundane tasks, allowing humans to focus on creative and strategic endeavors. In customer service, for example, AI chatbots handle routine inquiries, freeing human agents to resolve complex issues requiring empathy and nuanced communication. This partnership between humans and machines elevates productivity and job satisfaction, illustrating that AI is not a threat but a collaborator.

Another common misconception is that AI is the exclusive domain of large enterprises with deep pockets and vast resources. This belief fails to recognize the democratization of AI, particularly through accessible cloud-based solutions. Small and medium-sized businesses increasingly adopt AI to streamline operations, enhance customer experiences, and drive innovation. A local bakery, for instance, might use AI to predict demand patterns, optimize their ingredient purchases, and reduce waste. The notion that AI is only for the big players is outdated, as technology has leveled the playing field, making sophisticated AI tools available to businesses of all sizes.

These myths often originate from media portrayals that sensationalize AI's capabilities and potential threats. Movies and news outlets tend to focus on dystopian narratives where AI dominates, overshadowing the more nuanced reality of AI as a tool for empowerment. Additionally, a lack of understanding among non-technical audiences perpetuates these misconceptions. Without a clear grasp of AI's practical applications and benefits, fear and skepticism flourish—this gap in understanding highlights the need for education and informed discourse about AI's true potential.

In the business environment, informed decision-making is crucial. Decisions based on myths rather than facts can lead to costly mistakes. Businesses that avoid AI due to misconceptions risk falling behind competitors who embrace it. Accurate information enables leaders to leverage AI strategically, reaping its benefits and gaining a competitive edge. This means not only understanding what AI can do but also recognizing its limitations and ethical considerations. A balanced perspective allows for responsible AI implementation, aligning with both business goals and societal values.

AI is a transformative force, but its impact depends on how it's perceived and applied. By debunking these myths, business leaders can approach AI with confidence and clarity. They can make strategic decisions incorporating AI as a growth and innovation tool, rather than a source of fear and uncertainty. This approach opens doors to new opportunities, empowering businesses to thrive in an AI-driven world. As we continue to navigate the complexities of AI, let's focus on the facts, embrace informed decision-making, and harness AI's potential to create a brighter, more efficient future.

CHAPTER 2
STRATEGIC AI ALIGNMENT WITH BUSINESS GOALS

I magine a bustling logistics company that was struggling to meet delivery deadlines and customer expectations. They faced a myriad of challenges, from route inefficiencies to unpredictable supply chain disruptions. Enter AI, equipped with predictive analytics and real-time tracking. By integrating AI into their operations, the company was able to optimize delivery routes, anticipate potential delays, and adjust their strategies on the fly. This strategic alignment boosted their efficiency and significantly enhanced their customer satisfaction levels. This scenario underscores a vital point: aligning AI with your business goals is not just advantageous; it's transformative.

As you consider incorporating AI into your business, starting with a solid foundation is crucial. This begins with crafting a clear AI vision statement. A well-defined AI vision acts as a beacon, guiding your organization through the complexities of AI integration. It ensures that everyone, from the boardroom to the front line, is aligned and motivated towards a common goal. The purpose of an AI vision statement is twofold. First, it guides your overall AI strategy, ensuring every initiative aligns with your broader business objectives. Second, it aligns teams and stakehold-ers, fostering a unified approach to AI adoption.

Creating an effective AI vision statement involves several compo-nents. At its core, it should articulate your mission, goals, and values related to AI. These elements resonate with your organiza-tion's broader vision, ensuring consistency across all levels of your business. Your mission statement should communicate the purpose of your AI endeavors, reflecting the strategic goals you aim to achieve through AI. Your goals should be specific, measur-able, and aligned with your business needs, providing a clear roadmap for AI implementation. Your values should emphasize ethical AI practices, underscoring your commitment to respon-sible AI use and innovation.

To craft a compelling AI vision statement, engage stakeholders in workshops and brainstorming sessions. This collaborative approach ensures that diverse perspectives are considered, fostering a sense of ownership and commitment among your teams. Use these sessions to explore the potential of AI in your business, identifying opportunities for innovation and growth. Once you have a draft, refine it by seeking feedback and making necessary adjustments. The goal is to create a clear, focused state-ment that inspires and guides your organization.

Real-world examples can provide valuable insights into crafting your AI vision statement. Take Google, for instance. Their vision for AI centers on enhancing user experience, leveraging AI to make their products more intuitive and user-friendly. This vision aligns with their goal of organizing the world's information and making it universally accessible. Similarly, Amazon's AI vision focuses on logistics optimization, using AI to streamline their supply chain and enhance delivery efficiency. These examples illustrate how a well-crafted AI vision can drive strategic alignment, ensuring that AI initiatives support and enhance business objectives.

Crafting an AI vision statement is not just a strategic exercise; it's an opportunity to articulate your organization's aspirations for AI. It's a chance to rally your teams around a shared goal, fostering a culture of innovation and collaboration. As you embark on this journey, remember that your AI vision statement should be a living document, evolving as your business and the AI landscape change. By aligning your AI efforts with your business goals, you position your organization for success in the AI-driven future.

Reflection Section: Crafting Your AI Vision Statement

1. Engage Stakeholders: Organize workshops to gather diverse perspectives.
2. Draft and Refine: Develop a draft and seek feedback for refinement.
3. Align with Business Goals: Ensure your AI vision supports broader business objectives.
4. Incorporate Ethical Practices: Emphasize responsible AI use in your vision statement.

Consider how these steps can be applied within your organization to create a clear and inspiring AI vision statement that aligns with your strategic goals.

2.1 ALIGNING AI WITH CORPORATE STRATEGY: BEST PRACTICES

Imagine a thriving retail company that decided to implement AI-driven analytics to predict customer buying patterns. Their initial excitement quickly turned into frustration when the results fell short of expectations. The problem wasn't with the technology itself but with a lack of strategic alignment. This scenario underscores the critical importance of aligning AI initiatives with your corporate strategy. When AI is in sync with your broader business goals, you maximize its return on investment and amplify its impact. This alignment ensures that AI projects support sustainable growth rather than operating as isolated efforts with limited benefits.

Strategic alignment is not just about technology integration; it's about embedding AI into the fabric of your corporate strategy. This requires a concerted effort to involve cross-functional teams in AI planning. By bringing together diverse perspectives from marketing, operations, finance, and IT, you ensure that AI initiatives address real business challenges and opportunities. This collaborative approach fosters a sense of ownership and commitment across the organization, increasing the likelihood of successful AI adoption. Regularly updating your AI strategy is equally important. As your business evolves, so too should your AI initiatives. This dynamic approach allows you to adapt to changing market conditions and technological advancements, ensuring that AI remains a driving force in your strategic arsenal.

Several frameworks and tools can assist in aligning AI with corporate goals. The Balanced Scorecard approach, for instance, is a strategic management tool that offers a comprehensive view of your organization's performance. It helps you translate your vision and strategy into actionable objectives, integrating AI initiatives into your overall business plan. Another helpful tool is the AI Strategy Canvas, which provides a structured framework for developing and executing AI strategies. This canvas helps you identify key AI opportunities, assess your organization's readiness, and prioritize initiatives that align with your strategic goals. These tools are invaluable in ensuring that AI projects are not only technically feasible but also strategically relevant.

Real-world examples illustrate the power of strategic alignment in AI implementation. Take Zappos, for example. The online retailer successfully transformed its customer service operations by aligning AI initiatives with its core value of delivering exceptional customer experiences. By integrating AI-powered chatbots and support systems, Zappos enhanced its service capabilities while maintaining a human touch. This alignment resulted in improved customer satisfaction and increased loyalty. Similarly, Walmart leveraged AI to optimize its supply chain operations. By using AI to predict demand fluctuations and streamline logistics, Walmart achieved greater efficiency and cost savings. These examples demonstrate how strategic alignment can unlock the full potential of AI, driving business transformation and delivering tangible benefits.

Case Study Exercise: Reflecting on Strategic Alignment

Reflect on a past AI project within your organization. Consider the following questions:

1. How well was the project aligned with your corporate strategy?
2. Were cross-functional teams involved in the planning process?
3. Did the project adapt to changing business needs?
4. What tools or frameworks were used to ensure alignment?

Use these questions to identify areas of improvement and apply these insights to future AI initiatives.

2.2 AI FOR COMPETITIVE ADVANTAGE: STRATEGIES AND TACTICS

Consider the digital landscape, where businesses constantly race to outdo rivals. In this environment, securing a competitive advantage through AI is not just desirable—it's imperative. One of the most potent strategies involves leveraging AI to deliver personalized customer experiences. By analyzing customer data, AI systems can predict individual preferences and behaviors, allowing businesses to tailor their offerings to meet specific desires. This personalization enhances customer loyalty and distinguishes a brand in a crowded marketplace. Imagine a retail business using AI to offer customized product recommendations based on a customer's browsing history and past purchases. The result is a shopping experience that feels personal and engaging, increasing the likelihood of conversion and repeat business.

Another essential strategy for gaining a competitive edge is data-driven decision-making. AI excels at processing vast amounts of data quickly, providing insights that human analysis might miss. This capability allows executives to confidently make informed decisions, whether it's adjusting marketing strategies or optimizing supply chain logistics. For instance, a company might use AI-driven data analysis to identify emerging market trends, enabling it to pivot its product offerings before competitors catch on. This proactive approach enhances responsiveness and positions the business as a leader in innovation.

To implement these strategies effectively, specific AI tactics must be employed. One such tactic is the use of AI-driven recommendation engines. These systems analyze user interactions and preferences to suggest products or services that align with individual tastes. E-commerce giants have mastered this tactic, using it to boost sales and improve user satisfaction. By integrating these engines into their platforms, businesses can create a seamless and intuitive browsing experience that keeps customers engaged and eager to explore further.

Predictive analytics is another powerful tactic that enables businesses to anticipate market trends and consumer demands. By examining historical data, AI can forecast future behaviors, allowing companies to prepare and adapt their strategies accordingly. This foresight is invaluable in industries where timing and market positioning are crucial. A company utilizing predictive analytics can adjust inventory levels based on predicted demand, minimizing waste and maximizing profitability. This strategic foresight ensures that businesses are not just reacting to market changes but anticipating them, preserving their competitive edge.

Innovation plays a pivotal role in maintaining this advantage. Encouraging a culture of experimentation allows businesses to continually explore new possibilities and refine their AI applications. This culture fosters creativity and risk-taking, leading to breakthroughs that can redefine an industry. Investing in research and development is equally crucial, as it equips companies with the latest technologies and methodologies to stay ahead of the curve. Businesses that prioritize R&D are often the first to adopt new AI advancements, setting benchmarks that others strive to reach.

Leading companies exemplify these strategies and tactics in action. Netflix, for example, uses AI to power its content recommendations, a feature that has become central to its user experience. By analyzing viewing habits, Netflix delivers personalized content suggestions that enhance user engagement and satisfaction. This AI-driven approach not only retains subscribers but also attracts new ones, reinforcing Netflix's position as a leader in streaming. Similarly, Tesla's use of AI in autonomous driving technology showcases innovation at its finest. By integrating AI into its vehicles, Tesla has revolutionized the automotive industry, setting new standards for safety and efficiency. These examples illustrate how businesses can leverage AI to compete and lead, transforming industries and setting new benchmarks for success.

2.3 BUILDING AN AI ROADMAP: FROM VISION TO EXECUTION

Consider the AI roadmap as your business's compass, guiding you through the vast and often unpredictable terrain of AI implementation. It provides clear direction and establishes milestones that keep your team aligned and focused on the objective. Without a roadmap, the risk of veering off course increases significantly, potentially leading to wasted resources or stalled projects. A well-crafted roadmap not only charts the path forward but also facilitates the allocation and prioritization of resources, ensuring that your team has what it needs at each stage of the journey. By establishing concrete goals and timelines, you can better forecast expenses, allocate human resources efficiently, and set realistic expectations for stakeholders. This strategic tool is essential for maintaining momentum and ensuring that each phase of your AI initiatives delivers tangible value.

The first step in creating an AI roadmap is assessing your current capabilities and identifying any gaps hindering progress. This assessment requires a critical look at your existing technology, data infrastructure, and skill sets. Determine whether your current systems can support AI technologies or if upgrades are necessary. Consider conducting a skills audit to evaluate whether your team has the expertise required to develop and manage AI solutions. This gap analysis will inform your subsequent steps, allowing you to plan interventions that bridge the gaps and lay a solid foundation for AI integration. Once you clearly understand your starting point, you can set both short-term and long-term AI goals. Short-term goals might include pilot projects to test AI's potential in a controlled environment, while long-term goals could involve full-scale implementation across multiple departments.

Access to practical tools and templates is crucial for structuring your roadmap. Gantt charts, for example, are invaluable for visualizing timelines and dependencies, offering a clear picture of when specific tasks need to be completed and how they relate to each other. This visualization helps manage workloads and anticipate potential bottlenecks. Another useful resource is an AI Roadmap template, which outlines key milestones and deliverables at each stage of implementation. This template serves as a guide, ensuring that no critical component is overlooked and that progress is consistently measured against predefined criteria. Utilizing these tools allows you to maintain clarity and focus throughout the AI implementation process, adapting as needed while keeping your ultimate objectives in sight.

Real-world examples provide inspiration and practical insights into how an AI roadmap can be structured effectively. Microsoft, for example, has developed a robust AI roadmap for its cloud services, focusing on enhancing its AI capabilities to deliver innovative solutions to its customers. Their roadmap emphasizes continuous improvement and adaptation, allowing them to respond swiftly to technological advancements and market demands. Similarly, Uber's AI roadmap for ride-sharing optimization showcases how a structured plan can drive efficiency and innovation. By prioritizing AI initiatives that improve route optimization and customer experience, Uber has maintained its competitive edge in the highly dynamic ride-sharing market. These examples illustrate the importance of a well-defined AI roadmap in guiding successful implementation, from vision to execution, ensuring that AI initiatives align with broader business objectives and deliver measurable results.

2.4 KEY METRICS FOR AI SUCCESS: MEASURING ROI AND BUSINESS IMPACT

As you integrate AI into your business operations, understanding how to measure success becomes crucial. The metrics you choose will guide your evaluation of AI's impact, helping you refine strategies and justify investments. Return on Investment (ROI) stands as a fundamental metric, providing a straightforward financial perspective on AI's effectiveness. ROI measures the financial return generated by AI initiatives relative to their cost. This metric helps determine whether AI projects are financially viable and worth the continued investment. By calculating ROI, you gain insights into the direct financial benefits of AI, such as increased revenue or cost savings, allowing you to make informed decisions about future AI endeavors.

Customer satisfaction scores are another critical metric, offering a glimpse into how AI affects your customer relationships. These scores reflect the quality of customer interactions and the extent to which AI improves the overall customer experience. By analyzing customer satisfaction, you can assess whether AI-driven services, such as chatbots or personalized recommendations, are meeting customer expectations. High satisfaction scores indicate that AI enhances the customer journey, potentially leading to greater loyalty and repeat business. Conversely, low scores may signal areas for improvement, prompting you to adjust your AI strategies to serve your customers better.

To effectively measure these metrics, adopting robust methodologies is essential. Pre- and post-implementation analysis clearly compares performance before and after AI deployment. This method involves collecting baseline data prior to AI integration and comparing it with post-implementation results. By examining this data, you can identify improvements directly attributable to

AI, such as increased efficiency or enhanced service delivery. Additionally, utilizing AI performance dashboards offers a real-time, comprehensive view of AI's impact across various business functions. These dashboards consolidate key metrics into a single interface, allowing you to monitor AI performance continuously and make data-driven decisions swiftly.

However, measuring AI success is not without challenges. One major obstacle is attributing results specifically to AI initiatives. In complex business environments, multiple factors can influence outcomes, complicating the task of isolating AI's impact. To overcome this, it's important to establish clear baselines and control variables wherever possible. Another challenge lies in ensuring data quality and consistency. Inaccurate or incomplete data can skew results, leading to misguided conclusions. To address this, prioritize data governance practices, ensuring that data used for measurement is clean, accurate, and representative of business realities.

Real-world case studies provide valuable insights into how companies measure AI success. Salesforce, for example, experienced a significant increase in sales by leveraging AI to optimize its lead scoring process. By analyzing historical sales data, Salesforce developed AI models that accurately predicted lead conversion rates, allowing sales teams to prioritize high-potential leads. This strategic use of AI not only improved sales efficiency but also demonstrated a clear ROI, justifying further investment in AI technologies. Similarly, General Electric (GE) achieved substantial cost reductions by implementing AI solutions in its manufacturing operations. Using AI to predict equipment maintenance needs, GE minimized downtime and extended the lifespan of critical machinery. This operational efficiency translated into tangible financial savings, underscoring AI's value in driving business impact.

These examples highlight the importance of selecting appropriate metrics and methodologies for measuring AI success. By focusing on critical indicators such as ROI and customer satisfaction and employing robust measurement techniques, you can gain a comprehensive understanding of AI's impact on your business. This understanding validates your AI investments and informs future strategies, ensuring that AI continues to drive growth and innovation across your organization.

2.5 AVOIDING COMMON PITFALLS IN AI STRATEGY

Navigating the landscape of AI integration can be fraught with challenges, and recognizing common pitfalls is the first step to avoiding them. One of the most frequent mistakes organizations make is embarking on AI projects without clear objectives and key performance indicators (KPIs). AI initiatives can become aimless without a solid framework, leading to wasted resources and ambiguous outcomes. It's crucial to establish specific, measurable, achievable, relevant, and time-bound (SMART) goals that define what success looks like for your AI projects. Another significant oversight is underestimating the importance of data preparation. AI systems thrive on high-quality data, and neglecting this aspect can severely undermine project effectiveness. Comprehensive data management and governance are essential to ensure that the data feeding into AI systems is accurate, complete, and free from bias.

To avoid these pitfalls, start by setting SMART goals for your AI projects. These goals provide a clear direction and measurable targets, allowing your team to track progress and make necessary adjustments. Investing in robust data management and governance systems is equally vital. This means establishing protocols for data collection, cleaning, and maintenance, ensuring that your AI systems have the reliable data they need to deliver consistent results. Implementing a strong data governance framework not only enhances data quality but also addresses compliance and ethical considerations, safeguarding your organization against potential risks.

Stakeholder engagement is another critical element in the successful implementation of AI. Involving stakeholders from the outset ensures that AI projects align with business needs and gain the necessary support for execution. Engaged stakeholders are more likely to provide valuable insights, resources, and buy-in, which are essential for overcoming obstacles and driving projects forward. Their involvement also facilitates alignment between AI initiatives and broader business strategies, ensuring that AI projects contribute to the organization's overall objectives. When stakeholders understand the potential impact and benefits of AI, they become champions of innovation, fostering a culture of collaboration and acceptance.

Real-world examples of AI project failures offer valuable lessons. Consider IBM Watson Health, where implementation challenges stemmed from overpromising capabilities without adequate preparation. The ambitious project to revolutionize healthcare with AI faced hurdles due to data integration issues and unrealistic expectations. The lesson here is the importance of setting realistic goals and ensuring that data systems are robust and compatible. Another example is Amazon's experience with AI-driven recruitment tools, where they encountered problems with bias. The AI system inadvertently favored specific demographics, highlighting the critical need for diversity and bias mitigation in AI training data. These cases illustrate the importance of thorough planning, continuous monitoring, and ethical considerations in AI projects.

As you prepare to integrate AI into your business, understanding these pitfalls and implementing strategies to avoid them will position you for success. Clear objectives, robust data management, and stakeholder engagement are foundational elements that will guide your AI initiatives towards meaningful impact. In the next chapter, we'll explore practical AI implementation frameworks that build on these strategies, providing a structured approach to integrating AI into your business operations.

CHAPTER 3
PRACTICAL AI IMPLEMENTATION FRAMEWORK

P icture this: a mid-sized retail company grappling with inventory management, lost sales due to out-of-stock items, and excess stock wasting valuable resources. Frustrating, right? Imagine the same company embracing AI to transform its supply chain operations. By assessing their AI readiness, they identified gaps in their data infrastructure and talent capabilities, paving the way for strategic improvements. This assessment was the catalyst, enabling them to align resources effectively, ultimately optimizing their inventory and boosting profitability. This is the power of understanding where you stand before diving into AI projects.

Assessing AI readiness is a crucial first step for any business looking to leverage artificial intelligence effectively. It involves evaluating your organization's current capabilities and identifying areas that need enhancement to support AI initiatives. This assessment helps pinpoint strengths and weaknesses, enabling you to allocate resources where they are needed most. It ensures that your AI projects align with your strategic goals, maximizing their impact and increasing the likelihood of success. By understanding your readiness, you can make informed decisions about the scope and scale of AI implementation, avoiding costly missteps.

Several tools and frameworks are available to assist in this evaluation. One such tool is the AI Maturity Model, which assesses your organization's AI capabilities across various dimensions, such as data management, technology infrastructure, and talent. This model provides a comprehensive view of where you stand and highlights areas for growth. Another helpful tool is the AI Readiness Index, which gauges your preparedness to adopt AI solutions. This index evaluates factors like strategy, infrastructure, and culture, offering insights into your readiness level. Source 1 reveals that only 14% of companies are fully prepared for AI, underscoring the importance of this assessment.

Conducting an AI readiness assessment involves several steps. Start with a gap analysis to identify discrepancies between your current state and where you need to be to support AI initiatives. This analysis will reveal areas that require investment or improvement. Next, evaluate your data infrastructure, ensuring it can handle the demands of AI applications. Consider whether your existing systems can support the necessary data processing and storage. Simultaneously, assess your talent capabilities by examining your team's skills and identifying any gaps that need addressing through training or hiring.

Case studies provide valuable insights into successful AI readiness assessments. Take the example of a mid-sized retail company that conducted a thorough evaluation of its AI readiness. They identified a need for more data integration and more AI expertise within their team. By addressing these gaps, they were able to streamline their supply chain operations, resulting in significant cost savings and improved customer satisfaction. Similarly, a financial services firm conducted a gap analysis to assess its readiness for AI adoption. They discovered that their data infrastructure needed enhancement to support AI applications. By investing in upgrades and training their team, they were able to implement AI-driven risk management solutions, reducing losses and increasing profitability.

Interactive Element: AI Readiness Self-Assessment Checklist

To help you get started, here's a concise checklist for assessing your organization's AI readiness:

1. Gap Analysis: Identify gaps between your current capabilities and AI requirements.
2. Data Infrastructure: Evaluate your systems for data processing and storage capabilities.
3. Talent Assessment: Assess your team's skills and identify training needs.
4. Strategic Alignment: Ensure your AI initiatives align with your broader business goals.

Use this checklist as a starting point to evaluate your readiness for AI projects. Consider involving key stakeholders in this process to gain diverse perspectives and insights.

3.1 BUILDING THE AI BUSINESS CASE: JUSTIFYING INVESTMENT

Imagine you're at the helm of a growing company, eager to tap into AI's potential. You know it's not enough to want to innovate; you need to present a compelling case to secure investment. A strong AI business case is your blueprint for success. It demonstrates the potential return on investment (ROI), translating technological possibilities into financial terms that resonate with stakeholders. This clarity is essential for gaining their buy-in, ensuring they understand the tangible benefits AI can bring to your organization. It's not just about the technology itself; it's about how it aligns with your strategic goals and delivers value beyond the initial expenditure.

Crafting a compelling AI business case involves several key components that collectively tell your story. Start with an executive summary, a concise overview that captures the essence of your proposal. This section should be compelling enough to grab attention, summarizing the main points that will be expounded upon later. Follow with financial projections and ROI analysis, where you detail the expected financial impact of the AI project. Use concrete figures and forecasts to illustrate how AI will enhance efficiency, reduce costs, or drive revenue growth. These numbers aren't just for show; they form the backbone of your argument, providing a clear picture of the anticipated returns.

Developing the business case requires a methodical approach. Begin with market research and competitive analysis to understand the landscape. Identify where AI can provide a competitive edge, whether by filling gaps in the market or enhancing existing capabilities. This research will inform your understanding of the potential use cases and benefits AI can offer your business. Next, pinpoint the specific AI applications that align with your strategic goals. This could be anything from improving customer service with chatbots to optimizing supply chain logistics. The key is matching AI capabilities with your business needs, ensuring each proposed initiative has a clear purpose and expected outcome.

Successful examples abound of organizations that have effectively built their AI business cases. Consider a healthcare provider that sought to implement AI to streamline patient care. By focusing on reducing wait times and improving diagnostic accuracy, they presented a case that highlighted both cost savings and enhanced patient outcomes. This dual focus on efficiency and quality was instrumental in securing the necessary funding. Similarly, a logistics company justified its AI investment by demonstrating how predictive analytics could optimize delivery routes, reducing fuel costs and improving on-time performance. These examples underscore the importance of aligning AI initiatives with business objectives, presenting a clear value proposition that stakeholders can rally behind.

Building a business case is both an art and a science. It requires distilling complex technological concepts into language that resonates with decision-makers. It's about painting a picture of what the future could look like with AI as a driving force while also grounding that vision in reality with data and projections. Your business case should inspire confidence, showing that you've considered the risks and rewards and that you're prepared to lead the charge into an AI-enhanced future.

3.2 VENDOR SELECTION: HOW TO CHOOSE THE RIGHT AI PARTNER

Selecting the right AI vendor is a pivotal decision that can make or break your AI project. Imagine embarking on a journey without a reliable guide; the path is uncertain. Similarly, choosing an AI vendor aligns your project with its goals, ensuring that your vision translates into reality. The right partner provides specialized expertise and cutting-edge technology, enabling you to harness AI's full potential. They bring invaluable experience, having navigated similar landscapes, which helps avoid pitfalls and accelerates the implementation process. This alignment is crucial because it ensures the vendor understands your unique business needs and can tailor solutions accordingly. Several criteria are paramount when evaluating AI vendors. First, consider their technical capabilities and expertise. Does the vendor have the necessary skills and knowledge to address your specific requirements? Look for vendors with a proven track record in your industry, as they are more likely to understand the nuances and challenges you face. Client testimonials and case studies can provide insights into their past successes and failures, offering a glimpse into their reliability and performance. Another critical factor is the vendor's ability to align with your strategic goals. They should not only provide technology but also act as a strategic partner, helping you achieve your long-term objectives.

The vendor selection process begins with requesting proposals and conducting evaluations. Start by reaching out to multiple vendors, inviting them to submit detailed proposals outlining their capabilities and how they plan to meet your needs. Evaluate these proposals meticulously, assessing how well each vendor aligns with your project goals. Pay attention to their proposed timelines, costs, and the technologies they intend to use. This evaluation phase is crucial for narrowing down your options to a shortlist of potential partners. Once you have a shortlist, perform due diligence and reference checks. This step involves verifying the vendor's credentials, speaking with previous clients, and assessing their reputation in the industry. Ensuring that the vendor has a solid track record and the resources to deliver on their promises is essential. Reference checks provide firsthand accounts of the vendor's performance, highlighting their strengths and weaknesses. This comprehensive evaluation process ensures you make an informed decision, selecting a vendor that aligns with your business needs and objectives.

Consider the case of a retail company that successfully partnered with an AI vendor for a project aimed at enhancing customer experience. The retailer sought a vendor with expertise in AI-driven personalization, enabling them to tailor their offerings to individual customer preferences. After a thorough evaluation process, they selected a vendor with a strong track record in the retail sector. This partnership resulted in a personalized shopping experience, increasing customer satisfaction and boosting sales. Similarly, a finance firm sought a vendor to implement AI for fraud detection. They prioritized vendors with experience in the financial industry and a history of successful fraud prevention projects. By choosing a vendor with proven expertise, they were able to implement an AI solution that significantly reduced fraudulent activities, safeguarding their assets and reputation. These examples underscore the importance of selecting the right AI vendor. The right partner provides technical solutions and becomes an integral part of your strategic vision, helping you achieve your goals efficiently and effectively.

3.3 PHASED IMPLEMENTATION: MINIMIZING DISRUPTION AND MAXIMIZING ROI

Implementing AI in phases is a strategy that can significantly mitigate risks and manage the inherent changes that come with technological transformation. By rolling out AI gradually, you can address potential challenges in manageable segments rather than being overwhelmed by the complexities of a full-scale implementation. This approach allows your organization to make iterative improvements, learning from each phase to enhance the next. It's akin to building a house brick by brick, ensuring stability and quality at each stage. This method reduces the likelihood of disruption and increases the chances of achieving a favorable return on investment, as it enables you to correct course early if needed.

To effectively implement AI in phases, begin with a pilot project. This initial step is crucial as it allows you to test AI applications in a controlled environment before scaling them across the organization. Select a specific area of your business where AI can significantly impact, such as customer service or inventory management. Develop a prototype and gather feedback from stakeholders to evaluate its effectiveness. This feedback loop is vital as it provides insights into what works and what doesn't, enabling you to make necessary adjustments. Once the pilot proves successful, proceed to scale it across the organization. This involves refining the AI models and integrating them into existing systems, ensuring they align with your strategic goals and deliver the desired outcomes.

However, phased implementation has its challenges. One of the main obstacles is maintaining momentum and stakeholder engagement throughout the process. As the initial excitement of AI adoption wanes, keeping teams motivated and focused on the long-term benefits is essential. Regular updates and clear communication about the project's progress can help sustain enthusiasm and commitment. Another challenge lies in ensuring scalability and integration. As you expand AI applications, you may encounter issues with data compatibility and system interoperability. To overcome these obstacles, invest in robust IT infrastructure and prioritize cross-functional collaboration, ensuring that all departments are aligned and working towards common objectives.

Real-world examples illustrate the effectiveness of phased implementation strategies. Consider a company that deployed AI in its customer service department. They began with a small-scale pilot, introducing AI chatbots to handle basic inquiries. They refined the chatbot's capabilities by analyzing customer interactions and gathering feedback, gradually expanding its role to cover more complex queries. This phased approach allowed them to enhance customer satisfaction without overwhelming their support staff. Similarly, a logistics company adopted a gradual rollout of AI-powered supply chain solutions. They started with predictive analytics to optimize delivery routes, then expanded to include inventory management and demand forecasting. This step-by-step implementation minimized disruptions, improved operational efficiency, and maximized ROI. These examples demonstrate how a phased approach can lead to successful AI adoption, transforming business operations and delivering tangible benefits.

3.4 DATA COLLECTION AND PREPARATION: ENSURING HIGH-QUALITY INPUTS

In the realm of AI-driven business, the quality of your data is paramount. Think of data as the fuel for your AI engine. High-quality data enhances the accuracy and reliability of AI models, enabling them to make precise predictions and informed decisions. Without it, even the most sophisticated AI systems can produce flawed outputs. Poor data quality can lead to biased algorithms, resulting in unethical practices and skewed results. This is why it is crucial to focus on data integrity from the onset, ensuring that what you feed into your AI systems is both clean and relevant.

Effective data collection begins with establishing robust data governance frameworks. These frameworks serve as the backbone for managing data quality, ensuring that data is collected, stored, and processed in a way that maintains its integrity. They set the standards for data accuracy, completeness, and consistency, providing a clear structure for data management. In addition, safeguarding data privacy and compliance is non-negotiable. With regulations like GDPR and CCPA in place, businesses must ensure that their data collection practices comply with legal requirements. This involves implementing data anonymization techniques and obtaining explicit consent from data subjects, safeguarding both the organization and the individuals whose data they handle.

Once you have collected your data, the next step is data preparation. This process involves cleaning and preprocessing the data to eliminate inaccuracies and inconsistencies. Data cleaning is about removing duplicates, correcting errors, and filling in missing values, ensuring the data set is as accurate as possible. Preprocessing goes a step further by formatting the data into a structure that AI algorithms can easily analyze. This may involve normalizing data, transforming categorical variables into numerical values, or scaling features to a common range. Following this, data integration ensures that data from disparate sources is combined into a cohesive set, while transformation adapts it into formats suitable for analysis.

Consider the telecommunications company that faced significant customer churn due to inaccurate billing records. By implementing a rigorous data quality improvement initiative, they were able to clean and preprocess their data effectively. This involved correcting billing errors and consolidating customer information from various departments. As a result, their AI-driven customer retention strategies became more precise, reducing churn rates significantly and enhancing customer satisfaction. Similarly, an e-commerce platform sought to integrate data from multiple sales channels to gain a comprehensive view of customer behavior. By successfully integrating and transforming this data, they developed targeted marketing campaigns that increased conversion rates.

Visual Element: Data Preparation Infographic

To illustrate the data preparation process, consider this simplified infographic:

1. Data Cleaning: Remove duplicates, correct errors, and fill missing values.
2. Data Preprocessing: Normalize and scale data and transform variables.
3. Data Integration: Combine data from different sources into a cohesive set.
4. Data Transformation: Adapt data formats for AI analysis.

This step-by-step approach ensures that your data is ready for AI applications, boosting model accuracy and reliability.

3.5 INTEGRATING AI WITH EXISTING SYSTEMS: OVERCOMING TECHNICAL CHALLENGES

Seamlessly integrating AI with your existing systems is crucial for extracting maximum value from AI initiatives. By leveraging your current infrastructure and data, you can enhance AI's effectiveness without reinventing the wheel. This integration minimizes disruptions to your business operations, allowing you to continue delivering value to customers while adopting cutting-edge technology. The goal is to blend AI capabilities with your existing processes, creating a harmonious environment where new and old technologies complement each other. This synergy enhances operational efficiency and accelerates the realization of AI's benefits.

However, integrating AI is not without its challenges. Data silos often pose significant hurdles, where critical information is stored in disparate systems that don't communicate with each other. This lack of interoperability can hinder AI's ability to access and analyze comprehensive datasets, limiting its effectiveness. Additionally, legacy systems may need more flexibility to accommodate modern AI applications, creating bottlenecks in data flow and processing. These constraints can impede integration, leading to delays and increased costs. The challenge lies in bridging these gaps to ensure AI can operate seamlessly within your existing infrastructure.

To overcome these challenges, consider implementing application programming interfaces (APIs) and middleware. APIs serve as bridges that allow different software systems to communicate, facilitating data flow between AI applications and existing systems. Middleware acts as an intermediary layer that enables integration without requiring extensive modifications to your legacy systems. By deploying these solutions, you can enhance interoperability, ensuring AI has access to the data it needs to function effectively. Additionally, upgrading your legacy systems and infrastructure is another viable solution. This may involve modernizing outdated software or investing in scalable cloud platforms that support AI applications.

Examples from the field highlight the success of these integration strategies. A major corporation faced challenges integrating AI with its legacy enterprise resource planning (ERP) system. By implementing a robust middleware solution, they were able to connect their AI applications with the ERP system, enabling seamless data exchange and process automation. This integration not only improved efficiency but also enhanced decision-making by providing real-time insights into business operations. Similarly, a company in the customer service sector utilized middleware to link AI with its customer relationship management (CRM) system. This integration allowed them to leverage AI-driven insights for personalized customer interactions, improving service quality and customer satisfaction.

As you consider integrating AI with your existing systems, remember that the goal is to create a cohesive environment where AI complements and enhances your current capabilities. By addressing technical challenges with strategic solutions, you can unlock AI's full potential, transforming your operations and delivering greater value to your customers. This integration is a crucial step in your AI journey, setting the stage for future advancements and innovation.

CHAPTER 4
REAL-WORLD AI APPLICATIONS AND CASE STUDIES

I magine browsing online and receiving recommendations that feel tailor-made just for you—books you might want to read, music you might enjoy, or clothes that fit your style. It's as if the website knows you personally. This isn't magic; it's the power of AI in action, transforming how businesses engage with their customers. For entrepreneurs and business leaders, leveraging AI in marketing can revolutionize the way you connect with your audience, turning potential interest into genuine loyalty.

AI's role in modern marketing is profound, acting as a catalyst that enhances strategies and drives deeper customer engagement. It starts with customer segmentation and targeting, where AI analyzes data to identify distinct customer groups based on behavior, preferences, and demographics. This segmentation allows businesses to target their marketing efforts more accurately, delivering the right message to the right audience at the right time. Predictive analytics further enriches this approach by forecasting future customer behaviors. By understanding likely future actions, businesses can tailor their offerings, turning predictions into personalized experiences that resonate with each customer.

Creating personalized marketing campaigns using AI involves a detailed process that begins with data collection and analysis. Businesses gather data from various sources—social media interactions, purchase history, and even browsing habits. This data is then analyzed to uncover patterns and insights about customer preferences. With these insights, AI helps in crafting personalized content recommendations. Imagine an online retailer using AI to suggest clothing items based on a user's past purchases and current fashion trends. This personalized approach enhances the shopping experience and increases conversion rates by ensuring customers are more likely to find what they seek.

Real-world cases exemplify the successful application of AI in marketing. Netflix, known for its personalized content recommendations, uses AI to analyze viewing habits and suggest shows and movies tailored to individual tastes. This personalization keeps users engaged, increasing viewing time and subscriber retention. Similarly, Sephora employs AI-powered beauty assistants that provide personalized product recommendations and tutorials based on customer preferences and feedback. This AI-driven service enhances the customer experience, turning routine shopping into a personalized journey that feels unique and engaging.

AI also significantly impacts customer insights, providing businesses with more profound and more actionable data. With AI, you can conduct real-time customer feedback analysis, allowing you to respond swiftly to customer needs and preferences. This immediate feedback loop helps businesses adapt their strategies quickly, ensuring they remain relevant and responsive. Furthermore, AI enhances predictions of customer lifetime value by analyzing patterns in customer engagement and spending. This insight enables businesses to identify high-value customers and tailor strategies to nurture these relationships, ultimately boosting profitability.

Spotify's use of AI, as highlighted in SOURCE 1, provides another compelling example. Their AI-driven Spotify Wrapped feature analyzes user data to create personalized summaries and playlists. This engages users and enhances brand visibility and user loyalty, with 156 million users engaging with the feature in 2022 alone. The success of Spotify Wrapped demonstrates how AI can transform user interaction into a powerful marketing tool, driving brand engagement and customer satisfaction through personalized experiences.

Reflection Section: Applying AI to Your Marketing Strategy

1. Identify Data Sources: List the data sources you currently use for customer insights (e.g., social media, website analytics).
2. Analyze Customer Behavior: Consider how AI could improve your understanding of customer preferences and behaviors.
3. Explore AI Tools: Research AI tools that could enhance your marketing efforts, focusing on those that offer predictive analytics or personalization features.
4. Set Objectives: Define clear goals for integrating AI into your marketing strategy. What outcomes do you hope to achieve?

Consider how these steps can help you harness AI's potential to create more effective and personalized marketing campaigns that drive engagement and growth.

4.1 AI IN FINANCE: FRAUD DETECTION AND RISK MANAGEMENT

In today's digital world, financial institutions face the relentless challenge of fraud, with cybercriminals constantly evolving their tactics. AI has become indispensable in this battle, revolutionizing how banks and other financial entities detect and prevent fraudulent activities. Real-time transaction monitoring is one of the most significant contributions of AI to fraud detection. With its ability to analyze vast amounts of data at lightning speed, AI can spot suspicious patterns as they occur, allowing institutions to respond instantly. This immediacy is crucial in preventing fraudulent transactions and protecting the institution and its customers from potential losses. AI excels in pattern recognition and anomaly detection, identifying unusual behaviors that might indicate fraud. By continuously learning from new data, AI systems can distinguish between normal and suspicious activities, adapting to new fraud tactics more swiftly than traditional methods ever could.

Risk management in finance has also seen a transformation with AI at the helm. Machine learning, a subset of AI, plays a pivotal role in credit scoring, assessing the creditworthiness of applicants with a level of accuracy and fairness that was previously unattainable. Machine learning models can predict an individual's ability to repay loans more accurately than conventional methods by analyzing a wide array of data points, including transaction histories and spending behaviors. This precision reduces default rates and ensures that lending decisions are both profitable and responsible. Predictive analytics, another AI technique, is invaluable for market risk assessment. By analyzing historical market data and current economic indicators, AI systems can forecast potential market shifts, enabling financial institutions to develop proactive strategies to mitigate risks. This foresight is crucial in maintaining stability and protecting assets in an industry where uncertainty is a constant companion.

Real-world applications of AI in finance showcase its profound impact. Take PayPal, for instance, which utilizes AI-driven fraud prevention systems to secure its vast network of online transactions. By implementing machine learning algorithms, PayPal can detect fraudulent behavior in real-time, significantly reducing the incidence of fraud and enhancing customer trust. Similarly, JPMorgan Chase employs an AI-based risk management platform to navigate the complexities of financial risk. This platform analyzes market trends and economic data, providing insights that guide strategic decision-making, ensuring that the bank remains resilient in the face of market fluctuations. These examples attest to AI's transformative capability in safeguarding financial operations and enhancing the robustness of decision-making processes.

Incorporating AI into financial decision-making processes has brought about a paradigm shift, improving the precision and reliability of these decisions. AI enhances the accuracy of fraud detection, reducing the likelihood of false positives that can inconvenience customers and strain resources. This precision ensures that genuine transactions proceed smoothly, maintaining customer satisfaction and trust. Furthermore, AI's role in risk assessments ensures that decisions are grounded in comprehensive data analysis, reducing the margin for error. Faster and more reliable risk assessments allow institutions to respond to market changes swiftly, capitalizing on opportunities and mitigating threats before they escalate. This agility is crucial in the fast-paced financial sector, where the ability to make informed decisions quickly can mean the difference between profit and loss, success and failure.

Interactive Element: Fraud Awareness Checklist

1. Understand Key Indicators: Familiarize yourself with common signs of fraudulent activities in financial transactions.
2. Evaluate AI Solutions: Assess AI tools available for fraud detection and risk management in your organization.
3. Conduct Regular Reviews: Implement regular reviews of transaction monitoring systems to ensure they adapt to new fraud patterns.
4. Engage Stakeholders: Involve key stakeholders in discussions about AI implementation to enhance awareness and buy-in.

Consider these steps as you explore AI's potential to enhance your financial institution's security and decision-making capabilities.

4.2 AI IN OPERATIONS: OPTIMIZING SUPPLY CHAIN AND LOGISTICS

In the fast-paced world of supply chains and logistics, efficiency is king. AI technologies have become indispensable in streamlining these processes, transforming how businesses manage their operations. At the heart of supply chain optimization lies demand forecasting and inventory management. AI analyzes historical sales data, market trends, and even external factors like weather patterns to predict future demand with remarkable accuracy. This foresight allows businesses to adjust their inventory levels proactively, ensuring that they neither overstock nor understock. The result is a more efficient supply chain that minimizes waste and maximizes profitability, all while maintaining high service levels. AI's role continues beyond there. It extends to route optimization and logistics planning, where AI algorithms determine the most efficient routes for delivering goods. By considering variables such as traffic patterns, delivery windows, and fuel costs, AI enables companies to optimize their logistics networks, reducing delivery times and costs. This optimization ensures that goods reach their destinations faster and at a lower cost, enhancing customer satisfaction.

The techniques used in logistics optimization are a testament to AI's prowess. Predictive analytics is vital in demand forecasting, allowing businesses to anticipate customer needs and adjust their supply chains accordingly. By analyzing vast datasets, AI systems can identify patterns and trends that might elude human analysts. This capability ensures that inventory levels are aligned with demand, reducing the risk of stockouts or excess inventory. Machine learning, another critical technique, is used for route optimization. It analyzes past delivery data, learns from it, and suggests the most efficient routes for future deliveries. This approach not only saves time and fuel but also reduces the environmental impact of logistics operations. By continually learning and adapting, AI keeps logistics networks running smoothly and efficiently.

Real-world examples illustrate the transformative power of AI in supply chain and logistics. Amazon, a pioneer in AI-powered supply chain management, uses AI to streamline its vast network of warehouses and distribution centers. Through advanced robotics and machine learning algorithms, Amazon predicts demand, optimizes inventory placement, and automates the picking and packing processes. This integration of AI into their supply chain has enabled Amazon to offer rapid delivery times, setting new standards in customer service. Similarly, DHL employs AI-driven logistics optimization to enhance its operations. By leveraging AI for route planning and demand forecasting, DHL reduces delivery times and minimizes operational costs, improving customer satisfaction and a stronger competitive position.

The impact of AI on operational efficiency is profound, driving significant improvements in performance while reducing costs. AI reduces inventory holding costs by ensuring inventory levels are closely aligned with actual demand, minimizing the need for expensive warehousing. It also improves delivery times by optimizing routes and logistics processes, ensuring that goods reach customers quickly and efficiently. This enhancement in operational efficiency translates to higher customer satisfaction, as businesses can meet customer expectations consistently and reliably. AI's ability to streamline operations also frees up resources, allowing companies to focus on strategic initiatives and innovation. As businesses continue to adopt AI technologies, the potential for further improvements in operational efficiency and customer satisfaction is immense, promising a future where supply chains are more agile, responsive, and sustainable than ever before.

4.3 AI IN HR: ENHANCING RECRUITMENT AND EMPLOYEE ENGAGEMENT

AI is reshaping the recruitment landscape in innovative and efficient ways. Imagine the traditional recruitment process—sifting through countless resumes, conducting numerous interviews, and hoping to select the right candidate. AI changes this narrative by automating resume screening, allowing you to focus on candidates who truly fit the role. With AI, resumes are assessed in seconds, highlighting qualifications that match job requirements and filtering out those that don't. This automation speeds up the hiring process, reduces human error, and ensures a more objective review of applicants. Beyond initial screening, AI employs predictive analytics to assess candidate fit. By analyzing data from past hires, AI systems can predict which candidates are likely to succeed in specific roles, thereby improving the quality of hires and reducing turnover. This predictive capability ensures that you not only hire faster but also hire smarter, aligning talent acquisition with long-term business goals.

Once you have the right team in place, keeping them engaged and satisfied is paramount. AI steps in here as well, offering innovative techniques to enhance employee engagement and retention. Sentiment analysis is a powerful tool AI uses to gauge employee feedback. By analyzing texts from surveys, emails, and even social media, AI can detect underlying emotions and sentiments. This real-time feedback provides insights into employee morale and satisfaction, allowing you to address issues before they escalate. Moreover, predictive analytics helps you foresee potential employee turnover. By examining patterns such as declining performance or reduced engagement, AI can alert you to employees at risk of leaving, allowing you to intervene and retain valuable talent. These methodologies transform HR from reactive to proactive, ensuring that employee well-being and engagement remain at the forefront.

Unilever's approach to recruitment is a prime example of AI's transformative impact in HR. By partnering with Pymetrics, Unilever developed an AI-driven recruitment platform that evaluates candidates through online games assessing various skills and attributes. This innovative process reduced the time spent on initial assessments and enhanced the accuracy of candidate selection by matching profiles with those of successful employees. The AI system even provides feedback to all applicants, fostering a positive candidate experience. Similarly, IBM's AI-powered employee engagement platform uses AI to analyze employee interactions and feedback to tailor personalized development and engagement strategies. The result is a more satisfied and committed workforce, contributing to higher retention rates.

The impact of AI on HR practices is profound and multifaceted. The use of AI results in faster and more efficient hiring processes. Automated systems handle repetitive tasks, freeing HR professionals to focus on strategic functions like talent development and organizational planning. This efficiency reduces time-to-hire and ensures businesses are not missing out on top talent due to slow hiring processes. Additionally, AI enhances employee satisfaction and retention by providing insights that help tailor engagement strategies to individual needs. Businesses create a more supportive and motivating work environment by addressing concerns promptly and offering personalized development opportunities. This focus on individual needs not only boosts morale but also fosters loyalty, reducing turnover and the associated costs. AI transforms HR into a strategic partner in business, driving performance and growth through enhanced recruitment and engagement.

4.4 AI IN CUSTOMER SERVICE: CHATBOTS AND BEYOND

Navigating the complexities of customer service is a challenge many businesses face, but AI is transforming how we approach it. At the forefront are AI-powered chatbots, which have revolutionized customer support by providing instant, 24/7 assistance to users. These chatbots handle various tasks, from answering frequently asked questions to processing orders and troubleshooting technical issues. The beauty of AI chatbots lies in their ability to learn and adapt over time, becoming more efficient with each interaction. They reduce human agents' workload and ensure customers receive prompt service, enhancing overall satisfaction. Predictive analytics further complements this by analyzing customer interactions to anticipate issues before they arise. By identifying patterns in customer behavior, AI can suggest proactive solutions, thus preventing potential problems and improving the customer experience.

Implementing AI in customer service involves a series of strategic steps that begin with designing and deploying AI chatbots. This process requires understanding customer needs and determining how chatbots can address them effectively. Start by mapping out common customer queries and deciding which ones can be automated. Once you have a clear picture, develop a chatbot with a user-friendly interface that aligns with your brand's voice and personality. Deploy it on platforms where your customers frequently interact, such as your website or social media channels. The next step is integrating AI with existing customer service platforms. This integration ensures a seamless flow of information between AI systems and human agents, allowing for a cohesive customer experience. It also enables AI to access historical customer data, providing context for interactions and personalizing responses. Testing and refining the chatbot's capabilities are crucial to ensure it meets your service standards and adapts to changing customer needs.

Real-world examples illustrate the transformative impact of AI in customer service. H&M, the global fashion retailer, uses AI-driven chatbots to enhance customer support. These chatbots assist with everything from handling returns to offering style advice and providing customers with quick and personalized service. Implementing AI chatbots has streamlined H&M's customer support operations, freeing human agents to focus on more complex inquiries. American Express offers another compelling example with its AI-powered customer support system. By leveraging AI, American Express provides personalized financial advice to customers, helping them manage their accounts more effectively. The system analyzes customer data to offer tailored recommendations, enhancing the user experience and building trust. These cases highlight how AI can elevate customer service, making it more efficient and responsive.

The impact of AI on customer satisfaction is significant, as it addresses one of the most critical aspects of service: speed. Faster response times mean customers spend less time waiting for assistance, leading to higher satisfaction levels. AI also improves issue resolution by accurately diagnosing problems and suggesting effective solutions. This reduces the need for multiple interactions, streamlining the support process and enhancing customer convenience. Beyond efficiency, AI enhances personalization in customer interactions. By analyzing past behaviors and preferences, AI provides tailored responses and recommendations, making customers feel valued and understood. This personalized approach fosters stronger customer relationships and encourages loyalty, as customers are more likely to return to businesses that offer attentive and individualized service.

4.5 AI IN PRODUCT DEVELOPMENT: ACCELERATING INNOVATION

In the fast-paced world of product development, staying ahead of the competition requires innovation and speed. AI has emerged as a powerful ally in this quest, driving innovation and accelerating the development process. Imagine AI as a tool that transforms ideas into tangible products with unprecedented efficiency. AI-powered design and prototyping allow businesses to explore a multitude of design possibilities quickly. Through generative design, AI algorithms create hundreds of design variations based on specific parameters, such as material constraints and performance requirements. This not only reduces the time spent in the ideation phase but also enhances creativity by suggesting designs that might not occur to human designers. These AI-generated designs can then be prototyped rapidly, allowing teams to iterate and refine their products at a pace that was previously unimaginable.

Beyond design, AI plays a crucial role in understanding market trends and consumer needs, significantly influencing product development. Predictive analytics, powered by AI, analyzes vast datasets to forecast market trends and consumer preferences. This insight is invaluable for businesses seeking to align their products with market demands, ensuring their development meets consumer expectations. By leveraging AI to anticipate trends, companies can make informed decisions about product features, pricing strategies, and marketing approaches. This proactive stance not only reduces the risk of product failure but also positions companies to capitalize on emerging opportunities, securing a competitive edge in their industry.

Several companies have successfully implemented AI in their product development processes, demonstrating its transformative potential. Autodesk, for instance, has integrated AI-driven generative design tools into its workflow. These tools allow designers to input specific criteria and let AI explore a vast array of design possibilities. The result is innovative designs that optimize functionality and aesthetics, significantly enhancing product quality. Similarly, Procter & Gamble has harnessed AI-powered platforms to streamline its product development cycle. By using AI to analyze consumer feedback and market data, P&G can refine its products more efficiently, reducing time-to-market and ensuring alignment with consumer needs. These examples highlight how AI accelerates the development process and enhances the final product, delivering greater value to consumers.

AI's impact on innovation and time-to-market is profound. Faster product design and iteration cycles mean that businesses can move from concept to market-ready products in a fraction of the time. This acceleration reduces development costs and allows companies to respond quickly to changing market conditions. Moreover, AI ensures that products align with market needs and trends, reducing the risk of developing items that fail to resonate with consumers. This alignment is achieved through continuous analysis of consumer data and market dynamics, enabling businesses to adapt their products in real-time. As a result, companies not only innovate faster but also deliver products that are more likely to succeed in the marketplace.

Incorporating AI into product development is not just about speeding up processes; it's about enhancing the quality and relevance of products. By leveraging AI, businesses can push the boundaries of innovation, exploring new possibilities and creating products that meet the evolving needs of consumers. This innovative approach transforms product development from a linear process into a dynamic and iterative journey, where AI acts as both a catalyst and a guide. As we look to the future, the integration of AI in product development will continue to revolutionize the industry, offering endless opportunities for growth, creativity, and success. By embracing AI, businesses position themselves at the forefront of innovation, ready to lead in a competitive landscape.

CHAPTER 5
ETHICAL AI
IMPLEMENTATION AND
GOVERNANCE

C onsider the potential of a cutting-edge AI system designed to streamline hiring processes by sifting through thousands of resumes to find the perfect candidates. Now, imagine if this system inadvertently favored certain demographics over others due to biases in its training data. The implications would not only undermine trust in the technology but could also expose the company to legal risks and damage its reputation. This scenario underscores the critical importance of ethical AI implementation. As you venture into the realm of AI, adopting ethical principles that guide development and deployment is essential, ensuring fairness, transparency, accountability, and respect for privacy.

At the heart of ethical AI are three core principles: fairness, transparency, and privacy. Fairness demands that AI systems operate without bias, ensuring that all individuals are treated equally and that decisions are not influenced by factors such as race, gender, or age. This principle is crucial in recruitment or credit scoring applications, where biases can have significant real-world consequences. Transparency involves openness about how AI systems work, enabling users to understand the processes behind AI-driven decisions. This clarity fosters trust and accountability, as stakeholders can verify that the system operates as intended. Lastly, privacy is about safeguarding personal data, ensuring that AI systems comply with data protection regulations, and respecting individuals' rights. In an era where data is a valuable commodity, maintaining privacy is paramount for building trust and protecting user information.

To put these principles into practice, consider conducting ethical impact assessments as a foundational step in any AI project. These assessments involve evaluating potential ethical risks and impacts before deployment, ensuring that AI initiatives align with your organization's ethical standards. By identifying potential issues early, you can mitigate risks and make informed decisions that prioritize ethical outcomes. Implementing fairness-aware algorithms is another practical approach to ensuring ethical AI. These algorithms are designed to detect and reduce biases, promoting equitable decision-making. By embedding fairness into the algorithmic design, you can create AI systems that uphold ethical standards and deliver consistent, unbiased results.

Leadership plays a pivotal role in fostering an ethical AI culture within an organization. As a leader, your commitment to ethics sets the tone for the entire team, influencing how AI is perceived and implemented. By championing ethical practices, you encourage a culture where ethical AI is not just a checkbox but a core value. This commitment involves actively promoting ethical discussions, providing training on ethical AI practices, and holding teams accountable for upholding ethical standards. Encouraging a culture of ethical AI practices ensures that all team members understand the importance of ethics and are empowered to identify and address potential ethical risks. When ethical considerations are integrated into the fabric of your organization, AI initiatives are more likely to succeed and align with your values.

Several organizations have developed frameworks to guide ethical AI implementation. Google, for instance, has established a set of AI principles prioritizing fairness, transparency, and privacy. These principles serve as a foundation for all AI projects, ensuring that ethical considerations are at the forefront of development. Similarly, the Montreal Declaration for Responsible AI outlines guidelines for ethical AI use, emphasizing the importance of accountability, inclusivity, and respect for privacy. These frameworks provide valuable insights and benchmarks that can inform your own ethical AI efforts, helping you navigate the complexities of AI governance.

Reflection Section: Ethical AI Principles in Action

Consider how you can integrate these ethical principles into your AI initiatives:

1. Fairness: How can your AI systems ensure equal treatment for all individuals?
2. Transparency: What steps can you take to make AI processes clear and understandable?
3. Privacy: How will you protect user data and comply with privacy regulations?

Reflect on these questions and identify actionable steps to incorporate ethical principles into your AI projects. These considerations will not only guide ethical implementation but also enhance trust and accountability in your AI endeavors.

5.1 NAVIGATING REGULATORY COMPLIANCE: GDPR AND BEYOND

Imagine a company that has just launched a cutting-edge AI-driven marketing platform capable of analyzing user behavior to deliver personalized recommendations. Exciting, right? But then the company faces a massive fine due to non-compliance with data privacy regulations. Regulatory compliance is not just a bureaucratic hurdle; it's a critical aspect of AI projects that can make or break your business. Adhering to regulations is essential to avoid costly legal penalties and fines that can cripple even the most promising ventures. But beyond avoiding penalties, compliance builds trust with your customers and stakeholders. When people know their data is handled responsibly, they are more likely to engage with your services and products. This trust translates into loyalty, a precious commodity in today's competitive market.

The General Data Protection Regulation (GDPR) is one of the most comprehensive data protection laws, setting high standards for data privacy globally. Under GDPR, individuals have specific rights over their personal data, including the right to access, rectify, and erase their information. This means businesses must be transparent about how they collect and use data, and they must provide individuals with control over their personal information. Additionally, GDPR stipulates strict data breach notification obligations. In the event of a data breach, companies must notify the relevant authorities within 72 hours and inform affected individuals without undue delay. These requirements ensure that organizations remain accountable for protecting personal data and are prepared to act swiftly in the event of a security incident.

Meeting these regulatory requirements requires thoughtful strategies and proactive measures. One effective approach is implementing Data Protection Impact Assessments (DPIAs). These assessments help identify and mitigate risks associated with data processing activities, ensuring that privacy considerations are integrated into the design of AI systems from the outset. DPIAs are not just a legal requirement; they are a tool for understanding the impact of your data practices and making informed decisions that prioritize user privacy. Another strategy is appointing a Data Protection Officer (DPO). This role involves overseeing data protection policies, ensuring compliance, and serving as a point of contact for data protection authorities. A DPO provides expertise in navigating complex data protection landscapes, helping your organization stay on the right side of the law.

Consider a healthcare organization that successfully navigated GDPR compliance. Faced with the challenges of handling sensitive patient data, the organization implemented robust data protection measures, including conducting regular DPIAs and appointing a dedicated DPO. These steps ensured compliance and enhanced patient trust and confidence in the organization's services. Similarly, a tech company operating under the California Consumer Privacy Act (CCPA) demonstrated exemplary adherence to regulatory requirements. By implementing comprehensive data protection practices and fostering a culture of privacy awareness, the company maintained compliance and strengthened its reputation as a responsible data steward.

Regulatory compliance in AI is not merely about meeting legal obligations; it's about embedding privacy and security into the core of your operations. As regulations continue to evolve, staying informed and adapting your practices is crucial. By prioritizing compliance, you protect your organization from legal risks and foster a culture of trust and transparency with your customers and stakeholders.

5.2 MITIGATING ALGORITHM BIAS: TECHNIQUES AND TOOLS

Algorithm bias is a formidable challenge in AI development, stemming mainly from historical data biases that inadvertently creep into AI systems. These biases occur when the data used to train AI models reflects existing prejudices, whether based on race, gender, or socioeconomic status. When unchecked, these biases can lead to discriminatory outcomes, where AI systems unfairly disadvantage certain groups. The consequences are not merely theoretical; they manifest in real-world scenarios, tarnishing reputations and eroding trust. Imagine an AI-powered recruitment tool that consistently favors candidates from a particular demographic, skewing the diversity of talent. Such outcomes not only undermine the ethical principles of fairness but also expose organizations to reputational damage and potential legal repercussions. The root causes of algorithm bias lie in the datasets themselves, which often mirror the inequalities present in society. While vast and valuable, historical data carries the weight of past prejudices, which AI systems may inadvertently perpetuate if not addressed.

To tackle this challenge, a range of techniques and tools have been developed to detect and mitigate bias in AI algorithms. Fairness-aware machine learning techniques are at the forefront of this effort. These techniques involve designing algorithms that can identify and adjust for biases during the learning process, ensuring that the AI systems produce equitable outcomes. By incorporating fairness constraints into the model's training phase, these techniques proactively counteract biases before they influence decision-making. Additionally, bias detection tools and frameworks play a crucial role in identifying areas of concern. These tools analyze AI models for signs of bias, offering insights into where and how biases may be present. By pinpointing these areas, developers can make informed adjustments, refining algorithms to achieve more balanced results. The combination of fairness-aware techniques and bias detection tools empowers businesses to create AI systems that align with ethical standards and societal expectations.

A critical factor in reducing algorithm bias is the use of diverse and representative datasets. The diversity of data directly impacts the inclusivity of AI outcomes. When datasets encompass a wide range of demographics and perspectives, the resulting AI models are better equipped to make unbiased decisions. This diversity helps to avoid the perpetuation of existing biases, fostering AI systems that are equitable and just. It is essential to curate datasets meticulously, ensuring they capture the full spectrum of human experience. This means actively seeking out underrepresented groups and perspectives and balancing the scales to reflect a fairer reality. The importance of diverse data cannot be overstated, as it forms the foundation upon which fair AI systems are built. In industries like finance and healthcare, where decisions can significantly impact individuals' lives, the need for diverse datasets is paramount to prevent discriminatory practices.

Several organizations have made strides in mitigating algorithm bias, offering valuable lessons for others to follow. A notable example is a tech company that successfully reduced bias in its hiring algorithms. By thoroughly analyzing their recruitment data, they identified biases and implemented fairness-aware techniques to correct them. This proactive approach not only improved the fairness of their hiring process but also enriched the diversity of their workforce, enhancing innovation and collaboration. Similarly, in the financial sector, a company focused on ensuring fairness in its credit scoring models. By integrating bias detection tools and diverse datasets, they were able to develop credit models that accurately and equitably assessed applicants, removing the influence of historical prejudices. These examples underscore the importance of vigilance and innovation in addressing algorithm bias. They demonstrate that with the right tools and commitment, organizations can create AI systems that are not only technically robust but also ethically sound, paving the way for a more equitable future.

5.3 TRANSPARENT AI: BUILDING TRUST WITH STAKEHOLDERS

In the realm of AI, transparency is not just a buzzword—it's a necessity. At its core, transparency in AI means being open and clear about how AI systems operate and make decisions. This openness is crucial because it fosters trust and accountability among users and stakeholders. Imagine a customer service chatbot that provides automated responses. Users who understand how the chatbot processes queries and generates answers are more likely to trust its responses. This trust is built on transparency, which removes the mystery from AI processes, making them understandable and reliable. By demystifying AI, businesses can build stronger relationships with their customers, who feel reassured that the technology is being used ethically and responsibly.

Several practices can be employed to achieve AI transparency. One effective approach is to meticulously document AI decision-making processes. This documentation involves detailing the algorithms and data sets used, as well as the criteria for decision-making. By providing this information, businesses can demonstrate how AI systems reach their conclusions, offering users a window into the system's inner workings. Another critical practice is the development and deployment of explainable AI (XAI) models. Unlike traditional black-box models, XAI models are designed to provide clear and understandable explanations of their outputs. These models allow users to see the rationale behind AI decisions, empowering them to make informed judgments. By prioritizing XAI, businesses can enhance transparency and ensure that AI systems are accountable and trustworthy.

Effective stakeholder communication is another cornerstone of transparent AI. Clear and open communication with stakeholders —including customers, employees, and partners—is essential for building trust. This communication involves regularly updating stakeholders on AI initiatives, sharing insights into how AI is being used, and addressing any concerns or questions they may have. By fostering an environment of openness, businesses can enhance stakeholder understanding and engagement. Encouraging feedback from stakeholders is equally important, as it provides valuable insights into potential areas for improvement. Businesses can create a collaborative atmosphere where trust and transparency thrive by actively involving stakeholders in the AI process.

Several organizations have successfully implemented transparent AI practices, setting examples for others to follow. In healthcare diagnostics, some companies have embraced explainable AI to enhance patient trust. By providing clear explanations of AI-generated diagnoses, these companies help patients understand their medical conditions and treatment options, fostering confidence in the technology. In the financial services sector, transparency is equally crucial. Some financial institutions use transparent AI models to explain credit decisions to customers. These institutions build trust and demonstrate fairness in their AI-driven processes by offering insights into the factors influencing credit approvals or denials. These examples highlight the tangible benefits of transparent AI, showing how openness can enhance trust and accountability across various industries.

Transparency in AI is not just a technical challenge; it's an opportunity to build lasting relationships with stakeholders. By embracing transparency, businesses can demystify AI, making it accessible and understandable for all. This openness fosters trust and accountability, ensuring that AI is used ethically and responsibly. As AI continues to shape the future of business, transparency will remain a guiding principle, enabling businesses to navigate the complexities of AI with integrity and confidence.

5.4 AI AND PRIVACY: SAFEGUARDING DATA IN A DIGITAL AGE

In today's data-driven world, the significance of preserving privacy within AI cannot be overstated. As businesses leverage AI to gain insights and drive innovation, ensuring the protection of individual rights and freedoms becomes paramount. This commitment to privacy safeguards the trust that customers place in your organization, which is fundamental to long-term success. Protecting privacy also aligns your business with legal and regulatory requirements, such as those mandated by GDPR and other data protection laws globally. Non-compliance can lead to severe penalties, but more importantly, it can erode customer trust—the bedrock of any successful business relationship. As AI systems expand their reach, they often require access to vast amounts of personal data. Without stringent privacy measures, this data can be vulnerable to misuse or unauthorized access, leading to potential breaches that can harm individuals and damage reputations.

To ensure robust data privacy throughout the AI lifecycle, organizations must adopt best practices prioritizing data protection at every stage. Implementing data minimization principles is a crucial step in this process. This practice involves collecting only the data necessary for the specific AI task, reducing the volume of personal information handled, and minimizing exposure to risk. Anonymization and pseudonymization techniques further enhance privacy by altering personal data to prevent the identification of individuals. Anonymization removes personally identifiable information entirely, ensuring that the data cannot be traced back to any individual. Pseudonymization, on the other hand, replaces private identifiers with fictitious ones, allowing data to be re-identified only under specific conditions. These practices protect individual privacy and enable businesses to comply with legal standards and ethical norms, fostering trust and accountability.

Privacy-preserving AI technologies offer innovative solutions to enhance data protection. Differential privacy is one such technique that adds random noise to data sets, safeguarding individual privacy while preserving the overall utility of the data. This method allows AI models to learn from data without exposing sensitive information, ensuring that insights derived from the data cannot be traced back to specific individuals. Federated learning models also play a pivotal role in preserving privacy. By allowing AI models to be trained across multiple decentralized devices or servers without exchanging data, federated learning minimizes data transfer and reduces the risk of data exposure. These technologies represent a significant advancement in privacy protection, enabling businesses to leverage AI's capabilities while upholding the highest data privacy standards.

Real-world examples illustrate the successful implementation of privacy-preserving AI. In healthcare research, certain organizations have adopted differential privacy techniques to analyze patient data without compromising individual confidentiality. By applying these methods, researchers can extract valuable insights while maintaining patient trust and adhering to strict privacy regulations. Similarly, in AI-driven marketing campaigns, companies use anonymization techniques to analyze consumer behavior without infringing on personal privacy. By anonymizing data, businesses can personalize marketing efforts while respecting consumer rights, creating a balance between innovation and ethics. These examples demonstrate that with the right strategies and technologies, it is possible to harness AI's potential while safeguarding privacy, ensuring that data-driven advancements benefit both businesses and individuals alike.

5.5 ETHICAL AI CASE STUDIES: LESSONS LEARNED FROM INDUSTRY LEADERS

In the fast-evolving landscape of AI, ethical considerations have become paramount as they determine the trustworthiness and acceptability of AI solutions. Real-world case studies offer invaluable insights into ethical AI implementation, showcasing both triumphs and challenges. These examples provide a practical lens through which we can understand the complexities of ethical AI, highlighting best practices and potential pitfalls. By analyzing the experiences of industry leaders, we gain a deeper appreciation of the importance of ethics in AI development and deployment. These case studies serve as a guide, illuminating the path forward for businesses striving to integrate ethical principles into their AI strategies.

One notable case study revolves around Tesla's approach to ethical AI in autonomous vehicles. Tesla has been at the forefront of integrating AI into its self-driving cars, aiming to revolutionize transportation. However, this innovation brings ethical dilemmas, particularly concerning safety and decision-making. Tesla's challenge lies in programming AI systems to make split-second decisions that can impact human lives. The ethical considerations involve determining how the AI should prioritize safety in various scenarios, such as choosing between the safety of passengers and pedestrians. Tesla's experience underscores the need for continuous monitoring and evaluation of AI systems to ensure they adhere to ethical standards and prioritize human safety. This vigilance is crucial, as the implications of autonomous vehicle decisions extend far beyond technology, touching on legal, social, and moral dimensions.

Similarly, social media giant Facebook has faced ethical scrutiny over its use of AI in content moderation and data handling. The company utilizes AI algorithms to identify and manage harmful content, striving to create a safer online environment. However, the challenges surrounding AI ethics in social media are multifaceted. Facebook's AI systems must navigate the delicate balance between freedom of expression and content regulation. Additionally, concerns about data privacy and algorithmic bias have raised questions about the transparency and accountability of AI-driven decisions. Facebook's journey highlights the importance of cross-functional collaboration in ethical AI implementation. By engaging with diverse stakeholders, including policymakers, ethicists, and user representatives, Facebook can comprehensively refine its AI practices and address ethical concerns.

From these case studies, several key lessons emerge that can inform your own AI initiatives. First, the importance of continuous monitoring and evaluation must be considered. Ethical AI is not a one-time achievement but an ongoing process that requires regular assessment and adjustment. By establishing mechanisms for continuous monitoring, businesses can identify and address ethical issues as they arise, ensuring that AI systems remain aligned with ethical standards. Second, the need for cross-functional collaboration is paramount. Ethical AI requires input from various disciplines, including technology, law, ethics, and sociology. By fostering collaboration across departments and involving external experts, organizations can develop AI solutions that are ethically robust and socially responsible.

Based on these insights, I recommend that businesses establish an AI ethics committee tasked with overseeing ethical considerations throughout the AI development lifecycle. This committee should include representatives from diverse fields, ensuring a holistic approach to ethical AI. Additionally, conducting regular ethical audits and reviews can help identify potential ethical risks and guide the implementation of corrective measures. These audits should assess the impact of AI systems on stakeholders, evaluating factors such as fairness, transparency, and privacy. By adopting these practices, businesses can proactively address ethical challenges, fostering trust and accountability in their AI initiatives.

As we conclude our exploration of ethical AI implementation, it's clear that ethics must be an integral part of any AI strategy. By learning from industry leaders and adopting best practices, businesses can navigate the ethical complexities of AI, ensuring that their innovations benefit society while upholding the highest ethical standards. As we move forward, let us embrace the lessons learned and commit to advancing AI in an innovative and ethical manner, paving the way for a future where technology serves humanity responsibly.

CHAPTER 6
TALENT DEVELOPMENT AND ORGANIZATIONAL READINESS

T hink about a company on the brink of technological breakthroughs yet held back by a workforce that struggles to adapt. This scenario is all too common as artificial intelligence permeates business landscapes. As a leader, your ability to cultivate an AI-ready workforce is paramount. It's not just about deploying new technologies; it's about preparing your team to harness these tools effectively. The rapid pace of AI development demands continuous learning, making training and upskilling not just beneficial but essential. Bridging the skills gap is critical to remain competitive. AI is evolving at a blistering pace, and businesses that fail to keep their workforce updated risk falling behind. Training isn't a one-time event but a continuous journey that ensures your organization can adapt to new AI advancements and leverage them efficiently.

Developing AI capabilities within your organization begins with effective training programs. Online courses and certifications are a flexible way to build foundational knowledge. Platforms like Coursera and edX offer specialized AI courses that can be accessed anytime and anywhere, making it easier for employees to learn at their own pace. These courses often provide certifications that enhance individual skills and add value to your organization by fostering a culture of learning and growth. In-house workshops and boot camps offer another layer of training. These sessions are tailored to your company's specific needs, focusing on practical applications of AI that are relevant to your business. By bringing in experts to conduct hands-on training, you equip your team with the skills needed to tackle real-world challenges. This approach not only boosts technical proficiency but also encourages collaboration and innovation.

Partnering with AI training providers can further enhance your training initiatives. These partnerships bring specialized expertise and resources that may not be available internally. Collaborating with leading AI educators ensures that your team is exposed to the latest industry trends and technologies. These providers often offer customized training programs that align with your strategic goals, ensuring that your workforce is prepared to implement AI solutions effectively. Such collaborations also demonstrate your commitment to employee development, boosting morale and retention.

Cross-functional training is another crucial aspect of building an AI-ready workforce. It's not enough for only the IT department to understand AI; everyone in your organization should be equipped with basic AI literacy. This holistic approach ensures seamless collaboration between technical and non-technical teams, fostering a culture where AI initiatives are understood and supported across the board. Cross-functional training enhances organizational AI literacy, allowing employees from different departments to contribute to AI projects and initiatives. This inclusive approach encourages diverse perspectives and ideas, leading to more innovative and effective AI solutions.

Consider the AI training initiatives at Google and Microsoft. Google has implemented comprehensive AI training programs that empower employees across all levels to leverage AI in their roles. These programs focus on technical skills and broader AI literacy, ensuring everyone, from engineers to marketers, can understand and apply AI concepts. Similarly, Microsoft's AI Business School offers executive-level training designed to help leaders integrate AI into their business strategies. This program emphasizes strategic thinking and ethical AI use, equipping leaders with the skills needed to drive AI transformation.

Interactive Element: AI Skills Development Checklist

To ensure your organization is on the right track, consider this checklist for developing AI skills:

1. Identify Core Skills: Determine the essential AI skills needed for various roles within your organization.
2. Evaluate Training Needs: Assess current skill levels and identify gaps that need addressing.
3. Select Training Programs: Choose a mix of online courses, workshops, and partnerships that align with your goals.
4. Implement Cross-Functional Training: Ensure all departments have access to AI literacy training.

Use this checklist as a guide to develop a comprehensive training strategy that prepares your workforce for AI integration.

6.1 PARTNERING WITH ACADEMIA: CREATING AI TALENT PIPELINES

Imagine a business landscape where your company not only keeps pace with technological advancements but also leads in innovation. One effective way to achieve this is by partnering with academic institutions. Such collaborations are more than a strategic move; they're an investment in your company's future. By aligning with universities and research centers, you gain access to cutting-edge research and expertise that can propel your AI initiatives forward. Academic partnerships offer a direct line to the latest advancements in AI, allowing your company to stay ahead of the curve and adapt to a rapidly changing environment.

These partnerships also open doors to internships and collaborative projects, providing opportunities for real-world application and experimentation. Students bring fresh perspectives and innovative ideas, often viewing problems from angles seasoned professionals might overlook. By involving students in projects, you benefit from their insights and create a pipeline of trained talent familiar with your company's specific needs and culture. Internships serve as a testing ground where potential employees demonstrate their skills and fit within your organizational ethos, reducing the risks associated with new hires.

To establish such partnerships, consider sponsoring AI research and development initiatives within universities. By funding research projects, you foster innovation and gain early access to breakthroughs that could revolutionize your industry. Offering scholarships and grants for AI studies is another strategic move. Not only does this support the education of future experts, but it also positions your company as a leader committed to advancing AI knowledge and its ethical application. Creating joint AI labs and research centers further solidifies these relationships. These labs become hubs of innovation where academic and industry experts collaborate, driving both practical and theoretical advancements in AI.

Internships and cooperative education programs are pivotal in providing students with practical experience. They bridge the gap between academic learning and industry application, equipping students with the skills needed to thrive in professional environments. These programs are mutually beneficial: students gain hands-on experience and industry exposure while companies build a talent pipeline for future hiring. By investing in these initiatives, you cultivate a workforce ready to tackle the challenges of AI integration, ensuring your company remains competitive and innovative.

Consider IBM's collaboration with MIT, which exemplifies the power of academic partnerships. Together, they established a research lab focused on AI, fostering an environment of creativity and exploration. This partnership accelerates AI research and provides IBM with access to a pool of talented individuals trained in cutting-edge technologies. Similarly, Amazon's Machine Learning University, developed in partnership with leading academic institutions, offers employees and students the opportunity to learn and apply AI concepts in real-world scenarios. These examples demonstrate how strategic academic partnerships can drive innovation and talent development, ensuring your company is well-equipped to lead in the AI era.

6.2 ESSENTIAL AI SKILLS: WHAT YOUR TEAM NEEDS TO KNOW

As an entrepreneur or business leader, you're likely aware that the rise of AI in business demands a workforce equipped with specific skills. In the realm of AI, certain competencies are non-negotiable. For various roles within your AI team, data science and analytics stand at the forefront. These skills enable your team to interpret vast datasets, extracting actionable insights that drive decision-making. Understanding the intricacies of machine learning and deep learning is equally vital. These technologies form the backbone of AI, allowing systems to learn from data and improve over time. Moreover, AI ethics and governance must be considered. As AI becomes more integrated into business operations, ensuring its deployment aligns with ethical standards and governance policies is crucial. Each of these skills plays a distinct role in making AI a transformative force in your business.

However, more than technical prowess is required. A balanced skill set that includes both technical and non-technical abilities enhances your team's performance. Communication skills, for instance, are paramount. They ensure that team members can articulate complex AI concepts in a manner that stakeholders and non-technical colleagues can understand. This clarity fosters collaboration across departments, breaking down silos and encouraging innovation. Furthermore, integrating AI responsibly requires understanding ethical considerations, making it essential for team members to navigate potential biases and legal implications. This comprehensive approach ensures that AI initiatives are not only effective but also aligned with your company's values and long-term goals.

Developing these skills requires a strategic approach. Encourage your team to enroll in specialized AI courses and certifications. These programs provide structured learning paths covering the latest AI technology advancements. Additionally, participating in AI hackathons and competitions can be incredibly beneficial. These events offer a hands-on environment where team members can apply their knowledge, solve real-world problems, and collaborate with peers. They foster a spirit of innovation and problem-solving, essential traits in the fast-paced world of AI. Continuous learning and professional development should also be a priority. Encourage your team to attend conferences, webinars, and workshops, staying abreast of industry trends and emerging technologies. By fostering an environment of continuous learning, you ensure that your team remains agile and adaptable, ready to tackle the ever-evolving challenges that AI presents.

When we look to industry leaders for inspiration, companies like Facebook and NVIDIA demonstrate the power of well-rounded AI teams. Facebook's AI Research (FAIR) division is renowned for its innovative approach to AI development. They've cultivated a team that excels in machine learning, computer vision, and natural language processing, driving advancements that keep them at the cutting edge of technology. Similarly, NVIDIA, a leader in graphics processing and AI has built a team that combines deep technical expertise with strategic vision. Their ability to leverage AI across various applications, from gaming to autonomous vehicles, showcases the importance of a diverse skill set. These examples highlight that the success of AI initiatives hinges on having a team equipped with both the technical skills and the strategic insight necessary to drive innovation and growth.

6.3 OVERCOMING RESISTANCE TO AI ADOPTION: CHANGE MANAGEMENT STRATEGIES

In any organization, the prospect of integrating artificial intelligence can stir apprehension. One major hurdle is the fear of job displacement. Employees worry that AI will render their roles obsolete, leading to uncertainty about their future within the company. This fear isn't unfounded, as AI does automate certain tasks, but it's important to recognize that it also creates new opportunities for those willing to adapt. The key is to shift the narrative from replacement to augmentation, emphasizing how AI can enhance job roles by taking over mundane tasks, thus allowing employees to focus on more strategic and creative endeavors.

Another significant barrier is the lack of understanding and awareness about AI's capabilities and limitations. This knowledge gap can lead to misconceptions, with some employees viewing AI as a mysterious force rather than a tool designed to assist and improve business processes. Addressing this requires a concerted effort to educate and inform, ensuring that everyone in the organization understands what AI is and how it can benefit them. Providing clear, accessible information helps demystify AI, enabling employees to see its potential rather than its perceived threats.

Concerns about data privacy and ethics also contribute to resistance. As AI systems often rely on large datasets to function effectively, employees may worry about how their data—and that of customers—will be used and protected. These concerns are valid, especially given the increasing scrutiny around data privacy. To overcome this, organizations must prioritize transparent data practices and establish robust ethical guidelines. By demonstrating a commitment to ethical AI use, businesses can build trust and reassure employees that their privacy and ethical considerations are being taken seriously.

Clear and transparent communication is paramount to manage change effectively and overcome resistance. From the outset, articulate the reasons for adopting AI and the expected benefits for both the organization and its employees. This transparency helps alleviate fears and fosters a sense of inclusion. Involving employees in AI initiatives from the start is another powerful strategy. Encourage participation in planning and implementation phases, seeking their input and feedback. This involvement empowers employees and ensures that AI solutions are tailored to meet the needs of those who will use them.

Providing training and support is crucial in easing the transition to AI adoption. Equip employees with the skills and knowledge they need to work effectively alongside AI technologies. Offer workshops, seminars, and hands-on training sessions to build confidence and competence. This investment in human capital demonstrates that the organization values its workforce and is committed to their growth and development in the AI era.

Leadership plays a pivotal role in driving change and fostering a culture of acceptance for AI. Strong leaders lead by example, showing their commitment to AI initiatives and addressing concerns head-on. By openly discussing the challenges and opportunities that AI presents, leaders can dispel myths and build enthusiasm. Providing reassurance is equally essential. Leaders should emphasize that AI is a tool to assist, not replace and that the organization is committed to ethical, responsible AI use.

Consider the example of General Electric (GE), which successfully navigated the challenges of AI adoption by prioritizing change management. GE's leaders communicated the benefits of AI clearly and involved employees at every stage of the process. By providing comprehensive training and support, they addressed fears and built a skilled workforce ready to embrace AI. Similarly, PricewaterhouseCoopers (PwC) tackled resistance by fostering a culture of transparency and collaboration. They engaged employees in AI projects, seeking their input and addressing their concerns. This approach overcame resistance and empowered employees to see AI as an opportunity rather than a threat.

6.4 FOSTERING A CULTURE OF INNOVATION: ENCOURAGING AI EXPERIMENTATION

Consider a vibrant workplace where creativity and experimentation are not just encouraged but celebrated. This is the kind of culture that drives AI success. Embracing a culture of innovation is not merely about technological advancements; it's about creating an environment where new ideas can flourish. This culture is crucial for driving continuous improvement and innovation, both integral to staying competitive. When employees feel empowered to explore and experiment, they contribute to a cycle of innovation that keeps your company at the forefront of the industry. Moreover, such a culture is magnetic, attracting top talent eager to work in an environment that values creativity and forward-thinking. Talented individuals seek workplaces where they can challenge the status quo and push boundaries, and a culture of innovation provides just that.

To cultivate this environment, AI innovation labs should be established. These labs serve as dedicated spaces where teams can experiment with AI technologies without the constraints of day-to-day operations. They are incubators for new ideas, allowing teams to test hypotheses, explore different applications of AI, and develop solutions that could transform your business. Providing such a space signals to employees that innovation is a priority, fostering a sense of ownership and investment in AI initiatives. Encouraging cross-functional collaboration and idea-sharing is another powerful strategy. By breaking down silos and promoting interaction among different departments, you create a melting pot of perspectives and expertise. This diversity often leads to innovative solutions that a single team might not achieve. Facilitate regular brainstorming sessions and workshops where employees from various backgrounds can come together to discuss challenges and share ideas. This collaborative approach not only generates fresh insights but also strengthens team cohesion and morale.

Providing resources and support for AI projects is essential to sustain this culture of innovation. Ensure teams have access to the latest AI tools, technologies, and training necessary to explore new possibilities. Invest in professional development opportunities that allow employees to enhance their skills and stay updated with industry trends. By equipping your teams with the resources they need, you empower them to innovate confidently and effectively. Additionally, allocate time for experimentation, allowing employees to work on side projects or initiatives that align with their interests and expertise. This autonomy fosters creativity and can lead to unexpected breakthroughs.

Failure plays a vital role in the innovation process. Viewing failures not as setbacks but as valuable learning opportunities is important. Each failure provides insights that can refine and improve AI projects, leading to more robust and effective solutions. Encourage a growth mindset within your organization, where employees feel comfortable taking risks and learning from their mistakes. Celebrate these lessons learned and use them to iterate on AI projects, turning challenges into stepping stones for success. By fostering resilience and adaptability, you create a culture where innovation thrives, even in the face of setbacks.

Consider the AI innovation at Google's X lab, an example of a company that has successfully fostered a culture of experimentation. This lab encourages "moonshot" thinking, where teams pursue ambitious projects with the potential for significant impact. By embracing bold ideas and learning from failures, Google's X lab has developed groundbreaking technologies that have transformed industries. Similarly, Apple's innovation-driven culture emphasizes creativity and exploration. Their focus on design and user experience has led to revolutionary products that have set new standards in the tech industry. These companies demonstrate the power of a culture that values experimentation and innovation, illustrating how such an environment can lead to remarkable achievements.

6.5 LEADERSHIP IN THE AGE OF AI: NEW SKILLS FOR NEW CHALLENGES

The role of leadership is evolving dramatically with the advent of artificial intelligence. As a business leader, you are now tasked with not just overseeing operations but guiding the strategic vision of AI within your organization. This involves crafting a roadmap for AI integration that aligns with your company's goals and values. It's about seeing the bigger picture and understanding how AI can transform various facets of your business. An effective leader in this era must also ensure ethical and responsible AI practices are at the forefront of all initiatives. This means creating frameworks that govern how AI decisions are made, ensuring they are fair, transparent, and aligned with ethical standards. It's about setting the tone for your organization and modeling the behaviors and attitudes you wish to see in your team.

To successfully navigate these challenges, leaders need to develop a new set of skills. Data literacy and analytical thinking are fundamental. In a world where data drives decisions, being able to interpret and act on data insights is crucial. This doesn't mean you need to become a data scientist, but you should be comfortable with data-driven discussions and decisions. Technological fluency is another key skill. You must understand the basics of AI technologies, such as machine learning and natural language processing, to make informed decisions about their implementation and potential impact. Alongside these technical skills, ethical decision-making and governance are essential. You'll need to make choices that balance innovation with responsibility, addressing concerns about privacy, bias, and transparency. This involves staying informed about the latest ethical guidelines and ensuring your AI initiatives comply with them.

Developing these skills can seem daunting, but there are actionable steps you can take. Enrolling in executive education programs focused on AI is a great start. These programs offer insights into the strategic implications of AI and how to leverage it effectively in your organization. Participating in AI-focused leadership workshops and seminars is another way to enhance your understanding. These events provide opportunities to learn from experts and engage in discussions about the challenges and opportunities AI presents. Networking with AI experts and thought leaders can also be invaluable. Building relationships with those at the forefront of AI innovation allows you to exchange ideas, gain new perspectives, and stay updated on emerging trends and technologies. This network can be a resource for support and guidance as you navigate the complexities of AI leadership.

Figures like Satya Nadella at Microsoft exemplify successful AI leadership. Under his guidance, Microsoft has embraced AI as a core component of its strategy, focusing on ethical AI development and empowering every person and organization on the planet to achieve more. Nadella's leadership style emphasizes empathy, collaboration, and a commitment to innovation, setting a standard for AI-driven transformation. Similarly, Sundar Pichai at Google has championed an AI-first approach, integrating AI into Google's products and services to enhance user experience and efficiency. Pichai's vision for AI is rooted in accessibility and responsibility, ensuring that the technology benefits everyone. These leaders demonstrate how a clear vision, coupled with a commitment to ethical practices and continuous learning, can drive successful AI adoption and transformation.

In this chapter, we explored the evolving responsibilities of leadership in the age of AI, highlighting the skills necessary to guide organizations through this technological transformation. As we look forward, it's clear that effective leadership is central to leveraging AI's full potential. Equipping yourself with the right skills and strategies can lead your organization into an AI-driven future with confidence and foresight.

CHAPTER 7
SCENARIO-BASED LEARNING AND INTERACTIVE RESOURCES

I magine a bustling retail store, once the neighborhood's go-to shopping spot, now grappling with a surge in customer churn and dwindling foot traffic. The management team, aware of the shifting tides in consumer behavior, realizes that traditional marketing strategies are no longer effective. The challenge? High customer turnover and a lack of precise segmentation and targeting. This scenario is all too familiar to many retailers today, where the competition is fierce and customer loyalty is fleeting. What if AI could be the game-changer? This chapter explores how AI-driven strategies can transform marketing campaigns, turning data into personalized customer experiences and ultimately breathing new life into a struggling business.

The retailer's journey to revitalization began with an ambitious AI-driven marketing campaign. The first step was data collection —analyzing customer interactions and transactions in detail. The retailer amassed a rich dataset by leveraging data from purchase histories, online browsing behavior, and social media engagements. This data formed the backbone of their AI strategy, providing the insights needed to understand customer preferences and behaviors. With this foundation, machine learning algorithms could be applied to segment customers into precise groups based on shared characteristics and buying patterns. Marketing would no longer be a shot in the dark; instead, it would become a targeted endeavor, reaching the right audience at the right time with the right message.

With customer segments clearly defined, the next step involved creating personalized marketing content using AI algorithms. These algorithms analyzed data points to craft messages and offers tailored to each segment's unique needs and desires. Whether it was a personalized email offer for a loyal shopper or a targeted ad for a potential customer who had abandoned their online cart, AI ensured every interaction was meaningful and engaging. The power of AI lies in its ability to automate and optimize these processes, allowing marketers to focus on strategy rather than execution. This personalized approach increased engagement and fostered a deeper connection between the brand and its customers, leading to improved retention and satisfaction.

Integrating AI into the retailer's existing systems was crucial to the implementation process. The AI tools were seamlessly woven into the retailer's customer relationship management (CRM) system, enabling real-time data analysis and customer engagement. This integration allowed the marketing team to respond swiftly to customer interactions, adapting campaigns based on real-time feedback and performance metrics. AI-powered chatbots and virtual assistants were deployed to enhance customer service, providing instant support and personalized recommendations. This real-time engagement improved the customer experience and provided valuable insights into customer preferences and trends, driving continuous improvement in marketing strategies.

The outcomes of the AI-driven marketing campaign were transformative. Customer retention rates soared as personalized interactions made customers feel valued and understood. Sales increased as targeted campaigns converted potential leads into loyal customers. The retailer discovered the importance of high-quality data in AI effectiveness. Accurate, well-maintained data was pivotal in driving successful AI initiatives, highlighting the need for robust data management practices. This case underscores the transformative potential of AI in marketing, offering valuable lessons for businesses seeking to enhance their customer engagement and drive growth.

Reflection Section: AI in Marketing Implementation

Reflect on your own marketing strategies and consider the following prompts:

1. How can data collection be optimized to provide richer insights into customer behavior?
2. What steps can you take to integrate AI into your existing marketing systems, ensuring seamless operations?
3. How can personalized marketing content enhance customer engagement and retention in your business?

Use these questions as a guide to explore the possibilities of AI in transforming your marketing efforts.

7.1 SCENARIO 1: IMPLEMENTING AI FOR PREDICTIVE MAINTENANCE IN MANUFACTURING

Picture a bustling manufacturing plant, its machines working tirelessly to meet the demands of a competitive market. Yet, behind this facade of efficiency lies a challenge that many manufacturers face: frequent equipment breakdowns that disrupt production and inflate costs. These unexpected failures lead to high maintenance expenses and costly downtimes, affecting not only the bottom line but also the company's reputation for reliability. The company, renowned for its precision-crafted components, knew that its traditional maintenance strategies—reactive and often inefficient —were no longer sufficient. It was time to explore a more proactive approach, one that could anticipate problems before they occurred, saving both time and money. Enter AI-driven predictive maintenance, a solution that promises to transform their maintenance operations by leveraging cutting-edge technology and data analytics.

The strategy for implementing predictive maintenance began with installing Internet of Things (IoT) sensors on critical equipment throughout the plant. These sensors diligently monitored key performance indicators, such as temperature, vibration, and pressure, collecting vast amounts of data in real time. This data served as the foundation for the next step: using machine learning algorithms to analyze patterns and detect anomalies that might indicate potential equipment failures. By examining historical and current data, these algorithms could predict when a machine would likely break down, allowing the company to schedule maintenance activities proactively. This shift from reactive to predictive maintenance marked a significant change in how the company approached equipment management, focusing on preventing issues rather than simply responding to them.

Integrating AI into the existing maintenance workflow required thoughtful planning and execution. The first task was seamlessly incorporating AI tools into the company's maintenance management system, ensuring that data from IoT sensors could be processed and analyzed efficiently. This integration allowed maintenance teams to receive timely alerts and insights, enabling them to act swiftly and decisively. Alongside this technological upgrade, the company recognized the importance of equipping its maintenance staff with the skills needed to leverage AI effectively. Comprehensive training programs were introduced, guiding employees on interpreting AI-generated data and implementing data-driven maintenance strategies. This combination of technology and training empowered the workforce, transforming them into proactive problem solvers rather than reactive responders.

The outcomes of this AI-driven approach were transformative. Equipment downtime decreased significantly, as maintenance teams could address potential issues before they escalated into costly breakdowns. Maintenance costs also saw a substantial reduction, as the company optimized its maintenance schedules, focusing on tasks that genuinely needed attention while avoiding unnecessary interventions. The success of this initiative underscored a critical lesson: continuous monitoring and data analysis are paramount to the effectiveness of predictive maintenance. By maintaining a vigilant eye on equipment performance and regularly updating their predictive models, the company ensured that its maintenance strategies remained relevant and effective, adapting to the ever-evolving demands of the manufacturing environment.

Visual Element: Predictive Maintenance Workflow Diagram

To better illustrate the process, consider a workflow diagram outlining the steps of predictive maintenance:

1. Data Collection: IoT sensors monitor equipment in real time.
2. Data Analysis: Machine learning algorithms analyze collected data for patterns and anomalies.
3. Predictive Insights: Alerts and recommendations are generated for proactive maintenance.
4. Maintenance Execution: Informed decisions guide maintenance activities, reducing downtime and costs.

This visual representation provides a clear understanding of how predictive maintenance can be seamlessly integrated into manufacturing operations, highlighting the interplay between technology and human expertise.

7.2 SCENARIO 2: AI-POWERED TALENT MANAGEMENT IN A TECH COMPANY

In the bustling corridors of a leading tech company, where innovation is the currency of growth, the HR department faced a pressing challenge: high employee turnover. Skilled professionals were leaving at an alarming rate, taking with them their expertise and a piece of the company's future. Compounding this issue was the difficulty in identifying high-potential employees who could be nurtured into future leaders. These challenges were significant in a sector where talent is the lifeline of innovation. The company realized that more than traditional talent management strategies were needed. They needed a transformative approach, one that could not only identify the stars within their ranks but also foster an environment where employees felt valued and engaged. This realization led them to explore AI-powered solutions, leveraging technology to turn talent management into a strategic advantage.

The company embarked on an AI-powered talent management strategy to address these challenges. The first step involved collecting comprehensive data on employee performance and engagement. This data was gathered from various sources, including performance reviews, peer feedback, and employee surveys, creating a holistic view of each employee's contributions and satisfaction levels. With this data in hand, the company applied machine learning algorithms to conduct sophisticated sentiment analysis. These algorithms sifted through qualitative data, such as open-ended survey responses and internal communication patterns, to gauge employee sentiment and identify potential areas of concern. This analysis provided the HR team with valuable insights into employee morale and engagement, highlighting those at risk of leaving and those who were thriving.

Armed with insights from sentiment analysis, the company turned to predictive analytics to identify high-potential employees. By analyzing patterns in performance data and career progression, AI tools could predict which employees were likely to excel in leadership roles or take on more significant responsibilities. This predictive capability allowed HR to tailor development programs and succession plans, ensuring that high-potential employees received the training and opportunities needed to grow. The use of AI turned talent management from a reactive process into a proactive strategy, aligning employee growth with the company's long-term goals.

Implementing AI into the talent management workflow required a strategic integration with the company's existing HR management system. This integration ensured that AI tools could access and analyze employee data seamlessly, providing real-time insights and recommendations. To maximize the effectiveness of these tools, the company invested in training HR staff on using AI technology. This training equipped HR professionals with the skills to interpret AI-generated insights and apply them to talent management practices. By fostering a culture of data-driven decision-making, the company empowered its HR team to leverage AI to its fullest potential, transforming how they managed and developed talent.

The results of the AI-powered talent management strategy were significant. Employee retention improved as the company could identify and address potential issues before they led to resignations. Engagement levels rose as employees felt more connected to their roles and saw a clear path for career advancement. The ability to identify and nurture high-potential employees ensured a steady pipeline of future leaders, aligning talent development with strategic business objectives. This initiative underscored the importance of transparent and ethical AI practices. The company built trust in its AI-driven processes by ensuring that AI tools were used responsibly and with employee privacy in mind. This trust was crucial in fostering an environment where employees felt valued and engaged, contributing to the company's long-term success. In today's rapidly evolving tech landscape, this talent management approach addresses immediate HR challenges and positions the company as an employer of choice, attracting the best and brightest in the industry.

Case Study: AI-Driven Talent Management Success in Tech

Consider a major tech firm where AI-driven talent management transformed its workforce dynamics. By implementing predictive analytics, the firm reduced turnover by 20%, identifying employees at risk of leaving and offering targeted retention programs. This proactive approach not only stabilized the workforce but also improved overall morale and productivity. Such a case illustrates the potential of AI to revolutionize talent management, turning challenges into opportunities for growth and innovation.

7.3 SCENARIO 3: ENHANCING CUSTOMER EXPERIENCE WITH AI IN BANKING

In the bustling world of banking, customer service often makes or breaks a bank's reputation. This particular bank, despite its solid financial products, found itself grappling with long wait times and inconsistent service quality. Customers frequently voiced their frustration over delayed responses and varying levels of service, which eroded trust and impacted customer retention. In a market where customer experience is as crucial as interest rates, these issues were significant obstacles. The challenge was clear: the bank needed to reinvent its customer service not only to meet but exceed customer expectations. AI offers a solution that promises to streamline processes, enhance service quality, and provide a more personalized experience.

The strategy to overhaul customer experience began with implementing AI-powered chatbots. These intelligent systems were designed to handle routine inquiries and transactions, providing instant responses to common questions about account balances, transaction history, and loan applications. By automating these interactions, the bank aimed to free up human agents to focus on more complex issues, reducing wait times and improving overall service efficiency. Next, the bank harnessed the power of natural language processing (NLP) to make customer interactions more intuitive and human-like. NLP enabled the chatbots to understand and respond to customer queries in the same way a human would, ensuring that each interaction felt personalized and engaging.

Finally, the bank applied predictive analytics to offer customized banking services, analyzing customer data to predict needs and offer tailored financial advice. This proactive approach not only enhanced customer satisfaction but also helped identify cross-selling opportunities, boosting revenue.

Integrating AI into the bank's customer service operations required careful planning and execution. The first step was seamlessly incorporating AI tools into the existing customer service platform, ensuring they could access and process customer data in real time. This integration was crucial for providing accurate and timely responses, as well as for personalizing interactions based on customer history and preferences. Alongside this technological upgrade, the bank recognized the importance of training its customer service staff to work alongside AI tools. Comprehensive training programs were introduced to familiarize employees with AI functionalities and equip them with the skills to interpret AI-driven insights. By fostering a collaborative environment between humans and machines, the bank ensured that its customer service operations were not only efficient but also effective in meeting customer needs.

The outcomes of the AI-driven enhancements were significant. Wait times for customer support decreased dramatically as chatbots effectively managed routine inquiries and streamlined service flow. Customer satisfaction scores rose, reflecting the improved quality and consistency of service. Customers appreciated the rapid responses and personalized interactions, which made them feel valued and understood. The initiative highlighted the importance of continuous improvement and feedback loops. By regularly gathering customer feedback and analyzing service performance, the bank could identify areas for further enhancement and ensure that its AI systems remained aligned with customer expectations. This iterative approach allowed the bank to adapt its strategies and tools, continuously refining its customer service to maintain high standards of satisfaction.

As the bank continues to leverage AI for customer service, it remains committed to innovation and excellence. The lessons learned from this initiative underscore the transformative potential of AI in enhancing customer experience. By focusing on efficiency, personalization, and continuous improvement, banks can not only meet but exceed customer expectations, securing loyalty and driving growth in an increasingly competitive landscape. The future of banking lies in the seamless integration of technology and human touch, where AI serves as a powerful ally in delivering exceptional customer experiences.

7.4 INTERACTIVE LEARNING: QUIZZES AND DISCUSSION FORUMS

Imagine a lively discussion where ideas flow freely and individuals engage with each other, challenging assumptions and reinforcing understanding. This is the essence of interactive learning tools such as quizzes and discussion forums. They are not just educational supplements but integral components that deepen understanding and foster engagement. Quizzes provide an immediate feedback loop—correct answers validate comprehension, while incorrect ones offer learning opportunities. They reinforce key concepts and principles, ensuring that the knowledge sticks. Discussion forums, on the other hand, create a vibrant community of learners. They encourage active participation and collaboration, where sharing insights becomes a collective exercise that enriches everyone involved. These platforms allow for diverse perspectives, providing a broader understanding of complex topics.

The structure of AI-related quizzes is meticulously designed to cater to varying levels of expertise. They often start with multiple-choice questions that cover AI fundamentals, like defining key terms or explaining basic concepts. For example, a question might ask: "Which of the following best describes machine learning?" Such questions test foundational knowledge and ensure that core ideas are understood before moving on to more complex material. As learners progress, scenario-based questions come into play. These questions present hypothetical situations requiring the application of AI concepts to solve business challenges. An example could be: "How would you implement an AI solution to reduce customer churn in a mid-sized retail company?" This type of applied learning reinforces theoretical knowledge by demanding practical application, bridging the gap between understanding and execution.

Discussion forums play a complementary role, acting as a dynamic space for knowledge exchange. They facilitate peer-to-peer learning, where individuals can pose questions, offer solutions, and share experiences. This environment is invaluable for support, as participants learn from one another's successes and failures. Forums also encourage diverse perspectives, which are crucial for holistic understanding. For instance, a discussion topic might explore ethical AI practices, prompting participants to debate the implications of AI bias and privacy concerns. Such discussions can lead to a deeper appreciation of AI's complex ethical landscape, highlighting the importance of responsible and fair AI deployment. By engaging in these forums, learners develop critical thinking skills and a nuanced understanding of AI's impact.

Quiz questions and discussion topics are crafted to challenge and stimulate thought. For example, a quiz might include a question like: "What are the primary differences between supervised and unsupervised learning?" This encourages learners to differentiate between these two fundamental AI techniques. A discussion topic could delve into the societal implications of AI, asking: "How should businesses address the ethical challenges posed by AI to build trust with customers?" These examples illustrate how quizzes and forums can be used to deepen understanding and encourage critical engagement. By actively participating in these learning tools, you not only reinforce your knowledge but also contribute to a growing body of shared wisdom, collectively pushing the boundaries of what AI can achieve in business.

7.5 SUPPLEMENTARY ONLINE COURSES: EXTENDING YOUR LEARNING

Imagine the power of transforming your understanding of AI by diving deeper into its complexities through supplementary online courses. These courses are designed to expand both the depth and breadth of your AI knowledge, offering insights from industry experts and access to cutting-edge resources. One of the greatest benefits of these online courses is the flexibility they provide. You can learn at your own pace, fitting your studies around your busy schedule, whether you're at home, in the office, or even traveling. This flexibility means you can absorb the material when you're most focused, ensuring that the knowledge you gain is both meaningful and retained.

The landscape of AI-related online courses is diverse, catering to a wide range of interests and expertise levels. For those just starting, introductory courses cover the basics of AI, providing a solid foundation of understanding. These courses typically explore fundamental concepts, such as machine learning and neural networks, offering a comprehensive overview that equips you with the vocabulary and basic skills to engage with more complex material. For those ready to advance, courses delve deeper into machine learning and deep learning techniques, exploring detailed algorithms and their applications in real-world scenarios. Additionally, specialized courses focus on ethical AI and governance, addressing the critical importance of deploying AI responsibly and ethically within your business. These courses explore the balance between innovation and ethics, providing frameworks and strategies to ensure that your AI initiatives align with both legal requirements and societal expectations.

Integrating these online courses with the content of this book can significantly enhance your learning experience. Consider creating a study plan that aligns with the chapters of this book, ensuring that the concepts you encounter here are reinforced and expanded upon through your online studies. For example, as you work through the chapter on AI implementation frameworks, you might enroll in a course that offers a hands-on approach to building AI models, allowing you to apply theoretical knowledge in a practical context. You create a cohesive learning path that maximizes understanding and application by linking course content with specific chapters. This integration provides continuity and context, making your learning more comprehensive and actionable.

Several online courses stand out for their quality and relevance. "AI for Everyone" by Andrew Ng on Coursera is a highly recommended course that demystifies AI for non-technical audiences, offering clarity and confidence in understanding AI's potential and limitations. For those looking to dive deeper, the "Deep Learning Specialization" by Deeplearning.ai provides an in-depth exploration of deep learning technologies, offering practical insights into building and deploying AI models. These courses, among others, are invaluable resources that complement the material in this book, providing you with the tools and knowledge to implement AI strategies effectively within your organization.

As you progress through these courses, you'll find that they enhance your technical skills and broaden your perspective on AI's role in business. This dual enhancement prepares you to tackle AI challenges with a more informed and strategic approach, ensuring that you can leverage AI's full potential to drive growth and innovation. By integrating these supplementary courses with the insights gained from this book, you position yourself at the forefront of AI advancements, ready to lead your organization into the future with confidence and expertise.

CHAPTER 8
OVERCOMING CHALLENGES AND ENSURING LONG-TERM SUCCESS

C onsider a bustling e-commerce platform grappling with inaccurate recommendations and disgruntled customers. A deep dive into their operations reveals the root cause: poor data quality. This is a common challenge in the digital age, where businesses rely heavily on data to inform decisions. High-quality data isn't just a luxury; it's a necessity for successful AI projects. Good data enhances model accuracy and reliability, which are critical for making informed decisions. When data is flawed, AI models can produce skewed results, leading to misguided strategies. Moreover, high-quality data is vital for reducing biases, promoting ethical AI practices, and fostering trust in AI systems. With it, businesses can avoid alienating customers and stakeholders, undermining their competitive edge.

Ensuring data quality requires implementing robust data governance frameworks. These frameworks establish policies and procedures for maintaining data integrity, accuracy, and security. They help businesses manage data throughout its lifecycle, ensuring consistency and compliance with regulatory standards. Regular data auditing and cleansing are vital practices within these frameworks. Audits help identify inconsistencies and errors while cleansing processes remove inaccuracies and redundancies. These steps ensure that the data used in AI models is reliable and up-to-date, providing a solid foundation for decision-making.

Embracing technology is also crucial in managing data quality. Data profiling tools, for instance, play a significant role by identifying anomalies and inconsistencies within datasets. These tools scrutinize data attributes, helping businesses recognize patterns and outliers that may impact AI performance. Data cleansing software goes a step further, automating the correction of errors and removal of duplicates. This software streamlines the data preparation process, ensuring that datasets are pristine before feeding them into AI models. Additionally, data integration platforms are indispensable for consolidating data from disparate sources, creating a unified dataset that AI systems can leverage for analysis. These platforms facilitate seamless data flow across departments, enhancing collaboration and insight generation.

Several organizations have successfully tackled data quality challenges, setting benchmarks for others to follow. A global retail chain, for example, embarked on a comprehensive data quality initiative to improve its supply chain operations. By implementing advanced data profiling tools and a robust governance framework, the company significantly improved inventory management and customer satisfaction—similarly, a leading financial services firm prioritized data governance to enhance its risk management strategies. The firm employed data cleansing software to rectify inaccuracies in its financial datasets, resulting in more accurate risk assessments and improved decision-making processes.

Reflection Section: Evaluating Your Data Quality

Take a step back and evaluate your organization's current data quality practices. Consider the following questions to guide your reflection:

1. Data Governance: Have you established a robust data governance framework to manage data integrity and compliance?
2. Data Auditing: How frequently do you conduct data audits to identify and rectify inaccuracies?
3. Technology Utilization: Are you leveraging data profiling, cleansing, and integration tools to enhance data quality?
4. Continuous Improvement: What steps can you take to ensure continuous improvement in data quality management?

Reflecting on these questions can help identify areas for improvement and guide your organization toward achieving high data quality, ensuring AI initiatives are built on a solid foundation. As you address data quality challenges, remember that high-quality data is not just an operational requirement; it's a strategic asset that drives AI success and long-term business growth.

8.1 SCALING AI PROJECTS: STRATEGIES FOR SUSTAINABLE GROWTH

Scaling AI projects in an organization is akin to a small business transforming into a multinational corporation, a complex process fraught with challenges. Resource constraints and budget limitations often top the list of hurdles. Many businesses find themselves with ambitious AI plans but limited funding or personnel to execute them effectively. The costs of scaling AI can be substantial, encompassing technology, talent, and training. Additionally, technical hurdles and integration issues present significant barriers. Legacy systems may not seamlessly integrate with new AI technologies, creating bottlenecks that impede progress. The technical expertise required to navigate these complexities is often scarce, further complicating efforts. These challenges can stall AI initiatives, preventing them from reaching their full potential.

A phased implementation approach can be highly effective to overcome these obstacles and achieve sustainable AI growth. By breaking down the process into manageable stages, businesses can focus on incremental improvements, ensuring each phase is successful before moving on to the next. This method allows organizations to allocate resources more efficiently, minimizing risks and maximizing returns. Leveraging cloud-based AI platforms is another strategy that can significantly enhance scalability. These platforms offer flexible, on-demand resources that can be scaled up or down as needed, providing businesses with the agility to respond swiftly to changing demands. Cloud solutions also eliminate the need for costly infrastructure investments, freeing up capital for other strategic initiatives. Building cross-functional AI teams is equally important. By bringing together diverse expertise from across the organization, these teams can foster innovation and ensure AI projects align with broader business goals. Collaboration across departments enhances problem-solving capabilities and promotes a holistic view of AI's role within the company.

Organizational culture plays a pivotal role in the success of scaling AI projects. A culture that encourages innovation and experimentation is vital for fostering growth. Businesses must create an environment where employees feel empowered to explore new ideas and take calculated risks. This culture of innovation drives AI success and attracts and retains top talent eager to work at the cutting edge of technology. Promoting collaboration and knowledge sharing within the organization is another crucial aspect. When teams communicate effectively and share insights, they can build on each other's successes and learn from failures, accelerating the scaling process. An open and collaborative culture enhances the organization's ability to adapt to new challenges and seize emerging opportunities.

Several organizations have successfully navigated the complexities of scaling AI, setting examples for others to follow. A multinational tech company, for instance, implemented a phased approach to scale its AI initiatives. By starting with small, focused projects and gradually expanding, the company was able to build momentum and demonstrate value, securing additional resources and buy-in from stakeholders. This methodical approach allowed them to scale AI across various functions, from customer service to product development, enhancing efficiency and innovation. In the healthcare sector, a leading organization leveraged cloud-based AI platforms to scale its data analytics capabilities. By integrating AI into its operations, the organization improved patient outcomes and operational efficiency, demonstrating the transformative impact of AI when scaled effectively. These examples illustrate that with strategic planning and a supportive culture, scaling AI is not only possible but can also lead to significant competitive advantages.

8.2 DEMONSTRATING AI ROI: COMMUNICATING VALUE TO STAKEHOLDERS

Securing the trust and support of stakeholders hinges on effectively demonstrating the return on investment (ROI) of AI initiatives. This is not merely a financial exercise; it's about showing that the resources dedicated to AI are yielding tangible benefits. Demonstrating ROI is crucial for securing continued funding and support, which are the lifeblood of any long-term AI strategy.

When stakeholders see a clear return, they are more likely to back current projects and future endeavors. This trust is foundational, as it empowers leaders to push the boundaries of innovation with confidence, knowing they have the necessary backing.

Calculating the ROI of AI initiatives requires a meticulous approach. Pre- and post-implementation analysis is a starting point. By establishing a baseline of performance metrics before AI deployment, you can quantitatively assess improvements post-implementation. This involves comparing metrics such as cost savings, increased revenue, or enhanced efficiency to what was initially projected. The cost-benefit analysis further refines this by weighing the total costs against the benefits accrued from AI projects. Financial modeling can also provide deeper insights, projecting future returns based on current trends and outcomes. Additionally, incorporating key performance indicators (KPIs) and metrics into your analysis will provide a more comprehensive picture. Metrics might include time saved, error reduction, or customer satisfaction levels—each tailored to the specific goals of the AI project.

Communicating this value to stakeholders requires more than dry numbers. Crafting detailed ROI reports and dashboards can effectively encapsulate the data, turning complex figures into digestible insights. These tools highlight the areas where AI has driven success, linking outcomes directly to business objectives. Storytelling is another powerful strategy. By weaving AI success stories into your presentations, you humanize the data, transforming abstract figures into relatable narratives. These stories should showcase real-world examples of how AI has improved operations or solved critical business challenges. Regular updates and presentations are also vital. Keeping stakeholders informed builds trust and fosters a sense of shared ownership in the AI journey. Engaging stakeholders through interactive sessions, where they can ask questions and provide input, strengthens their connection to the project and reinforces their commitment to its success.

Consider the example of a global financial institution that successfully communicated the ROI of its AI initiatives. By implementing a sophisticated AI-driven fraud detection system, they not only reduced fraudulent transactions but also saved millions in potential losses. This success was communicated through detailed reports and compelling narratives that highlighted the system's impact on customer trust and financial security. Similarly, a manufacturing company demonstrated AI value by showcasing increased production efficiency and decreased downtime due to predictive maintenance technologies. Their approach involved presenting ROI metrics alongside stories from the production floor, illustrating how AI transformed daily operations and empowered employees.

These examples underscore the importance of not just calculating but effectively communicating AI ROI to stakeholders. By blending rigorous analysis with engaging storytelling, you can build trust, secure support, and drive forward your AI initiatives with the confidence of knowing that everyone is aligned and invested in the outcomes.

8.3 CONTINUOUS IMPROVEMENT: KEEPING YOUR AI INITIATIVES RELEVANT

In the fast-paced world of business, the only constant is change. This is especially true for AI, where technologies evolve rapidly, and what works today might be obsolete tomorrow. Continuous improvement in AI is not just a best practice; it's a necessity. Adapting to changing business needs and technologies ensures that your AI initiatives remain valuable and aligned with your strategic goals. Without ongoing enhancement, AI systems can quickly become outdated, leading to missed opportunities and inefficiencies. The relevance of AI to your business is directly linked to your ability to iterate, learn, and refine these systems continually.

Strategies for maintaining and enhancing AI initiatives are crucial for long-term success. Regular performance monitoring and evaluation are foundational to this process. By continuously tracking the performance of AI systems, you can identify areas that require improvement and make data-driven adjustments. This proactive approach allows for the timely detection of issues before they escalate into significant problems. Implementing feedback loops and user testing further bolsters AI systems. Encouraging users to provide feedback creates a dynamic inter- action between the system and its users, leading to more person- alized and effective AI solutions. Through regular testing, you can validate the effectiveness of updates and ensure that changes meet user expectations. Encouraging a culture of learning and iteration within your organization is equally important. Innovation thrives when employees are empowered to experi- ment and learn from successes and failures. This culture fosters an environment where continuous improvement is not just encouraged but expected.

AI governance plays a critical role in overseeing these enhance- ments. Establishing AI oversight committees ensures a dedicated team is responsible for monitoring AI systems and guiding their development. These committees provide strategic direction, ensuring that AI initiatives align with broader business objectives. Regular AI audits and reviews are vital for maintaining account- ability and transparency. By conducting thorough evaluations of AI systems, businesses can ensure compliance with ethical stan- dards and industry regulations while also identifying opportuni- ties for improvement. This governance framework is crucial for maintaining trust and confidence in AI initiatives, both within the organization and among external stakeholders.

Several organizations exemplify the benefits of continuous improvement in AI projects. A tech startup, for example, has maintained its competitive edge by continuously enhancing its AI-driven customer service platform. The startup has improved customer satisfaction and retention by regularly updating algorithms based on user feedback and market trends. This iterative approach has allowed them to adapt swiftly to changing customer needs, solidifying their market position. In the retail sector, a company has successfully implemented iterative AI development to refine its inventory management systems. Through continuous improvement, they have optimized stock levels, reduced waste, and increased overall efficiency. This commitment to iteration has resulted in significant cost savings and improved service delivery.

The importance of continuous improvement in AI cannot be overstated. The engine drives AI success, ensuring that systems remain relevant, effective, and aligned with business goals. By fostering a culture of learning, implementing strategic monitoring and feedback mechanisms, and establishing robust governance frameworks, businesses can navigate the complexities of AI and unlock its full potential. Continuous improvement is not just about keeping pace with technology; it's about leading the way in innovation and excellence.

8.4 AI INNOVATION LABS: FOSTERING CONTINUOUS EXPERIMENTATION

Imagine a bustling hub where ideas come to life, the energy of innovation is palpable, and every corner of the space buzzes with the promise of groundbreaking discoveries. This is the essence of an AI innovation lab—a dedicated environment explicitly designed for AI research and development. These labs are not just about housing advanced technology but about creating a fertile ground for creativity and exploration. By providing a space solely focused on AI, organizations can foster an atmosphere where experimentation is not only encouraged but expected. The freedom to test, iterate, and refine ideas without the constraints of daily operational pressures allows teams to push the boundaries of what's possible. This is where theoretical concepts meet practical application, driving projects that can transform industries and redefine business norms.

The advantages of having such a dedicated space for AI experimentation are manifold. First and foremost, AI innovation labs accelerate research and development cycles, enabling faster progression from ideation to implementation. With dedicated resources and infrastructure, these labs facilitate rapid prototyping and testing, reducing the time it takes to bring new AI solutions to market. Furthermore, they serve as magnets for top talent, attracting individuals who are passionate about being at the forefront of technological advancement. For organizations, this means not only access to cutting-edge ideas but also the ability to retain skilled professionals who are eager to work in an environment that values innovation. The collaborative nature of these labs encourages cross-disciplinary interactions, where experts from varied fields can come together to solve complex problems, leading to richer insights and more innovative solutions.

Establishing and managing an AI innovation lab requires careful planning and execution. The first step is securing the necessary funding and resources. This involves financial investment and acquiring the technological infrastructure and tools needed to support advanced AI research. Once resources are in place, the next step is to build a multidisciplinary team. Diverse expertise is crucial, as AI projects often require input from data scientists, engineers, ethicists, and industry specialists. This diversity ensures that the lab can tackle a wide range of challenges and opportunities. Establishing clear goals and metrics for success is also essential. These objectives guide the lab's activities, providing a framework for evaluating progress and impact. Metrics might include the number of successful prototypes developed, the speed of product development cycles, or the level of innovation in project outcomes. By setting these benchmarks, organizations can measure the lab's effectiveness and adjust strategies as needed.

Several organizations have set exemplary standards in establishing AI innovation labs. Google's AI innovation lab, for example, stands as a beacon of innovation and excellence. It has been instrumental in developing technologies that have reshaped industries, from natural language processing advancements to breakthroughs in computer vision. By fostering a culture of experimentation, the lab has continually pushed the envelope in AI research, producing solutions that are both impactful and ethical. Similarly, a leading automotive company has leveraged its AI research lab to pioneer advancements in autonomous driving technology. Through extensive testing and collaboration with academic institutions, the lab has accelerated the development of self-driving cars, setting new benchmarks for safety and efficiency. These labs demonstrate dedicated AI spaces' transformative potential when backed by strategic vision and robust management.

AI innovation labs are more than just physical spaces; they are the heart of an organization's AI strategy. By fostering a culture of continuous experimentation, they empower businesses to stay ahead of the curve, anticipate industry shifts, and lead in technological advancements. These labs catalyze change, turning ambitious ideas into tangible realities that can drive growth, enhance competitiveness, and create new avenues for success.

8.5 THE FUTURE OF AI IN BUSINESS: PREPARING FOR WHAT'S NEXT

As we look to the horizon of technological advancement, AI stands at the forefront, poised to redefine industries and reshape business landscapes. One of the most exciting developments is the progression in deep learning and neural networks. These technologies are becoming more sophisticated, enabling machines to perform tasks that require human-like understanding. Imagine a world where AI systems can interpret complex legal documents, provide medical diagnoses with remarkable accuracy, or compose music that resonates on an emotional level. Such capabilities are no longer confined to the realm of science fiction. They are on the cusp of becoming integral to daily operations across various sectors, promising to enhance productivity and innovation.

Another emerging trend is the increased adoption of AI in edge computing. This approach processes data closer to where it is generated, reducing latency and improving responsiveness. Businesses in sectors like manufacturing and logistics can benefit immensely from edge computing. For instance, smart factories equipped with edge AI can monitor machinery in real time, predicting maintenance needs and preventing downtime. This not only boosts efficiency but also significantly cuts costs. As more devices and applications leverage edge computing, companies that integrate AI at the edge will find themselves better positioned to respond to market demands swiftly and effectively.

To capitalize on these advancements, organizations must prepare strategically. Investing in research and development is crucial. Businesses can stay ahead of competitors by dedicating resources to exploring new AI technologies and applications and driving innovation. Continuous learning is equally important. Encouraging employees to upskill and stay informed about AI trends ensures that the organization remains agile and adaptable.

Building strategic partnerships with AI innovators can also provide access to cutting-edge technologies and insights. Collaborating with startups, research institutions, or tech giants allows businesses to leverage external expertise and accelerate their AI initiatives. Lastly, adopting a flexible and adaptive AI strategy is vital. This includes regularly reviewing and updating AI goals and processes, allowing for quick pivots in response to technological changes or market shifts.

The transformative potential of AI extends across industries. In manufacturing, AI-driven automation is set to revolutionize production lines. Robots equipped with AI can perform complex tasks with precision, increasing output and reducing errors. This shift enhances product quality and allows human workers to focus on more strategic roles. In retail, AI-enhanced personalization is elevating customer experiences. AI systems can tailor recommendations, promotions, and services to individual consumers by analyzing shopping behaviors and preferences. This level of personalization fosters customer loyalty and drives sales, giving retailers a competitive edge.

Forward-thinking organizations are already laying the groundwork for these changes. A leading financial services firm, for example, is future-proofing its operations by investing heavily in AI talent and infrastructure. By integrating AI into its core processes, the firm can offer personalized financial advice and services, enhancing customer satisfaction and retention. In the healthcare sector, a major organization is preparing for AI advancements by collaborating with tech companies to develop AI-powered diagnostic tools. These tools promise to improve patient outcomes through early detection and personalized treatment plans, setting new standards for healthcare delivery.

As AI continues to evolve, its impact will resonate across every facet of business. To thrive in this future, organizations must embrace innovation, foster adaptability, and remain vigilant in their pursuit of excellence. The path forward is one of opportunity, where those prepared to seize the moment will lead the vanguard of change.

CONCLUSION

As we conclude this journey into the world of AI in business, it's vital to recognize the foundational role that understanding AI fundamentals plays. These fundamentals are not just technical details; they are the keys to unlocking AI's potential in your organization. AI is more than a buzzword—it's a transformative tool capable of driving growth, enhancing efficiency, and offering a significant competitive edge when integrated thoughtfully and strategically.

Strategic alignment of AI initiatives with your business goals is the cornerstone of successful implementation. Throughout this book, we've explored how aligning AI with overarching strategies maximizes its impact. This alignment ensures that AI does not function in isolation but works in tandem with your business objectives, creating synergy and driving innovation.

We've introduced you to a Practical AI Implementation Framework, designed to guide you step-by-step through the AI integration process. This framework is your roadmap, minimizing disruption and maximizing return on investment through a phased approach. Taking small, manageable steps can build confidence, demonstrate value, and pave the way for more extensive AI projects.

Real-world applications and case studies have illustrated AI's profound impact across industries. From marketing to finance, operations to human resources, AI is revolutionizing how businesses operate. These examples provide a practical lens through which you can envision AI's role in your own business, offering tangible insights and inspiration.

Ethical AI implementation and governance are not optional; they are essential. As leaders, it is your responsibility to ensure that AI technologies are deployed responsibly, transparently, and equitably. Establishing governance frameworks and adhering to regulatory compliance safeguard against biases and ensure trust among stakeholders.

Developing AI talent and fostering organizational readiness are critical to sustaining AI initiatives. Building a workforce equipped with the right skills and fostering a culture of innovation will empower your organization to harness AI's full potential. Encourage continuous learning and stay informed about the latest AI trends and technologies to maintain a competitive edge.

Scenario-based learning and interactive resources provided throughout the book serve as practical tools to deepen your understanding. These resources are designed to reinforce key concepts and offer hands-on experience, helping you apply AI insights effectively within your business context.

Implementing AI comes with challenges, from data quality issues to integration hurdles. Yet, with the solutions and strategies outlined here, you can overcome these obstacles and ensure long-term success. Start by assessing your AI readiness and crafting an

AI vision statement. These foundational steps will set the stage for successful AI adoption.

As you embark on your AI journey, I encourage you to be proactive and innovative. Foster a culture of experimentation and collaboration within your organization. Support AI projects and share success stories to build a community of practice. Engage with supplementary online courses and interactive resources to continue learning and growing in your AI expertise.

Thank you for investing your time and interest in this book. My journey and passion for AI in business stem from a desire to help leaders like you navigate the complexities of AI. I am committed to supporting you in harnessing AI's transformative potential. Please feel free to connect with me on professional networks for further insights and support.

Remember, AI is a powerful ally when strategically and ethically implemented. It promises to transform how you do business, opening doors to new opportunities and driving lasting growth. With this knowledge and guidance, you are equipped to lead your organization into a future where AI is not just a tool but a catalyst for innovation and success. Stay curious, stay informed, and let AI be the force that propels your business forward.

KEEPING THE AI ADVANTAGE ALIVE

Now that you've got the tools you need to bring AI into your business, it's time to share what you've learned with others looking for the same boost.

By leaving your honest review on Amazon, you'll help other curious business owners discover how *The AI in Business Advantage* can guide them in their journey too. Your thoughts could make all the difference for someone else who's ready to learn but doesn't know where to start.

Thank you for your support. The power of AI in business grows when we share our knowledge — and with your review, you're helping me keep that mission going.

Scan to leave a review and see my entire library of books!

-Samuel Thorpe

REFERENCES

GFT. (n.d.). *10 winning strategies for successful AI integration in your business.* https://www.gft.com/int/en/blog/10-winning-strategies-for-successful-ai-integration-in-your-business

Intel. (n.d.). *Machine learning business examples and applications.* https://www.intel.com/content/www/us/en/artificial-intelligence/machine-learning-examples.html

Aberdeen. (n.d.). *AI analytics vs. traditional analytics: 3 essential differences.* https://www.aberdeen.com/blog-posts/blog-ai-analytics-vs-traditional-essential-differences/

McKinsey & Company. (2023). *The state of AI in 2023: Generative AI's breakout year.* https://www.mckinsey.com/capabilities/quantumblack/our-insights/the-state-of-ai-in-2023-generative-ais-breakout-year

Tidio. (n.d.). *35 inspiring mission and vision statement examples.* https://www.tidio.com/blog/mission-and-vision-statement-examples/

MIT Sloan Management Review. (n.d.). *Strategic alignment with AI and smart KPIs.* https://sloanreview.mit.edu/article/strategic-alignment-with-ai-and-smart-kpis/

Focus4Ward. (n.d.). *Case studies on successful AI implementation: Learn from real-world examples.* https://focus4wardcourses.com/case-studies-on-successful-ai-implementation-learn-from-real-world-examples/

The New Stack. (n.d.). *Creating a strategic roadmap for effective AI implementation.* https://thenewstack.io/creating-a-strategic-roadmap-for-effective-ai-implementation/

Cisco. (n.d.). *AI readiness assessment.* https://www.cisco.com/c/m/en_us/solutions/ai/readiness-index/assessment-tool.html

Salesforce. (n.d.). *5 steps to building a compelling AI business case.* https://partners.wsj.com/salesforce/bringing-trust-to-ai/5-steps-to-building-a-compelling-ai-business-case/

Built In. (n.d.). *64 artificial intelligence (AI) companies to know.* https://builtin.com/artificial-intelligence/ai-companies-roundup

Catanzariti, A. (n.d.). *Implementing AI with a phased approach.* https://www.linkedin.com/pulse/implementing-ai-phased-approach-angel-catanzariti-ohuvf

Content Grip. (n.d.). *AI marketing tools: Case studies and success stories.* https://www.contentgrip.com/ai-marketing-tools-case-studies-success-stories/

Infosys BPM. (n.d.). *AI-powered financial fraud detection in banking.* https://www.infosysbpm.com/blogs/bpm-analytics/fraud-detection-with-ai-in-banking-sector.html

ThroughPut. (n.d.). *Artificial intelligence (AI) in supply chain and logistics.* https://throughput.world/blog/ai-in-supply-chain-and-logistics/

Marr, B. (n.d.). *The amazing ways how Unilever uses artificial intelligence to recruit, train thousands of employees.* https://bernardmarr.com/the-amazing-ways-how-unilever-uses-artificial-intelligence-to-recruit-train-thousands-of-employees/

Harvard Business Review. (2020, October). *A practical guide to building ethical AI.* https://hbr.org/2020/10/a-practical-guide-to-building-ethical-ai

CNIL. (n.d.). *AI: Ensuring GDPR compliance.* https://www.cnil.fr/en/ai-ensuring-gdpr-compliance

Brookings. (n.d.). *Algorithmic bias detection and mitigation: Best practices and policies to reduce consumer harms.* https://www.brookings.edu/articles/algorithmic-bias-detection-and-mitigation-best-practices-and-policies-to-reduce-consumer-harms/

Marr, B. (2024, May 3). *Building trust in AI: The case for transparency.* Forbes. https://www.forbes.com/sites/bernardmarr/2024/05/03/building-trust-in-ai-the-case-for-transparency/

U.S. Department of Energy. (n.d.). *Supercharging America's AI workforce.* https://www.energy.gov/cet/supercharging-americas-ai-workforce

CIO. (n.d.). *How university partnerships are priming tech talent pipelines.* https://www.cio.com/article/219668/how-university-partnerships-are-priming-tech-talent-pipelines.html

DataCamp. (n.d.). *AI for leaders: Essential skills and implementation.* https://www.datacamp.com/blog/ai-for-leaders

Marr, B. (2024, May 10). *11 barriers to effective AI adoption and how to overcome them.* Forbes. https://www.forbes.com/sites/bernardmarr/2024/05/10/11-barriers-to-effective-ai-adoption-and-how-to-overcome-them/

Learn Courses. (n.d.). *Case studies: Success stories of brands using AI-driven marketing automation.* https://medium.com/@LearnCourses/case-studies-success-stories-of-brands-using-ai-driven-marketing-automation-88f7c39f8085

Alastair, P. (n.d.). *AI case study Saturday: Predictive maintenance in manufacturing.* https://www.linkedin.com/pulse/ai-case-study-saturday-predictive-maintenance-alastair-ppt6e

Gleeson, B. (2024, June 11). *Revolutionizing talent management and employee development with AI.* Forbes. https://www.forbes.com/sites/brentgleeson/2024/06/11/revolutionizing-talent-management-and-employee-development-with-ai/

Mosaicx. (n.d.). *AI in banking: How artificial intelligence can personalize customer experiences.* https://www.mosaicx.com/blog/ai-in-banking

Mad Devs. (2024). *Top data quality management tools to choose in 2024.* https://maddevs.io/blog/data-quality-management-tools/

McKinsey & Company. (n.d.). *Scaling AI for success: Four technical enablers for sustained impact.* https://www.mckinsey.com/capabilities/mckinsey-digital/our-insights/tech-forward/scaling-ai-for-success-four-technical-enablers-for-sustained-impact

Twilio. (n.d.). *How to estimate and measure the ROI of AI investments.* https://www.twilio.com/en-us/blog/ai-roi

Lenovo. (n.d.). *AI lab insights: Where innovation meets intelligence.* https://www.lenovo.com/us/en/glossary/ai-lab/?

MASTER CHATGPT EFFORTLESSLY

THE SIMPLE WAY TO UNDERSTAND NATURAL LANGUAGE PROCESSING, BOOST EFFICIENCY THROUGH AUTOMATION, AND WRITE POWERFUL PROMPTS

SAMUEL THORPE

INTRODUCTION

In 1956, an engineer named Arthur Samuel wrote a computer program that could play checkers. It was one of the earliest examples of a machine learning to perform a task, something that would lay the groundwork for what we now call artificial intelligence. Fast forward to today, and AI has woven itself into our daily lives, from suggesting what movie to watch next to diagnosing diseases. Among these advancements, one tool stands out: ChatGPT. For many, it is a glimpse into a future where machines understand and converse with humans seamlessly.

But what is ChatGPT, really? And how can it benefit you? This book, "Mastering ChatGPT Effortlessly: The Simple Way to Understand Natural Language Processing, Boost Efficiency through Automation, and Write Powerful Prompts," seeks to answer those questions. The purpose here is straightforward: to make ChatGPT accessible to beginners and guide you in tapping into its vast potential.

The vision for this book is to be a conversation starter. It is not about getting lost in technical jargon but about understanding how ChatGPT can be applied in everyday life and work. Think of it as a guide to crafting prompts that resonate, whether you're writing a business email or exploring creative storytelling.

Who is this book for? It's for adults and teens curious about technology but who might feel overwhelmed by it. It's for those who want to explore new ways to boost efficiency in business and personal projects. It's for artists and writers looking for a new tool to unlock creativity. In essence, it's for anyone who has ever wondered how to make technology work better for them.

As we navigate this digital landscape, understanding the cultural and ethical implications of AI is crucial. This book encourages you to think critically about the role of AI in society. It urges you to consider not just what AI can do but what it should do. This is especially important as these technologies continue to evolve and integrate into our lives.

Allow me to introduce myself. I am Samuel Thorpe. My passion lies in helping people, particularly those new to technology, overcome challenges and find clarity in the ever-evolving digital world. I've spent years researching and guiding others to make technology accessible and useful.

The structure of the book is designed to guide you from the basics to more complex applications. We start with an introduction to ChatGPT, explaining what it is and how it works. As you progress, you'll find detailed and versatile prompts, exercises to practice, and applications across various fields. By the end, you'll have a toolkit to use ChatGPT effectively in your projects.

The research for this book draws from multiple sources. It includes insights from experts in AI, practical examples from everyday users, and my own experiences. This blend ensures a well-rounded perspective, offering both theoretical knowledge and actionable advice.

While the subject matter is advanced, I've made an effort to keep the tone engaging and approachable. You won't find dense technical manuals here. Instead, the goal is to make learning enjoyable, mixing advanced ideas with clear explanations. This book also includes examples, stories, and analogies to keep the content relatable. Interactive elements like quizzes offer a chance to test your knowledge as you go. These features make the book not just a read, but an experience.

In conclusion, this book is an invitation. An invitation to explore a fascinating tool that can transform the way you work and create. A call to examine the possibilities and embrace the challenges that come with new technology. I invite you to join me on this journey, to discover how ChatGPT can become an invaluable part of your toolkit. Let's explore what it means to truly understand and utilize this remarkable technology. The journey begins now.

CHAPTER 1
GETTING STARTED WITH CHATGPT

In late November 2022, a curious group of engineers at OpenAI released a seemingly innocuous tool into the wild. Its name was ChatGPT, and it carried with it modest expectations. Yet, what happened next was nothing short of a phenomenon. Within weeks, ChatGPT captured the imaginations of millions, becoming a viral success and sparking a global conversation about artificial intelligence. How does a piece of technology achieve such prominence? And more importantly, why should you care? The answers lie in understanding ChatGPT, where it came from, and what it can do for you in your daily life.

1.1 WHAT IS CHATGPT? AN OVERVIEW

To grasp the significance of ChatGPT, we must first explore its origins. OpenAI, the innovative organization behind it, was founded with a bold mission: to ensure that artificial general intelligence benefits all of humanity. This mission is not just a corporate tagline; it's a guiding principle that drives every project they undertake. From the inception of GPT-1 to the refined capabilities of GPT-3.5, ChatGPT emerges as a testament to their relentless pursuit of progress in the field of natural language processing (NLP).

The journey of ChatGPT began with GPT-1, which laid the foundation for understanding language patterns. It was soon followed by GPT-2, a model that astonished researchers with its ability to generate coherent text. However, it was GPT-3, released in 2020, that truly pushed the boundaries. GPT-3.5, the backbone of ChatGPT, builds on this legacy with enhanced capabilities and refined algorithms. Each iteration marks a significant leap forward, bringing us closer to machines that can genuinely understand and respond to human language in meaningful ways. ChatGPT represents the culmination of these advancements, a fine-tuned marvel poised to engage with users in more nuanced and sophisticated interactions.

The core functionalities of ChatGPT are what make it truly remarkable. At its heart, ChatGPT excels in generating human-like text. Whether you're composing an email, crafting a story, or brainstorming ideas, ChatGPT can assist with a level of fluency that feels natural. It's also adept at answering questions and providing insights and information on a wide range of topics. Beyond mere text generation, ChatGPT engages in conversation, responding to prompts with contextually relevant replies. This conversational prowess allows it to simulate dialogue and even perform specific tasks based on carefully crafted prompts. In essence, ChatGPT operates as a digital assistant, poised to augment your capabilities in both mundane and creative endeavors.

The technology powering ChatGPT is both complex and fascinating, yet it can be understood in simpler terms. At its core lies the Transformer model, a groundbreaking architecture in NLP that uses a mechanism called self-attention. This allows ChatGPT to weigh the importance of different words in a sentence, leading to more accurate and context-aware text generation. The process begins with pre-training, where the model learns from vast datasets, followed by fine-tuning, which refines its capabilities based on specific tasks. Tokenization, another key aspect, involves breaking down text into manageable pieces, enabling the model to generate coherent and cohesive responses.

Despite its impressive capabilities, ChatGPT has limitations. Its strength lies in content generation, where it can produce high-quality text rapidly. However, it sometimes struggles with understanding complex contexts, leading to less accurate responses. Additionally, ethical considerations must be taken into account. ChatGPT, like all AI models, can inadvertently perpetuate biases present in its training data. OpenAI acknowledges these challenges, consistently working to improve the model's accuracy and fairness.

As you explore ChatGPT further, it becomes clear that while it is a powerful tool, it is not infallible. It requires thoughtful prompts and careful consideration of its outputs. Yet, its potential is undeniable, offering a glimpse into a future where technology and human creativity converge in unprecedented ways.

1.2 SETTING UP YOUR CHATGPT ACCOUNT

Creating a ChatGPT account is your first step towards unlocking a world of possibilities with AI. You begin this process by visiting the OpenAI website. Upon reaching the website, you'll find a straightforward layout guiding you to the registration section. Here, you can create an account using your email address or through third-party options like Google, Microsoft, or Apple. The choice is yours, but using a personal email is often recommended for ease of access. Once you've entered your details, OpenAI will send you a verification email. It's a simple step, yet crucial, as it ensures that your account is secure and that you are the rightful owner. Look for the email in your inbox, and click the verification link. This action will confirm your account and grant you access to the ChatGPT environment.

Upon setting up your account, you will encounter various access levels and subscription options. OpenAI provides a free tier, which is perfect for getting acquainted with ChatGPT's basic functionalities. This tier allows you to explore the platform without any financial commitment, offering a range of features that cater to casual users. However, for those seeking enhanced capabilities, there is the ChatGPT Plus subscription, which is priced at a monthly rate. This premium option comes with benefits such as faster response times and priority access, making it ideal for users who rely heavily on the tool for professional or frequent use. Considering the cost against the value it provides, many find the premium features well worth the investment, especially if they use ChatGPT for business or creative projects.

Once your account is verified and you've chosen your subscription plan, the next step involves configuring your settings to optimize your ChatGPT experience. Start by setting your preferences, which allows you to tailor the interface and functionality to your liking. You can adjust notification settings to ensure you only receive alerts relevant to you. This customization helps in managing information flow and prevents unnecessary distractions. Additionally, understanding privacy settings is paramount. These settings control what information you share with OpenAI and how your data is handled, allowing you to use ChatGPT confidently and knowing your privacy is respected.

With your settings configured, it's time to familiarize yourself with the user dashboard. The dashboard is your control center, where you'll find all the tools and features ChatGPT offers. The navigation menu is intuitive, providing easy access to different sections of the platform. Here, you can initiate new chats, explore settings, or review past interactions. Key features are prominently displayed, making it simple for you to utilize ChatGPT's capabilities efficiently. Additionally, the dashboard includes links to help and support resources. These resources are invaluable, especially when you encounter questions or require further guidance on specific functionalities.

Interactive Element: Quick Start Checklist

- Visit the OpenAI website and navigate to the registration section.
- Create an account using your preferred method (email, Google, etc.).
- Verify your account via the email link sent by OpenAI.
- Choose between the free tier or ChatGPT Plus subscription.
- Configure your account settings, including preferences and privacy.
- Explore the user dashboard, familiarizing yourself with key features.

The journey of setting up a ChatGPT account is not merely about logging in; it's about creating a tailored experience that aligns with your needs and preferences. Each step, from verification to exploring the dashboard, is designed to empower you to make the most of this remarkable tool. With your account ready, you are now poised to explore the expansive world of possibilities that ChatGPT offers.

1.3 NAVIGATING THE CHATGPT INTERFACE

Engaging with ChatGPT begins with understanding its user interface, a space designed to facilitate clear and efficient interaction. At the center of this digital realm lies the main chat window, the heart of your conversations. This area displays the ongoing dialogue, where your prompts appear alongside ChatGPT's responses. It's the dynamic canvas where creativity and inquiry unfold, providing a seamless flow of interaction that mimics face-to-face communication. To the side, the sidebar navigation offers a gateway to different functionalities, keeping you oriented as you explore. This section houses shortcuts to your chat history, allowing you to revisit past exchanges, as well as links to settings and support. The sidebar serves as your compass, guiding you through the landscape of options available at your fingertips. Below the chat window, the input and output sections are where the magic happens. You type your prompts here, and ChatGPT's responses materialize in the output, a space that adapts to your inquiries with remarkable fluency.

Interactivity is a cornerstone of the ChatGPT experience, and the interface reflects this through various features. The toolbar, positioned strategically, offers functionalities that enhance your usage. Here, you can access options to adjust the session, clear the conversation, or export the chat for future reference. These tools are designed to streamline your workflow, providing quick solutions to common needs. Shortcut commands further augment this efficiency. By learning a few simple keystrokes, you can navigate the interface with ease, whether it's initiating a new conversation or switching themes. Another valuable asset is the help icon, a small but mighty tool that connects you to a wealth of resources. Clicking it opens a portal to guides, FAQs, and troubleshooting tips, ensuring that assistance is always within reach when you encounter a challenge or have a question.

Personalization is key to making ChatGPT truly yours, and the interface offers several ways to tailor your environment. One of the most immediate changes you can make is switching between light and dark modes, adjusting the theme to match your preference or reduce eye strain. This simple toggle can transform your interaction space, making it more comfortable for extended use. Additionally, you can adjust text size and font, ensuring that the display aligns with your reading habits and visual needs. Configuring layout settings allows for further customization. You can choose how elements are arranged, optimizing the interface for your workflow and ensuring that the tools you use most frequently are readily accessible.

For those who seek a deeper level of control, the command line offers an intriguing avenue. This feature, often associated with more advanced users, provides a direct method to execute specific operations and access settings beyond the standard interface. Basic command line operations include running scripts and executing commands that automate tasks or retrieve detailed information. This functionality can be handy for users who wish to integrate ChatGPT into larger projects or systems. By accessing advanced settings via the command line, you can tap into features that offer greater precision and customization, perfect for tailoring the tool to specialized needs. This level of control empowers you to mold ChatGPT into a versatile assistant that responds to your queries and adapts to your unique workflow and requirements.

By understanding and leveraging these interface elements, you position yourself to interact with ChatGPT in ways that maximize its potential. Whether crafting an intricate query or simply exploring the tool's capabilities, the interface serves as your guide and canvas, ready to adapt to your needs and enhance your experience.

1.4 BASIC COMMANDS AND INTERACTIONS

Understanding the basic commands of ChatGPT is akin to learning the fundamental tools in a new language. These are your building blocks, the starting point from which you can explore the vast landscape of possibilities this AI offers. Begin with asking questions. This command is straightforward yet powerful. You type a question, and ChatGPT responds with an answer. Whether you're seeking information on a historical event or the meaning of a word, this function is your gateway to acquiring knowledge. Think of it as having a digital encyclopedia at your fingertips, ready to provide insights with just a few keystrokes. Generating text is another core function. Here, you provide a prompt, and ChatGPT produces a coherent piece of text. This is particularly useful for tasks like writing essays, crafting stories, or even drafting messages. It's like having a skilled writer on standby, ready to assist with your creative and professional needs. Additionally, you can request summaries. This function distills lengthy articles or reports into concise summaries, saving you time and effort. It's perfect for when you're short on time but need to grasp the essence of a document. Finally, ChatGPT can translate text, opening up a world of communication across languages. This feature is invaluable for those engaged in international correspondence or simply curious about different languages.

Interactive conversations with ChatGPT are where the tool truly shines. Initiating dialogue is as simple as typing a greeting or a question. The AI responds, and thus a conversation begins. What sets ChatGPT apart is its ability to follow up on previous exchanges, creating a dynamic and engaging interaction. This isn't just a static question-and-answer session; it's an evolving dialogue that adapts to the context you provide. For instance, imagine you're brainstorming ideas for a project. You pose a question, receive a response, and then build on that response with further inquiries. ChatGPT keeps track of the conversation's flow, allowing for a more natural and intuitive exchange. This capability enhances its utility as a brainstorming partner or a sounding board for ideas. You can refine the interaction by using conversational context, making it more relevant and targeted. It's like having a conversation with a knowledgeable colleague, where each response builds on the previous one, leading to deeper insights and understanding.

When it comes to task-specific commands, ChatGPT proves itself to be a versatile assistant. Writing emails is one such task. You can provide a brief outline of what you wish to convey, and ChatGPT can draft a professional email for you. This feature is a time-saver and helps ensure clarity and professionalism in your communication. Creating lists is another practical application. Whether it's a to-do list, a grocery list, or a list of potential project ideas, ChatGPT can organize your thoughts into structured formats. Drafting reports is yet another area in which ChatGPT excels. Provide the necessary data points and context, and it can help compile these into a coherent report, complete with sections, headings, and conclusions. These task-specific commands transform ChatGPT into a multi-functional tool capable of assisting with a wide range of professional and personal tasks.

Despite its capabilities, using ChatGPT effectively hinges on understanding its limitations and best practices. Clear and concise prompts are crucial for obtaining accurate and helpful responses. When your input is straightforward and unambiguous, ChatGPT can more easily comprehend and generate relevant outputs. Avoiding ambiguous language is equally important. Vague or complex phrasing can confuse the AI, leading to less accurate responses. Instead, aim for simplicity and precision in your prompts. Also, don't hesitate to iterate on prompts for better results. Sometimes, the first response might be different from what you need, and refining your input can yield improved outcomes. This process of iteration is akin to refining your questions in a conversation to extract more information from a knowledgeable source. By embracing these best practices, you can maximize the effectiveness of ChatGPT, turning it into a reliable and invaluable tool in your digital toolkit.

1.5 TROUBLESHOOTING COMMON SETUP ISSUES

Setting up ChatGPT should be a straightforward process, but like all things digital, it sometimes comes with hiccups. One of the most frequent challenges users face is account verification failures. Imagine eagerly setting up your account, only to find that the verification email never arrives. This can happen for several reasons, such as the email landing in your spam folder or a typo in your email address during the registration process. It's a simple oversight, but it can stall your progress. Another common issue is connectivity problems, particularly if you're in an area with spotty internet service. A stable internet connection is crucial for interacting with ChatGPT, as any interruptions can disrupt the flow of information. Subscription and billing issues also arise, especially when users accidentally select the wrong plan or encounter errors during payment processing. It's frustrating to be ready to explore ChatGPT's features only to find that a billing issue stands in your way.

Now, let's address these problems with some practical solutions. If you're facing account verification failures, the first step is to check your spam or junk folder, as verification emails sometimes get diverted there. If that doesn't work, resending the verification email is your best bet. Most platforms, including ChatGPT, offer an option to resend verification emails on their login or sign-up page. For connectivity issues, ensure that your internet connection is stable. You can do this by checking your router and restarting it if necessary. Sometimes, simply switching to a different network or using a wired connection can solve the problem. For subscription and billing concerns, contacting OpenAI's support team is advisable. They can provide guidance on resolving payment errors or adjusting your subscription plan to align with your needs. Having your account details and any error messages ready will help the support team assist you more efficiently.

Knowing where to find help can make all the difference when you encounter difficulties. OpenAI offers a range of support resources that you can access with ease. The OpenAI support center is a comprehensive hub for troubleshooting guides, offering step-by-step solutions to common issues. It's your first stop when things go awry. Community forums are another invaluable resource, providing a platform where users share experiences and solutions. Engaging with the community can offer insights into how others have resolved similar problems, and you may find answers to questions you hadn't thought of asking. The Frequently Asked Questions (FAQs) section is a trove of information covering everything from account setup to advanced features. Browsing through the FAQs can preemptively address concerns and enhance your understanding of ChatGPT's functionalities.

Prevention, as they say, is better than cure. By taking proactive steps, you can minimize the likelihood of encountering setup issues in the first place. Keep your software updated to ensure compatibility with the latest features and security protocols. Regular updates not only enhance performance but also resolve known bugs and glitches. Employ strong passwords to protect your account from unauthorized access. A combination of letters, numbers, and special characters makes for a robust password. It's a simple measure that goes a long way in safeguarding your digital presence. Regularly reviewing your account settings is also beneficial. It allows you to confirm that your preferences, notifications, and privacy settings are aligned with your intentions. This habit keeps your account streamlined and reduces the possibility of unexpected disruptions.

In the dynamic world of technology, challenges are inevitable. However, with the right tools and mindset, they become manageable. Each step you take to troubleshoot or prevent issues is an investment in a smoother, more efficient experience with ChatGPT. By being prepared, you can navigate these challenges with confidence, ensuring that your interaction with this powerful tool remains seamless and productive.

1.6 ETHICAL CONSIDERATIONS IN AI USAGE

As we delve deeper into the realm of artificial intelligence, the ethical implications of tools like ChatGPT become increasingly important. These concerns aren't just theoretical—they affect real-world applications and decisions. Privacy sits at the forefront of these issues. With AI systems handling vast amounts of personal data, the risk of breaches looms large. Users may wonder how their information is stored and used, and rightfully so. Data security is critical, as any vulnerability can lead to unauthorized access or misuse. Such breaches not only compromise individual privacy but also erode trust in technology. Equally significant is the potential for bias in AI responses. These systems learn from existing data, and if that data reflects societal biases, AI outputs might unintentionally perpetuate them. This can manifest in various ways, from skewed information dissemination to reinforcing stereotypes.

Using ChatGPT responsibly involves several key practices. First, respecting user privacy is paramount. Always be conscious of the data shared with AI systems, and ensure that interactions are limited to non-sensitive information whenever possible. This approach minimizes exposure risks and promotes user confidence. Another critical aspect is avoiding the misuse of AI-generated content. With great power comes great responsibility, and using AI outputs ethically is essential. Whether crafting content or generating ideas, the intention should always align with honesty and integrity. Transparency in AI interactions fosters trust and understanding. Users should be aware of AI capabilities and limitations, preventing misconceptions about what these systems can and cannot do.

Fairness in AI applications is not a luxury but a necessity. Addressing biases involves actively working to minimize them in AI outputs. Diverse training data is vital, as it broadens the context and reduces the likelihood of skewed results. Diverse data ensures that AI systems reflect a more comprehensive view of society, capturing the nuances and variations that exist. Encouraging equitable AI practices means going beyond mere functionality; it requires a commitment to inclusivity and fair representation across all AI applications. This commitment must be reflected in the design, testing, and deployment of AI systems.

Structured frameworks and standards have been established to guide ethical AI usage. OpenAI, for instance, has developed ethical guidelines that outline best practices and principles for AI development and deployment. These guidelines serve as a roadmap, ensuring that AI systems are used in a manner that upholds ethical standards. Industry standards and best practices also play a crucial role, providing a foundation for organizations to build upon as they implement AI solutions. Case studies of ethical AI deployment offer valuable insights, showcasing how ethical considerations can be integrated into real-world applications. These examples highlight the positive impact of aligning AI usage with ethical principles, demonstrating the potential for AI to be a force for good when managed responsibly.

In considering these ethical dimensions, the goal is to ensure that AI remains a tool for empowerment and progress. It should be a catalyst for innovation, not a source of inequality or harm. As we continue exploring AI's potential, we are responsible for navigating these ethical complexities with care and foresight. By prioritizing ethical considerations, we can embrace AI's benefits while safeguarding against its potential pitfalls. In doing so, we not only enhance the technology itself but also pave the way for a more equitable and transparent digital future.

CHAPTER 2
WRITING EFFECTIVE PROMPTS

I magine standing at the door of a grand library. The shelves are brimming with endless volumes, each one eager to share its tales and knowledge. Yet, to unlock these treasures, you need the right key—a prompt. In the realm of ChatGPT, your prompt is that key. It is not merely an input but the foundation of a dialogue between you and the AI, setting the stage for the responses you receive. Understanding prompts is crucial, as they guide the AI in generating relevant and meaningful content. This chapter will explore what makes a prompt effective, how to craft one, and why it matters.

A prompt is your initial input text to the AI—a question, a directive, or a request. It's the seed from which the AI draws its responses. Think of it as a conversation starter, a way to engage with ChatGPT's capabilities. The prompt serves as the basis for generating responses and determining the direction and depth of the AI's output. This process mirrors a dialogue, where the clarity and specificity of your words shape the conversation's course. Just as a well-phrased question can elicit a thoughtful answer from a friend, a carefully crafted prompt can draw out insightful and precise responses from ChatGPT.

The importance of a good prompt cannot be overstated. A well-crafted prompt is essential for obtaining accurate and useful responses. Clarity in communication is paramount; it reduces ambiguity and ensures that the AI understands your intent. A clear prompt is like giving someone a map with a precise route, rather than vague directions. This precision enhances the relevance of answers, allowing ChatGPT to provide information that aligns with your needs. A prompt that clearly articulates the task at hand helps the AI focus its resources on producing the most appropriate response, thereby improving the overall quality of the interaction.

Prompts come in various forms, each serving a unique purpose. Open-ended questions invite expansive answers, encouraging the AI to explore different angles and possibilities. These prompts are ideal for brainstorming or when seeking comprehensive insights. Specific task requests, on the other hand, are more focused. They direct the AI to perform a particular action, whether it's composing an email or summarizing an article. These prompts are precise, targeting a clear outcome. Contextual prompts provide background information or set the scene for the AI, helping it generate relevant and tailored responses to your situation. Each type of prompt has its place, and understanding when to use each one is key to effective communication with ChatGPT.

The prompt-response cycle is the engine that drives the interaction with ChatGPT. It begins with you inputting a prompt and setting the stage for the AI to process and generate a response. This cycle is dynamic, with each step influencing the next. ChatGPT analyzes your input, drawing on its vast knowledge base to craft a reply that aims to meet your needs. Once the AI generates a response, the cycle enters the evaluation phase. Here, you assess the accuracy and usefulness of the answer, using this feed-back to refine future prompts. This iterative process is akin to a conversation, where each exchange builds on the previous one, leading to a richer and more informed dialogue.

Interactive Element: Prompt Evaluation Checklist

- **Clarity**: Is the prompt clear and unambiguous?
- **Relevance**: Does the response align with your expectations?
- **Specificity**: Is the task or question precisely defined?
- **Context**: Have you provided enough background information?
- **Outcome**: Does the response meet your needs or require refinement?

Understanding prompts is an essential skill for anyone looking to engage effectively with ChatGPT. The ability to craft and refine prompts opens up a world of possibilities, transforming the tool from a simple novelty into a valuable resource. As you explore the nuances of prompt writing, you'll discover the power of clear communication and its impact on the quality of AI interactions.

2.1 CRAFTING CLEAR AND CONCISE PROMPTS

Imagine trying to have a conversation with someone who speaks in riddles or uses overly complex language. You'd likely find it frustrating and confusing. The same principle applies when you're crafting prompts for ChatGPT. Clarity is your best ally. A clear prompt uses simple and direct language, devoid of unnecessary jargon or convoluted terms. This simplicity ensures that ChatGPT understands exactly what you're asking, leading to more precise responses. When you eliminate ambiguity, you're essentially paving a direct path for the AI to follow. It's like giving directions with clear street names instead of vague landmarks. The more straightforward your prompt, the more likely you are to receive useful and accurate information in return.

Being specific in your prompts is another key to unlocking the full potential of ChatGPT. Specificity provides the AI with a detailed map, guiding it to deliver the precise information you seek. This means including all necessary details—such as dates, locations, or other relevant specifics—within your prompt. For instance, asking "Tell me about the weather" is quite broad, but adding specifics like "What's the weather like in New York on March 12th?" gives ChatGPT the context it needs to provide a focused answer. By honing in on the specifics, you not only make it easier for ChatGPT to understand your request but also enhance the relevance and usefulness of the response it generates.

It's easy to fall into the trap of asking overly broad questions, hoping to cover all the bases in one go. However, this often leads to general or unfocused responses that may not meet your needs. Limiting the scope of your prompts helps to avoid this pitfall. Think of it as narrowing the lens through which the AI views your question. Instead of asking a sweeping question encompassing multiple themes, break down your query into smaller, more manageable parts. This approach is akin to solving a puzzle one piece at a time rather than trying to see the whole picture at once. Focusing on one aspect at a time allows ChatGPT to provide more targeted and meaningful insights.

Grammar and punctuation might seem like minor details, but they are crucial in prompt crafting. Proper grammar ensures that your prompts are structured in a way that ChatGPT can easily interpret. Imagine reading a sentence without any punctuation—it can quickly become a confusing jumble of words. Similarly, punctuation clarifies meaning, guiding the AI on how to process your request. It acts as a roadmap, indicating where one thought ends and another begins. Ensuring that your prompts are grammatically sound and punctuated correctly reduces the risk of misinterpretation, thus improving the quality of the AI's responses.

When you combine all these elements—clarity, specificity, focus, and proper grammar—you create a prompt that ChatGPT can engage with effectively. This combination transforms your interaction from a guessing game into a precise and productive exchange. As you refine your approach, you'll find that the AI becomes a more reliable partner, capable of assisting you in a multitude of tasks with greater accuracy and depth. The key is in the details, and by paying attention to how you frame your prompts, you unlock a world of possibilities with ChatGPT.

2.2 EXAMPLES OF EFFECTIVE PROMPTS FOR BEGINNERS

When you're just getting started with ChatGPT, simple prompts are your best friends. They serve as straightforward introductions to the capabilities of this tool, allowing you to quickly grasp how it functions. For instance, asking, "What is the weather like today?" is a direct and uncomplicated query. It teaches you how the AI retrieves current information and responds with relevant data. Similarly, a light-hearted prompt like "Tell me a joke" illustrates the AI's ability to generate creative and humorous content. These prompts are easy to understand and offer immediate feedback, making them perfect for beginners who want to explore ChatGPT's basic functionalities without diving into complex instructions.

Moving beyond the basics, context-based prompts add depth and richness to your interactions with ChatGPT. By providing context, you give the AI a framework within which to operate, leading to more nuanced and tailored responses. Take, for example, the prompt, "Explain the water cycle to a 10-year-old." Here, you specify not only the topic but also the complexity level appropriate for a young audience. This added context helps ChatGPT adjust its language and explanations to suit the intended reader. Similarly, asking the AI to "Summarize the plot of 'To Kill a Mockingbird'" provides it with a straightforward task and context, guiding it to deliver a concise yet informative response. These prompts demonstrate how context can transform a generic query into a precise and insightful exchange, enhancing your understanding of ChatGPT's versatility.

When you're looking for ChatGPT to perform specific tasks, task-specific prompts come into play. These prompts provide clear directives, enabling you to leverage ChatGPT's capabilities for practical applications. For instance, you might ask, "Write a professional email to a client." This prompt instructs ChatGPT to focus on crafting a formal communication, allowing you to see how it can assist in business-related tasks. Another example is "Generate a list of healthy dinner recipes," which showcases the AI's ability to compile information from various sources to meet your culinary needs. Task-specific prompts are particularly useful for those with clear objectives and want to see how ChatGPT can streamline their workflow or enhance their productivity through automation.

Iterative prompts are an excellent way to refine your inquiries and gain deeper insights. They involve a process of continual improvement, where you adjust your prompts based on the initial responses you receive. For example, if you ask, "What are the top tourist attractions in Paris?" and find the response too broad, you can refine it by specifying, "What are the top tourist attractions in Paris for art lovers?" This iterative approach allows you to hone in on the exact information you need, teaching ChatGPT to respond with more precision over time. As you iterate, you'll notice that the AI becomes more attuned to your specific preferences and requirements, leading to increasingly relevant and valuable interactions. This process not only improves the quality of the responses but also enhances your skills in crafting effective prompts, empowering you to unlock the full potential of ChatGPT in various contexts.

2.3 COMMON MISTAKES TO AVOID IN PROMPT WRITING

When interacting with ChatGPT, clarity is your ally. One of the most common pitfalls in prompt writing is ambiguity. Imagine asking someone, "Can you help?" without specifying what kind of help you need. Such a vague prompt can lead to confusion and irrelevant responses from ChatGPT. For instance, a prompt like "Tell me about the weather" could yield a broad range of information unless you specify a location or date. To clarify ambiguous prompts, focus on the details. Instead of saying, "Tell me about the weather," try, "What's the weather forecast for tomorrow in San Francisco?" By adding specificity, you guide the AI to deliver a response that aligns closely with your expectations. This specificity transforms a general query into a targeted request, significantly enhancing the quality of the interaction.

Overloading prompts with multiple requests is another mistake that can hinder effective communication with ChatGPT. Consider a scenario where you're asking, "Can you tell me about the weather in Paris, the history of the Eiffel Tower, and the best French cuisine?" Such a prompt is overloaded and can overwhelm the AI, leading to fragmented or incomplete responses. The key is to break down complex prompts into simpler, manageable parts. You could start by asking about the weather, then inquire separately about the Eiffel Tower, and finally explore French cuisine. This approach makes each prompt more digestible and allows you to obtain detailed responses for each specific question. By simplifying your requests, you enable ChatGPT to focus on one task at a time, fostering clearer and more coherent outputs.

Neglecting to provide context is another challenge that can lead to unsatisfactory results. Imagine walking into a conversation halfway through and trying to contribute without knowing the background. Prompts that lack context leave ChatGPT guessing at your intentions, often resulting in generic or off-target responses. For example, asking "Why is it important?" without any context could leave the AI grasping at straws. To improve accuracy, always provide sufficient background information. Instead of a context-less prompt, you might say, "Why is it important for students to learn coding in today's digital age?" By embedding context, you arm ChatGPT with the necessary information to tailor its responses to your specific needs. This simple addition can dramatically improve the relevance and depth of the answers you receive.

Ignoring feedback from the AI is a missed opportunity to refine your prompts. ChatGPT's responses are a reflection of your input, and paying attention to these outputs can reveal patterns and areas for improvement. If the AI consistently misinterprets your queries, it might be time to adjust your prompt structure. Consider an iterative approach: begin with a basic prompt, evaluate the response, and refine the prompt based on what you receive. Suppose your initial question about historical events yields an answer that is too broad. In that case, you could narrow it down by specifying a particular era or event. This iterative process helps you fine-tune your prompts, leading to more precise and satisfactory interactions. Recognizing the nuances in AI responses and adapting your prompts accordingly can unlock a more effective and rewarding experience with ChatGPT.

2.4 ADVANCED PROMPT STRUCTURING TECHNIQUES

When you think about crafting prompts, consider it an art that combines creativity and precision. One powerful technique you can use is incorporating conditional statements. Imagine setting up an "if-then" scenario to guide ChatGPT through a decision-making process. For instance, you might prompt it with, "If the weather is sunny, suggest outdoor activities; if it's rainy, recommend indoor pastimes." This approach helps get targeted responses and enables the AI to handle multiple potential outcomes. Similarly, multiple-choice prompts can streamline interactions, offering predefined options that guide ChatGPT to a specific area of focus. For a project, you might say, "Choose the best marketing strategy: A) Social Media, B) Email Campaign, C) Influencer Partnership." This can simplify decision-making, especially when you're juggling complex options and need quick, precise answers.

Layering prompts is another technique that can take your interactions with ChatGPT to a new level. Think of it as building a narrative, one question leading to the next, each deepening the context and enhancing the detail of the responses. Sequential questioning involves asking a series of related questions that build on each other, like peeling layers off an onion to get to the core. You might start by asking, "What are the benefits of exercise?" followed by, "How does it improve mental health?" and then, "What are some effective routines for beginners?" This layered approach allows you to explore a topic comprehensively, encouraging the AI to provide more detailed and contextually rich answers. It's beneficial when you're tackling complex subjects that require nuanced understanding.

Embedding specific instructions within your prompts can also refine the responses you receive. This method involves clearly stating the format or constraints you desire. For example, instruct ChatGPT to "Provide a summary in 50 words" or "List three benefits of a plant-based diet." By embedding these instructions, you set clear boundaries for the AI, ensuring it delivers information in the exact form you need. It's like giving a painter a canvas and a specific color palette; the artist can still be creative, but there's a framework to guide the creation. This technique is especially effective when you need concise and structured information, whether for reports, presentations, or personal projects.

Balancing open-ended and close-ended prompts is critical to maximizing the utility of ChatGPT. Open-ended prompts invite exploration and creativity, allowing the AI to expand on ideas without constraints. They are ideal when you're seeking inspiration or brainstorming, such as asking, "How can technology improve education?" This can lead to a wide range of perspectives and insights. On the other hand, close-ended prompts are more focused, often requiring a straightforward answer. They are useful for fact-checking or when you need a specific piece of information, such as, "Is the capital of France Paris?" Balancing these two types of prompts allows you to harness the full spectrum of ChatGPT's capabilities, from generating broad ideas to pinpointing exact information.

Understanding and applying these advanced techniques can significantly enhance your interactions with ChatGPT. Each method offers a unique way to engage with the AI, providing you with the tools to tailor responses to your specific needs. Whether you're exploring a topic in-depth or seeking quick, accurate answers, these strategies can help you make the most of ChatGPT's potential, turning it into an indispensable tool in your digital toolkit.

2.5 CUSTOMIZING PROMPTS FOR SPECIFIC TASKS

Tailoring prompts to suit different tasks is like choosing the right tool for a job. Each prompt should be crafted with its purpose in mind, allowing ChatGPT to deliver relevant and precise responses. Let's explore how to customize prompts for various tasks, starting with content creation.

When it comes to writing articles, blogs, or social media posts, clarity and engagement are key. Consider a prompt such as, "Draft a blog post on the benefits of remote work." This prompt guides ChatGPT to focus on a well-defined topic, encouraging it to explore various angles like productivity, work-life balance, and environmental impact. Similarly, crafting a social media caption, such as "Create a social media caption for a summer sale," requires brevity and appeal to capture the audience's attention. These prompts should inspire creativity while maintaining a clear focus, ensuring that the content aligns with your intended message and audience.

In the business world, prompts play a crucial role in streamlining communication and decision-making processes. For instance, "Generate a market analysis report" directs ChatGPT to compile data and insights into a structured format, providing valuable information for strategic planning. The AI can sift through trends and statistics, offering a comprehensive overview that aids in making informed business decisions. Meanwhile, prompts like "Write an email response to a customer complaint" require a balance of professionalism and empathy. Here, ChatGPT can assist in drafting a response that addresses the customer's concerns while maintaining a positive tone, ensuring the communication is both effective and courteous.

Educational prompts serve as powerful tools for learning and teaching. When you ask ChatGPT to "Explain the Pythagorean theorem," you're tapping into its ability to simplify complex concepts into understandable explanations. This can be incredibly helpful for students who need clear and concise information. Similarly, a prompt such as "Create a study guide for World War II history" allows the AI to organize key events and figures into a coherent format that facilitates study and retention. These prompts are designed to support educational goals, providing learners with resources that enhance their understanding and engagement with the material.

Creativity knows no bounds, and neither should your prompts for artistic endeavors. A prompt like "Write a short story about a space adventure" invites ChatGPT to tap into its storytelling capabilities, weaving narratives that capture imagination and intrigue. This can be an excellent exercise for aspiring writers looking to explore new genres or themes. Similarly, "Generate a prompt for a digital art project" can spark inspiration for artists seeking fresh ideas. The AI can suggest themes, concepts, or even specific techniques, providing a springboard for creativity that artists can adapt and build upon.

By customizing prompts to fit specific tasks, you can unlock ChatGPT's full potential, transforming it from a general tool into a specialized assistant tailored to your needs. Whether crafting content, conducting business, learning new concepts, or exploring creative projects, the right prompt can make all the difference. As you develop this skill, you'll find that your interactions with ChatGPT become more productive and rewarding, opening up new possibilities for innovation and growth.

As we conclude this chapter, remember that prompts are not just inputs, but bridges to more meaningful and effective interactions with ChatGPT. By tailoring them to your specific needs, you create opportunities for the AI to assist you in ways that are both insightful and practical. Next, we'll explore the practical applications of these prompts in daily life, showing you how to integrate ChatGPT into your routines for enhanced productivity and creativity.

CHAPTER 3
PRACTICAL APPLICATIONS IN DAILY LIFE

I magine waking up to a perfectly organized day, where tasks align seamlessly with your goals, and productivity flows effortlessly. This is not a distant dream but a reality made possible with ChatGPT. As a digital assistant, ChatGPT offers more than just answers; it provides a structured approach to daily life, making it a powerful ally in personal productivity. Whether you're a student juggling assignments or a professional managing multiple projects, ChatGPT's capabilities can simplify your routine and enhance your efficiency. Let's explore how it transforms everyday tasks into streamlined processes, ensuring you make the most of each day.

3.1 USING CHATGPT FOR PERSONAL PRODUCTIVITY

To begin, consider task management, a vital component for maintaining order and reducing stress. ChatGPT helps you craft daily to-do lists, ensuring nothing slips through the cracks. Imagine asking, "Create a to-do list for today with tasks like grocery shopping, replying to emails, and preparing a presentation." The AI swiftly organizes your tasks, prioritizing them based on urgency and relevance. This structured approach not only clarifies your day but also boosts productivity by minimizing decision fatigue. With ChatGPT, setting up a weekly schedule becomes a breeze. It assists in allocating time blocks for work, exercise, and relaxation, promoting a balanced lifestyle. By integrating these tasks into a cohesive plan, you regain control over your time, paving the way for a more focused and fulfilling day.

Goal setting and tracking are crucial for personal growth, and ChatGPT excels in this area. It guides you in establishing SMART goals—specific, measurable, achievable, relevant, and time-bound —ensuring your objectives are clear and attainable. For instance, when you ask, "Help me set SMART goals for my fitness routine," ChatGPT provides tailored recommendations based on your current fitness level and aspirations. Additionally, it tracks your progress, offering insights on milestones achieved and areas needing improvement. Suppose your target is to finish twelve books this year; ChatGPT can monitor your reading habits, reminding you to stay on track and celebrating your achievements as you reach each goal.

Time management is another domain in which ChatGPT offers valuable insights. Suggesting productivity tips for various scenarios empowers you to work smarter, not harder. If you're working from home, you might ask, "Give me productivity tips for working from home." ChatGPT responds with strategies like setting boundaries, creating a dedicated workspace, and scheduling regular breaks to maintain focus. Moreover, it provides techniques to combat procrastination, such as breaking tasks into smaller, manageable parts and setting deadlines to create a sense of urgency. By incorporating these strategies, you optimize your workflow and enhance your ability to meet deadlines.

Automating repetitive tasks is one of ChatGPT's standout features, saving you time and effort on mundane activities. Imagine asking it to "Draft a daily journal entry summarizing my activities and reflections." ChatGPT compiles your day's events into a coherent narrative, allowing you to focus on more pressing matters. Similarly, it generates email templates for routine correspondence, streamlining communication and ensuring consistency in your messages. This automation increases your efficiency and frees up mental space for more creative and strategic tasks, enabling you to concentrate on activities that truly matter. With ChatGPT, the monotony of repetitive tasks fades away, replaced by a sense of accomplishment and forward momentum.

Interactive Element: Daily Productivity Checklist

- **Create a To-Do List**: Use ChatGPT to outline daily tasks and prioritize based on urgency.
- **Set SMART Goals**: Define specific, measurable, achievable, relevant, and time-bound objectives.
- **Track Progress**: Monitor achievements and adjust strategies as needed.
- **Automate Routine Tasks**: Streamline activities like journaling and email drafting.

ChatGPT's integration into your daily life transforms how you manage time and achieve goals. By leveraging its capabilities, you streamline tasks, enhance productivity, and create a balanced lifestyle. This AI tool becomes a personal productivity coach, guiding you through the complexities of modern life with ease and efficiency.

3.2 ENHANCING DAILY COMMUNICATION WITH CHATGPT

In today's fast-paced world, effective communication is more crit-ical than ever. Whether you're coordinating with colleagues, reaching out to friends, or engaging with an online audience, ChatGPT can be your secret weapon. Imagine needing to send a professional email to a client. You want to strike the right balance between formality and friendliness, ensuring your message is clear and compelling. With ChatGPT, you can compose an email requesting a meeting, with the AI suggesting phrasing that captures both your intent and your tone. It might structure the email with a polite greeting, clearly state the purpose, and end with a courteous sign-off. This not only saves time but ensures your communication remains professional and effective. On a lighter note, suppose you're planning a weekend get-together and want to invite friends. ChatGPT can help craft a friendly email, suggesting language that feels warm and inviting. Tailoring the message to fit the occasion ensures you convey enthusiasm and hospitality, setting the tone for a joyful gathering.

Beyond emails, text messaging is another area where ChatGPT shines. Picture this: you need to reschedule an appointment, and clarity is paramount to avoid misunderstandings. ChatGPT can draft a concise message that communicates your need to change the date while expressing appreciation for the recipient's flexibil-ity. By choosing words carefully, it helps maintain a positive rapport. Similarly, when you want to express gratitude for a thoughtful gift, ChatGPT assists in writing a thank-you message that feels genuine and heartfelt. It can suggest including specific details about why the gift was meaningful, adding a personal touch that enhances the recipient's appreciation. These examples illus-trate how ChatGPT streamlines communication and enriches the personal connections we nurture through our words.

Social media is a vibrant space where engaging content reigns supreme. Crafting posts that capture attention and convey your message can be challenging, yet ChatGPT simplifies this process. Suppose you've landed a new job and want to share the news on Facebook. ChatGPT can draft a post that highlights your excitement and gratitude, encouraging your network to celebrate with you. It might suggest a blend of professional achievements and personal reflections, creating a well-rounded announcement. For visual platforms like Instagram, where captions complement images, ChatGPT helps generate catchy captions that resonate with your audience. If you're sharing a vacation photo, it can propose a caption that captures the essence of your experience, drawing viewers into your adventure. This versatility ensures that no matter the platform, your social media presence remains engaging and authentic.

In conversations, whether at networking events or family gatherings, having a few conversation starters up your sleeve can make all the difference. ChatGPT can suggest topics that help break the ice, fostering meaningful interactions. For a business networking event, ask about recent industry trends or seek advice on professional growth, sparking insightful discussions. At a family dinner, it could suggest discussing a recent travel experience or a shared hobby, creating moments of connection and laughter. By providing these conversation starters, ChatGPT equips you to navigate social settings with confidence, ensuring that you leave a lasting impression. This ability to facilitate engaging dialogue extends beyond formal scenarios, enriching everyday interactions with those around you.

3.3 CHATGPT FOR EDUCATIONAL PURPOSES

Imagine sitting at your desk, a daunting pile of homework staring back at you. The clock ticks, and your patience wears thin. This is where ChatGPT steps in, transforming your study sessions into streamlined experiences. Let's start with homework help. When you're grappling with complex concepts, like the principles of photosynthesis, ChatGPT becomes your personal tutor. You can ask it to break down these scientific processes into digestible bits, making it easier to grasp the core ideas. Need help with math? You may be stuck on calculating the area of a circle with a radius of 5 cm. Simply input your query, and ChatGPT will guide you through the formula, providing the answer and the steps involved in solving the problem. This interactive assistance can demystify challenging topics, helping you build confidence in your academic abilities.

Creating study guides and summaries is another area where ChatGPT shines. Preparing for an exam on the American Revolution? ChatGPT can help you summarize key points, offering a concise overview of significant battles, political changes, and influential figures. This not only saves time but also ensures you focus on the most critical information. Similarly, if you're tackling Harper Lee's "To Kill a Mockingbird," ChatGPT can aid in creating a study guide for its first chapter. It organizes themes, character insights, and plot developments, making it easier to understand and analyze the text. This structured approach transforms how you study, allowing you to engage with material more effectively and retain information longer.

Language learning is often a daunting task, but ChatGPT makes it more accessible and enjoyable. Whether you're planning a trip or simply aiming to broaden your linguistic skills, this AI tool becomes an invaluable resource. Suppose you're curious about how to say, "Where is the nearest train station?" in Spanish. ChatGPT can provide an accurate translation, ensuring you communicate effectively in a foreign language. Beyond translation, it offers lists of common phrases, such as essential French expressions for travelers. By familiarizing yourself with these phrases, you gain confidence to navigate new environments, enhancing your travel experiences and cultural interactions. This capability to learn languages on the go can be a game-changer for both casual learners and dedicated students.

Research assistance is another powerful application of ChatGPT, particularly for students and professionals conducting in-depth investigations. When tasked with a research paper on climate change, you might wonder where to start. ChatGPT can suggest credible sources and recommend databases or online journals, providing a solid foundation for your work. It can also generate outlines for projects, like a history presentation on Ancient Egypt. By proposing a structured framework, ChatGPT ensures your research is organized and comprehensive, streamlining the writing process. This guidance helps you focus on analysis and interpretation rather than getting bogged down by sourcing information. The ability to support research efforts is invaluable, enabling you to tackle complex topics with clarity and purpose.

These educational applications of ChatGPT demonstrate its versatility as a learning tool. From simplifying homework to enhancing language skills, it offers tailored support to meet diverse academic needs. Whether you're a student navigating school assignments or an adult pursuing lifelong learning, ChatGPT provides resources that empower you to achieve your educational goals with confidence and efficiency. It's more than just a digital assistant; it's a partner in your learning journey, equipped to guide you through the complexities of education with ease and reliability.

3.4 MANAGING FINANCES WITH AI ASSISTANCE

Navigating the world of personal finance can feel daunting, with numbers and decisions looming large. Yet, with ChatGPT as your digital assistant, managing your finances becomes less about stress and more about strategy. Budget planning is the cornerstone of financial stability, and ChatGPT excels in helping you create a budget that aligns with your lifestyle. Imagine you have a household income of $5,000 a month. By asking ChatGPT to "Create a monthly budget," you receive a detailed breakdown of expenses, savings, and discretionary spending. This helps in organizing your finances and highlights areas where adjustments can lead to savings. If you're looking to tighten the purse strings further, ChatGPT can suggest practical ways to cut expenses. It might propose reducing dining out, finding cheaper utility providers, or setting a cap on non-essential purchases, providing a clear path to save more each month.

Tracking expenses is another critical aspect of financial management, and ChatGPT simplifies this process. Think of it as a digital ledger, ready to log daily expenses with precision. You might ask, "Help me log today's expenses: $50 on groceries and $20 on gas." Instantly, ChatGPT records these transactions, keeping a running tally of your spending. At the end of the week, it can generate an expense report summarizing where your money went. This transparency allows you to identify spending patterns and make informed decisions. By having a clear picture of your financial habits, you gain control, enabling you to adjust and allocate your budget more effectively. This proactive approach to expense tracking ensures that you remain on top of your finances, avoiding unnecessary debt and fostering a healthier financial future.

When it comes to investments, ChatGPT acts as a knowledgeable guide, offering insights into the complex world of stocks and bonds. You might wonder about the fundamental differences between these two investment types. ChatGPT can explain that stocks represent ownership in a company, with the potential for high returns and risks, while bonds are loans to corporations or governments, offering steady income with lower risk. For beginners, ChatGPT can suggest investment strategies that align with your financial goals, such as diversifying your portfolio to minimize risk or focusing on index funds for long-term growth. It provides a foundation of understanding that empowers you to make informed investment decisions. While ChatGPT offers general advice, it's important to remember that consulting with a financial advisor is wise for personalized investment strategies.

Setting and tracking financial goals is a crucial step toward achieving long-term financial stability, and ChatGPT can play a pivotal role in this process. Consider setting a savings goal to buy a car in two years. ChatGPT can help you calculate the amount needed each month to reach this target, taking into account your current savings and potential interest earnings. By providing regular updates on your progress, ChatGPT keeps you motivated and focused. Similarly, if you're planning for retirement, ChatGPT can assist in tracking your contributions and projecting future savings growth. This continuous monitoring ensures that you stay on track, offering peace of mind and confidence in your financial planning. With ChatGPT, setting and achieving financial goals becomes a structured and attainable endeavor, transforming aspirations into reality.

Incorporating ChatGPT into your financial routine offers a strategic advantage, turning complex tasks into manageable actions. Whether you're budgeting, tracking expenses, seeking investment advice, or setting financial goals, ChatGPT provides the tools and insights needed to navigate your financial landscape with confidence and clarity. As you engage with this AI assistant, you discover a newfound ease in managing your finances, empowering you to make informed decisions and build a secure financial future. Through its capabilities, ChatGPT not only simplifies financial management but also enhances your understanding, equipping you with the knowledge to thrive financially.

3.5 CHATGPT IN HEALTH AND WELLNESS

Incorporating fitness into your routine can be daunting, especially if you need help figuring out where to start. Here, ChatGPT becomes your virtual personal trainer, tailoring workout plans to fit your needs. Suppose you ask it to "Create a weekly workout plan for a beginner." ChatGPT can suggest a balanced regimen that includes cardio, strength training, and flexibility exercises, ensuring a comprehensive approach to fitness. If you're interested in improving cardiovascular health, you might inquire, "Suggest exercises for improving cardiovascular health." ChatGPT could recommend activities like brisk walking, cycling, or interval training, each designed to elevate your heart rate and boost endurance. By providing structured guidance, ChatGPT helps you embark on a fitness path that aligns with your goals, making exercise an achievable and enjoyable part of your life.

Diet and nutrition often seem complex, with countless advice and diet trends vying for attention. ChatGPT simplifies this by offering personalized meal-planning assistance. If you're exploring plant-based eating, you could ask, "Generate a meal plan for a vegetarian diet." The AI might suggest a variety of dishes rich in protein and nutrients, from lentil soups to quinoa salads, ensuring you receive a balanced intake of essential vitamins and minerals. Curious about the benefits of a balanced diet? Ask ChatGPT to "Explain the benefits of a balanced diet," and it will outline how diverse nutrients support bodily functions, improve energy levels, and enhance overall health. By demystifying nutrition, ChatGPT empowers you to make informed dietary choices that promote well-being.

Mental health is just as crucial as physical health, and ChatGPT offers valuable insights into maintaining a healthy mind. Managing stress is a common challenge, and you might seek advice by asking, "Suggest relaxation techniques for reducing stress." ChatGPT can provide a range of options, from mindfulness meditation to progressive muscle relaxation, helping you identify methods that resonate with you. Improving sleep quality is another area where ChatGPT can assist. You could inquire, "Provide tips for improving sleep quality," and receive suggestions like establishing a bedtime routine, minimizing screen time before bed, and creating a calming sleep environment. These strategies not only enhance your sleep but also contribute to better mental resilience and emotional balance, fostering mental clarity and peace of mind.

Monitoring health metrics is integral to understanding your wellness journey, and ChatGPT simplifies this process. Imagine wanting to track your hydration levels; you might ask, "Log my daily water intake." ChatGPT can assist in setting reminders and keeping a record of your consumption, ensuring you meet your hydration goals. Similarly, if you're participating in a fitness challenge, you could request, "Track my progress in a 30-day fitness challenge." ChatGPT can help chart your workouts, note improvements in strength or endurance, and keep you motivated to reach your objectives. By providing a clear picture of your health metrics, ChatGPT supports your commitment to wellness, helping you stay accountable and motivated on your health journey.

3.6 LEVERAGING CHATGPT FOR HOME AUTOMATION

Imagine stepping into a home where everything works in harmony with your needs. ChatGPT makes this vision a reality through its seamless integration with smart home devices. It's like having a conductor orchestrating your daily routines with precision. Picture this: you wake up to a gentle glow from your smart lights, perfectly timed to ease you into the day. ChatGPT has set them to turn on just as your coffee maker begins brewing that perfect cup. Such synchronization transforms mornings into a symphony of efficiency. Beyond just lights and coffee, ChatGPT can manage your thermostats and security systems too. Imagine controlling these with simple voice commands, adjusting the temperature, or checking the security status without lifting a finger. It adapts to your preferences, ensuring comfort and safety are always at your fingertips.

Managing daily tasks efficiently is crucial, and ChatGPT excels in setting automated reminders. Consider this scenario: it's easy to forget mundane but necessary tasks like taking out the trash. With ChatGPT, you can set a reminder every Monday evening to ensure you never miss waste collection day. Similarly, it can remind you to water your plants every three days, keeping your greenery thriving with minimal effort. These reminders, though simple, free up your mental space for more important decisions, reducing the cognitive load of remembering trivial tasks. This level of automation keeps your household running smoothly and liberates you from the cycle of constant reminders, letting technology shoulder the burden of routine.

Household management often feels like juggling multiple responsibilities. ChatGPT helps balance these tasks effortlessly. Consider the weekly chore of cleaning. You can instruct ChatGPT to generate a cleaning schedule, breaking tasks into manageable weekly segments. It could suggest vacuuming on Mondays, dusting on Wednesdays, and mopping on Fridays, ensuring your home remains tidy without overwhelming your schedule. Similarly, when planning meals for the week, ChatGPT can create a grocery list based on your meal plans. This organization streamlines shopping, ensuring you have everything you need while minimizing waste. By taking charge of these logistical tasks, ChatGPT transforms household management from a chaotic endeavor into a structured routine.

Entertainment is the spice of life, and ChatGPT enhances this aspect by personalizing your leisure activities. Imagine settling in for a movie night but unsure of what to watch. ChatGPT can suggest movies or TV shows tailored to your preferences, considering past likes and current mood. It might recommend a gripping thriller if you're in the mood for excitement, or a heartwarming comedy for a light-hearted evening. Beyond just recommendations, ChatGPT can craft playlists for any occasion. Whether you're hosting a dinner party or unwinding after a long day, it curates music that sets the right tone, enriching your experience. This personalized touch transforms ordinary moments into memorable ones, making entertainment effortlessly enjoyable.

Textual Element: Smart Home Setup Checklist

- **Morning Routine**: Automate smart lights and coffee makers.
- **Voice Commands**: Control thermostats and security systems.
- **Automated Reminders**: Set reminders for trash collection and plant watering.
- **Cleaning Schedule**: Organize weekly chores into a manageable plan.

- **Grocery List**: Generate based on meal plans for efficient shopping.
- **Entertainment**: Get personalized movie and music recommendations.

ChatGPT's role in home automation extends beyond simple commands; it integrates into your lifestyle, enhancing comfort and efficiency. By taking charge of routine tasks and personalizing your environment, you are free to focus on what truly matters. With technology handling the details, you can enjoy a home that adapts to your needs, ensuring every day runs smoothly and with less effort. This chapter has explored the ways ChatGPT can revolutionize your living space, making it smarter and more responsive. As we move forward, we'll delve into how these innovations impact professional settings, transforming the way we work and collaborate.

CHAPTER 4
PROFESSIONAL USE
CASES

P icture a bustling marketing department, where ideas flow as freely as the coffee, and every team member is constantly on the lookout for that next big campaign. In the heart of this creative chaos, ChatGPT emerges as a digital ally, ready to revolutionize how marketing professionals brainstorm, personalize content, and stay ahead of industry trends. You might be a seasoned marketer or a novice just entering the field. Either way, understanding how to leverage AI like ChatGPT can elevate your approach, making your campaigns not only more effective but also more innovative.

Let's consider the challenge of creating engaging campaigns. The pressure to captivate audiences is immense, especially when targeting savvy groups like millennials. Here, ChatGPT steps in as a brainstorming partner, generating fresh ideas for social media campaigns that resonate with this demographic. Imagine being stuck in a creative rut, and with a simple command, ChatGPT offers a range of innovative strategies—from interactive polls to influencer partnerships—that align with millennial interests. It doesn't stop at brainstorming. When launching a new product, ChatGPT can assist in drafting a press release that captures attention, ensuring your message is clear, concise, and compelling. By integrating AI into the creative process, you open the door to new possibilities, turning potential roadblocks into stepping stones for success.

Personalization is the cornerstone of effective marketing, and ChatGPT excels in tailoring content to fit diverse audience segments. Consider the challenge of crafting personalized email templates for various customer personas. Each persona has unique needs and preferences, and ChatGPT helps you navigate this complexity by generating emails that speak directly to those differences. Whether addressing a young professional seeking career advice or a retiree exploring travel options, the AI ensures that each message feels personal and relevant. Similarly, when writing targeted ad copy, ChatGPT adjusts the language and tone to appeal to specific demographics, enhancing engagement and conversion rates. This level of customization not only streamlines your marketing efforts but also builds stronger connections with your audience, fostering brand loyalty and trust.

In the digital age, mastering search engine optimization (SEO) is crucial for ensuring your content reaches its intended audience. ChatGPT offers invaluable assistance in this area, helping you optimize your content for search engines. Imagine needing to generate a list of relevant keywords for a blog post on digital marketing. ChatGPT swiftly analyzes current trends and suggests keywords that boost visibility and drive traffic. Additionally, when crafting meta descriptions for your website pages, ChatGPT provides concise summaries that encapsulate the essence of your content while enticing potential visitors. This strategic use of AI in SEO enhances your online presence and ensures your content stands out in a crowded digital landscape, making it easier for people to discover what you have to offer.

Understanding and analyzing marketing trends is another area where ChatGPT proves invaluable. As the digital landscape evolves, staying informed about the latest trends is essential for maintaining a competitive edge. ChatGPT can summarize the latest developments in influencer marketing, providing insights into emerging platforms and strategies that are shaping the industry. ChatGPT helps you adapt your strategies to maximize reach and effectiveness by analyzing social media algorithms' impact on engagement rates. Whether you're exploring new trends or evaluating existing ones, ChatGPT serves as a critical tool for making informed decisions, ensuring that your marketing efforts remain relevant and impactful.

Interactive Element: Marketing Strategy Brainstorming

- **Campaign Ideas**: Use ChatGPT to generate fresh concepts for social media campaigns that target specific demographics.
- **Press Release Drafting**: Utilize ChatGPT to craft clear and engaging press releases for product launches.
- **Email Personalization**: Guide ChatGPT in creating personalized email templates for different customer personas.
- **SEO Optimization**: Leverage ChatGPT to suggest keywords and meta descriptions that enhance search visibility.
- **Trend Analysis**: Ask ChatGPT to summarize and analyze current marketing trends to inform your strategies.

Incorporating ChatGPT into your marketing toolkit transforms how you approach challenges, providing innovative solutions that enhance creativity, personalization, and strategic planning. As you explore these applications, you'll discover new ways to connect with your audience and elevate your marketing efforts, positioning yourself at the forefront of industry innovation.

4.1 STREAMLINING CUSTOMER SERVICE WITH CHATGPT

Imagine stepping into a bustling customer service center, where voices blend into a cacophony of inquiries and resolutions. Here, efficiency is key, and ChatGPT emerges as a powerful ally in streamlining operations. Automated response systems powered by ChatGPT can transform how you handle customer interactions. Picture drafting responses to common inquiries—those repetitive questions that flood your inbox daily. Whether it's a query about shipping times or return policies, ChatGPT crafts precise and polite replies, ensuring consistency and saving precious time. But it doesn't stop there. When faced with frequently reported issues, ChatGPT assists in generating comprehensive troubleshooting guides. These guides empower customers to resolve problems independently, reducing the load on service agents and enhancing customer satisfaction. This automation not only boosts efficiency but also ensures your team can focus on more complex, high-value interactions.

Personalization in customer service is more than a nicety; it's a necessity. ChatGPT excels in enhancing interactions by tailoring responses to individual customers. Imagine greeting each customer with a personalized message, acknowledging their unique history with your business. ChatGPT can craft these greetings, making each interaction feel special and valued. It analyzes customer purchase history to tailor responses, offering relevant solutions or upsell opportunities. For instance, if a customer frequently buys a specific product, ChatGPT suggests complementary items, creating a personalized shopping experience. This level of customization fosters loyalty, as customers appreciate the attention to detail and feel more connected to your brand. By leveraging ChatGPT, you transform generic interactions into personalized experiences, building stronger relationships with each customer.

Round-the-clock availability is a game-changer in customer service. ChatGPT enables you to provide 24/7 support, ensuring no inquiry goes unanswered, regardless of the hour. Setting up an AI chatbot to handle after-hours inquiries means customers receive immediate assistance, even when your team is offline. This chatbot can manage various requests, from FAQs to product information, ensuring customers find the answers they seek. For common support tickets, ChatGPT drafts thoughtful responses, maintaining a consistent and helpful tone. This seamless support system assures customers that help is always available, enhancing trust and satisfaction. In a world where instant gratification is expected, offering continuous support sets your service apart, demonstrating your commitment to customer care.

Understanding customer feedback is critical for continuous improvement, and ChatGPT plays a pivotal role in this analysis. Imagine sifting through mountains of surveys and reviews, where valuable insights lie hidden in plain sight. ChatGPT summarizes this feedback efficiently, highlighting key themes and concerns. It identifies areas where customers are delighted and pinpoint issues needing attention. From this analysis, ChatGPT generates action plans, offering strategic recommendations for enhancement. Whether it's improving a product feature or refining service processes, these insights guide informed decisions, driving your business forward. This capability ensures you remain attuned to customer needs, adapting and evolving in response to their feedback.

By integrating ChatGPT into your customer service operations, you unlock a new level of efficiency and personalization. It empowers you to handle inquiries swiftly, tailor interactions to individual customers, and provide unwavering support around the clock. Additionally, you gain valuable insights that inform strategic improvements by analyzing customer feedback. As you embrace these innovations, your customer service evolves, meeting the demands of modern consumers with agility and foresight.

4.2 USING CHATGPT IN CONTENT CREATION

Imagine the challenge of consistently producing high-quality content in a digital age where attention spans are fleeting and competition is fierce. ChatGPT stands as a remarkable ally for content creators, offering a wealth of tools to streamline and enhance the creation process. Whether you're drafting blog posts or crafting engaging social media content, this AI can be your creative partner. When tackling blog writing, for instance, ChatGPT assists in structuring ideas into coherent outlines. Suppose you're working on a blog post about remote work productivity. ChatGPT can help design an outline highlighting key points such as time management, workspace organization, and work-life balance. This structured approach not only organizes your thoughts but also ensures a logical flow that captivates readers.

Beyond outlines, crafting the opening lines of an article often sets the tone for the entire piece. Let's say you're tasked with writing about sustainable living. ChatGPT can draft the first paragraph, introducing the topic with clarity and intrigue and setting the stage for a compelling narrative that draws readers in. Imagine the potential: you input a few key themes, and ChatGPT generates a polished introduction that captures the essence of the topic. This capability saves time and sparks inspiration, allowing you to focus on refining and expanding upon the content.

The realm of social media demands concise yet impactful communication. Here, ChatGPT excels at generating engaging posts that resonate with audiences across platforms. Consider the challenge of composing a Twitter thread on the benefits of AI in business. ChatGPT can suggest succinct points, each building upon the last, to create a cohesive narrative. This ability to distill complex ideas into bite-sized insights makes your message accessible and engaging, ensuring it stands out in a crowded feed. Similarly, when crafting Instagram captions for a travel brand, ChatGPT offers creative suggestions that capture the spirit of adventure and allure, enticing followers to explore further.

Video content is another area where ChatGPT proves invaluable. Writing scripts for videos requires a balance of information and entertainment, a task ChatGPT handles with finesse. Suppose you're creating a YouTube tutorial on using ChatGPT itself. The AI can draft a script that guides viewers step-by-step, explaining features and functionalities in an approachable manner. It ensures clarity and coherence, maintaining viewer engagement throughout the video. Additionally, when introducing a company in a promotional video, ChatGPT can craft an introduction that highlights core values and unique selling points, setting the tone for a persuasive and memorable presentation.

Content creation doesn't end with the initial draft. Editing and proofreading are critical to ensuring clarity and coherence, tasks where ChatGPT offers support. Imagine finalizing a blog post, and you're wondering if the grammar is spot-on or if the flow is just right. ChatGPT can proofread the text, identify grammatical errors, and suggest improvements that enhance readability. It acts as a second set of eyes, meticulously reviewing content to ensure it aligns with your voice and message. This support not only elevates the quality of your writing but also boosts confidence, knowing your content is polished and professional.

With ChatGPT as your creative partner, content creation transforms from a solitary endeavor into a collaborative process. Its capabilities streamline drafting, enhance creativity, and ensure precision, allowing you to focus on what matters most—delivering valuable and engaging content to your audience. Whether you're a seasoned writer or a novice exploring new territories, ChatGPT offers a versatile and dynamic toolset that adapts to your needs, empowering you to elevate your content creation efforts to new heights.

4.3 CHATGPT FOR MARKET RESEARCH AND ANALYSIS

In the fast-paced world of business, staying ahead of the competition requires a keen understanding of the market landscape. ChatGPT proves to be an invaluable tool in conducting competitor analysis. Picture yourself tasked with generating a competitor analysis report for the tech industry. This is where ChatGPT's ability to process vast amounts of data becomes crucial. It can sift through news articles, industry reports, and social media mentions to compile a detailed overview of your competitors. By summarizing the strengths and weaknesses of a competing brand, ChatGPT helps you identify areas where your business can differentiate itself. It might highlight a competitor's strong customer service reputation but also point out their less robust product range. Such insights allow you to strategize effectively, capitalizing on opportunities they might have overlooked.

Keeping a pulse on market trends is equally vital for making informed business decisions. ChatGPT excels in identifying and summarizing these trends. Imagine you're exploring the renewable energy sector, a rapidly evolving field with a plethora of factors at play. ChatGPT can analyze current articles, research papers, and industry forecasts to provide a comprehensive view of the landscape. It identifies emerging technologies, regulatory changes, and shifts in consumer preferences, helping you navigate this complex environment with confidence. Similarly, understanding consumer behavior trends is crucial for tailoring products and services to meet market demands. ChatGPT highlights patterns in purchasing habits, preferences, and emerging interests, offering a clearer picture of where the market is heading. Armed with this information, you can align your strategies to meet these evolving needs, ensuring your business remains relevant and competitive.

Surveys are a powerful tool for gathering direct feedback from consumers, yet crafting effective questions and analyzing responses can be daunting. ChatGPT simplifies this process by assisting in survey creation and analysis. Suppose you're developing a customer satisfaction survey. ChatGPT can suggest precise questions that target key areas of interest, ensuring you gather actionable insights. Questions range from rating product satisfaction to suggestions for improvement, each crafted to elicit valuable feedback. Once the survey responses are in, ChatGPT helps analyze the data, generating a summary report that highlights trends and areas of concern. It might reveal that customers love the product quality but find delivery times lacking. This analysis guides your next steps, enabling you to address issues and capitalize on strengths. By streamlining this process, ChatGPT allows you to focus on implementing changes that enhance customer satisfaction and loyalty.

Industry reports serve as a cornerstone for strategic planning, providing a deep dive into sector-specific trends and forecasts. ChatGPT can generate these reports with remarkable efficiency.

Imagine needing an industry report on the future of e-commerce. ChatGPT collects data from various sources, including economic forecasts, technological advancements, and consumer behavior analysis, compiling them into a cohesive document. It outlines potential growth areas, challenges, and innovations shaping the industry. Furthermore, ChatGPT can summarize key insights from recent market studies, distilling complex data into understandable and actionable information. This ability to synthesize vast amounts of information into concise, readable reports empowers you to make informed decisions, ensuring you stay ahead in your industry. With ChatGPT handling the bulk of the analysis, you can focus on strategic planning and execution, leveraging insights to drive your business forward.

4.4 ENHANCING TEAM COLLABORATION WITH AI

Imagine stepping into a bustling office where teamwork is key to success. Here, ChatGPT shines as a tool that streamlines collaboration, making it easier to keep everyone on the same page. One of its standout features is generating concise summaries of team meetings. After a project kickoff meeting, for instance, ChatGPT can sift through notes and discussions to highlight key points. It organizes these insights into a clear and concise summary, ensuring that everyone knows the project's goals and initial decisions. This clarity reduces misunderstandings and keeps the team focused on shared objectives. Similarly, after a brainstorming session, ChatGPT can draft follow-up action items. It captures the creative energy of the meeting and translates it into actionable steps, ensuring ideas don't get lost once the session ends.

Collaborative document creation is another area where ChatGPT proves invaluable. In projects that require input from multiple team members, it acts as a facilitator. Imagine working on a project proposal. ChatGPT helps integrate contributions from various colleagues into a cohesive document, keeping the language consistent and the arguments aligned. This not only saves time but also enhances the quality of the final proposal. When preparing a report on quarterly performance, ChatGPT assists by compiling data and insights from different departments. It ensures that the report reflects a unified perspective, presenting the company's achievements and areas for improvement in a clear and engaging manner. By streamlining the drafting process, ChatGPT frees team members to focus on analysis and strategy rather than getting bogged down in document logistics.

Internal communication is the lifeblood of any organization, and ChatGPT significantly enhances this by automating routine messages. Suppose it's time to draft weekly team updates and announcements. ChatGPT can craft these messages with a tone that aligns with corporate culture, ensuring they are informative and engaging. It might include highlights of the week, upcoming deadlines, and motivational quotes to keep morale high. In a similar vein, ChatGPT helps create templates for internal memos and notices. Whether it's a policy change or a reminder about an upcoming event, the AI ensures that the message is clear, concise, and consistent with organizational standards. This automation reduces the time spent on repetitive tasks, allowing team members to concentrate on more strategic initiatives.

When it comes to task delegation and tracking, ChatGPT serves as a reliable assistant. Imagine assigning tasks based on team member strengths. ChatGPT can analyze skills and past performance to recommend who might be best suited for each responsibility. This ensures tasks are allocated efficiently, maximizing productivity and job satisfaction. Additionally, ChatGPT generates progress reports on ongoing projects, offering a snapshot of where things stand. It highlights completed tasks, pending items, and potential roadblocks, providing managers with the insights needed to make informed decisions. These reports are invaluable for keeping projects on track, ensuring that deadlines are met and objectives achieved. By handling these logistical elements, ChatGPT lets team leaders focus on motivating and guiding their teams rather than getting lost in day-to-day minutiae.

4.5 CHATGPT IN PROJECT MANAGEMENT

Imagine standing at the helm of a project with a multitude of tasks demanding your attention. Project management is the art of juggling these responsibilities efficiently, and ChatGPT steps in as an adept assistant, easing the burden of planning and execution. When creating a detailed project plan, ChatGPT can assist in drafting a comprehensive timeline. It outlines key milestones and deadlines, ensuring that every phase of the project is accounted for. This clarity helps visualize the project from inception to completion, making it easier to anticipate potential bottlenecks. Additionally, ChatGPT can generate a risk assessment report for new projects. It identifies possible challenges, evaluates their impact, and suggests mitigation strategies. This proactive approach equips you with the foresight needed to navigate uncertainties, enhancing your ability to steer the project toward success.

Resource allocation is another critical aspect of project management where ChatGPT proves invaluable. Imagine planning a marketing campaign with resources scattered across teams and departments. ChatGPT can help you create a resource allocation plan, detailing how personnel, time, and budget will be distributed. It ensures that each aspect of the campaign has the necessary support, optimizing efficiency and effectiveness. Furthermore, when drafting a budget proposal for project resources, ChatGPT can assist in itemizing costs, evaluating financial constraints, and proposing adjustments. This meticulous approach not only streamlines budgeting but also ensures that financial resources are aligned with project goals. By leveraging ChatGPT for resource allocation, you transform a complex task into a manageable process, facilitating smoother project execution.

Once a project is underway, tracking progress becomes paramount. ChatGPT excels in monitoring and reporting on project milestones. It can generate weekly project status updates, providing a snapshot of where things stand. These updates highlight completed tasks, pending actions, and any deviations from the plan, offering invaluable insights for decision-making. Additionally, ChatGPT can summarize project deliverables and completion rates, ensuring stakeholders are informed of achievements and progress. This transparency fosters accountability and keeps the project aligned with its objectives. By effectively tracking progress, you can make informed adjustments, ensuring the project remains on track and within scope.

Effective communication with stakeholders is vital to project success, and ChatGPT enhances this by streamlining interactions. Imagine needing to update stakeholders on project developments. ChatGPT can draft project update emails, articulating key achievements and upcoming goals. These communications are clear, concise, and tailored to the audience, ensuring stakeholders remain engaged and informed. Additionally, ChatGPT can assist in creating presentations that summarize project achievements, offering a visual and compelling overview of progress. This enhances stakeholder understanding and reinforces confidence in your management capabilities. By utilizing ChatGPT for stakeholder communication, you ensure that all parties are aligned with the project's vision and trajectory, fostering a collaborative and supportive environment.

Through these applications, ChatGPT becomes an indispensable tool in project management. It aids in planning, resource allocation, progress monitoring, and stakeholder communication, transforming how projects are executed and managed. As you integrate ChatGPT into your project management processes, you unlock efficiencies and insights that enhance your ability to deliver successful outcomes. This chapter has explored the multifaceted role ChatGPT plays in professional settings, and as we continue, we'll delve into the creative and artistic realms, where AI opens new horizons for innovation and expression.

CHAPTER 5
CREATIVE AND ARTISTIC APPLICATIONS

I magine unlocking a hidden world where words dance on the page, each sentence a brushstroke painting vivid scenes in the mind's eye. This is the realm of creative writing, where stories and poetry breathe life into our imaginations. ChatGPT is your guide, ready to transform your creative ideas into structured narratives and evocative verse. Whether you're crafting the next great mystery novel or composing a haiku that captures the essence of a fleeting moment, this tool bridges the gap between inspiration and creation, offering support and guidance at every step.

5.1 WRITING STORIES AND POETRY WITH CHATGPT

Creating a compelling story often begins with an outline, a structured map that guides your narrative journey. ChatGPT excels in helping you develop detailed story outlines, providing a framework to flesh out ideas into a coherent plot. Imagine you're setting your story in a quaint, mysterious small town. You might prompt ChatGPT to "Generate a plot outline for a mystery novel set in a small town." The AI can suggest a series of intriguing events, such as a mysterious disappearance or a hidden secret waiting to be uncovered, setting the stage for suspense and intrigue. Alongside plot development, character profiles breathe life into your story. You can request to "Create character profiles for the main protagonist and antagonist," and ChatGPT will help you flesh out their backgrounds, motivations, and conflicts. This foundation not only aids in storytelling but also ensures your characters resonate with readers, drawing them into the narrative world you've crafted.

Dialogue is the heartbeat of any story, capturing the essence of characters and driving the plot forward. Crafting realistic and engaging dialogue can be a challenging task, yet ChatGPT offers a helping hand. Consider a scene where tensions run high, like a heated argument between two characters. By instructing ChatGPT to "Write a dialogue exchange between two characters in a heated argument," you receive a vivid conversation that captures the emotional intensity of the moment. Alternatively, for a more nurturing interaction, you might ask for "Generate a conversation between a mentor and their mentee." Here, ChatGPT can craft a dialogue that conveys wisdom, encouragement, and personal growth, bringing depth and authenticity to your characters' interactions. These examples illustrate how ChatGPT serves as a dialogue coach, helping you refine the nuance and tone of your characters' voices.

Poetry is the art of distilling emotions and ideas into rhythm and meter, creating verses that resonate with readers on a profound level. ChatGPT's capabilities extend to poetry generation, offering a creative partner for exploring various poetic forms. You might be inspired to "Compose a haiku about the changing seasons." In response, ChatGPT will generate a three-line poem that captures the ephemeral beauty of nature's transitions, evoking imagery that lingers in the mind. Consider a sonnet on the theme of love for a more classical approach. By prompting ChatGPT to "Generate a sonnet on the theme of love," you'll receive a fourteen-line poem that weaves together emotion and structure, showcasing the enduring power of poetic expression. These poetic endeavors highlight ChatGPT's ability to transform abstract ideas into tangible art, enriching your creative repertoire.

In the realm of creative writing, editing, and refinement are crucial steps in polishing your work. ChatGPT offers valuable insights for enhancing your writing, acting as an editor who provides constructive feedback. Suppose you need help with the opening paragraph of a short story. You could ask ChatGPT to "Suggest improvements for a short story's opening paragraph." The AI can offer suggestions to enhance clarity, create intrigue, or refine your narrative voice. Similarly, when working on a poem, you might seek advice on the rhythm and flow. By requesting ChatGPT to "Provide feedback on the rhythm and flow of a poem," you'll receive tailored guidance to ensure your verses achieve the desired impact. This collaborative editing process empowers you to elevate your writing, transforming drafts into polished pieces that captivate and inspire.

Interactive Element: Creative Writing Exercise

- **Prompt for Plot Development**: Write a brief outline for a story set in your favorite location. Include a protagonist, an antagonist, and at least three key events.
- **Dialogue Practice**: Create a dialogue exchange between two characters experiencing a misunderstanding. Focus on how they resolve the conflict.
- **Poetry Exploration**: Compose a four-line stanza about a cherished memory. Experiment with different poetic forms and styles.

In leveraging ChatGPT's creative writing capabilities, you open doors to new possibilities, where your stories and poems flourish, guided by an AI that understands and enhances your artistic vision.

5.2 GENERATING VISUAL ART PROMPTS

Visual art is a language of its own, speaking through colors, shapes, and forms. If you're looking to fuel your creativity, ChatGPT can generate prompts that inspire drawing and sketching. Imagine being tasked with creating a futuristic cityscape, a scene that captures the awe of advanced architecture and vibrant urban life. ChatGPT might suggest envisioning towering skyscrapers with neon lights, hovering vehicles zipping between them, and bustling streets filled with diverse characters from all walks of life. Such a prompt can ignite your imagination, encouraging you to explore new techniques and perspectives in your art. Similarly, if you're venturing into character design for a fantasy novel, ChatGPT can provide prompts that challenge you to explore unique traits and qualities. You might find yourself sketching a character with ethereal wings, a mysterious aura, or a mischievous glint in their eye, each detail adding depth to their persona and enriching your visual narrative.

When it comes to brainstorming concepts for visual art projects, ChatGPT becomes an invaluable partner. Consider the possibilities for a series of paintings based on the four elements—earth, water, air, and fire. ChatGPT can help you explore how each element might be depicted, suggesting motifs, colors, and compositions that embody their essence. You might paint swirling water currents, fiery explosions, serene landscapes, or ethereal skies, each canvas capturing the unique qualities of its element. For a sci-fi themed digital art piece, ChatGPT can generate ideas that push the boundaries of imagination. Picture a world where technology and nature coexist, with cyborg creatures roaming lush landscapes or futuristic cities built within towering trees. These concepts encourage experimenting with new styles and themes, broadening your artistic horizons.

Art challenges and exercises are crucial for honing your skills, and ChatGPT has the tools to keep you motivated. Imagine embarking on a 30-day drawing challenge, each day presenting a new prompt to stretch your artistic muscles. ChatGPT could suggest themes like "draw a mythical creature" or "create a portrait using only geometric shapes," pushing you to explore different techniques and subjects. If you're focused on improving specific skills like shading and perspective, ChatGPT can recommend targeted exercises. You might practice rendering light and shadow on spherical objects or sketching urban scenes to perfect your understanding of depth and dimension. These challenges foster growth, providing the structure and inspiration needed to take your art to the next level.

Collaboration in art can lead to unexpected creativity, and ChatGPT facilitates this process easily. When generating themes for a collaborative mural, ChatGPT might propose ideas that resonate with shared values or community stories. Imagine creating a mural that celebrates cultural diversity, each section depicting elements of various traditions and histories. ChatGPT can offer prompts that guide participating artists in contributing their unique perspectives, ensuring a cohesive and meaningful final piece. For a group art project exploring cultural diversity, ChatGPT might suggest prompts that encourage participants to reflect on their heritage, share personal experiences, and express these through visual art. This collaborative approach enriches the creative process and fosters connection and understanding among artists.

5.3 ENHANCING ARTISTIC TECHNIQUES WITH CHATGPT

Artistic growth often hinges on learning new techniques and refining existing skills. ChatGPT is a valuable resource for artists of all levels, offering tutorials and tips that cater to your learning style. If you're new to oil painting, asking ChatGPT to "Explain the basics of oil painting for beginners" will provide you with foundational knowledge. You'll learn about essential supplies like brushes, palettes, and canvases and discover techniques such as layering and blending that define this medium. For digital artists, ChatGPT's guidance on "Mastering digital illustration" can introduce you to software tools, brush settings, and methods for creating dynamic compositions. These insights help demystify complex processes, empowering you to experiment with confidence and creativity.

Improving existing skills requires practice and dedication, and ChatGPT can suggest targeted exercises to enhance your artistic abilities. You may be looking to refine your anatomy drawing skills. By requesting "Generate practice exercises for improving anatomy drawing," you'll receive detailed suggestions like drawing skeletal structures or studying muscle groups from different angles. These exercises encourage you to observe and understand the human form more deeply, translating anatomical knowledge into more accurate and expressive art. Similarly, if you're aiming to deepen your understanding of color theory, ChatGPT can offer techniques for "Enhancing color theory knowledge." You might explore exercises like creating harmonious color palettes or experimenting with contrasting hues to evoke specific emotions. By engaging with these prompts, you cultivate a more nuanced approach to color, enriching your artistic expression.

Constructive feedback is invaluable in the artistic process, providing fresh perspectives and highlighting areas for improvement. ChatGPT can serve as an objective critic, offering suggestions on your work. Suppose you've completed a landscape painting and are seeking feedback. By asking ChatGPT to "Provide feedback on a completed landscape painting," you might receive insights on composition balance, color harmony, or how to enhance focal points. This guidance helps you refine your techniques, ensuring your work resonates with viewers. Similarly, ChatGPT's ability to "Suggest improvements for a graphic novel panel layout" can be instrumental for those working on graphic novels. It might advise on panel flow, dialogue placement, or visual pacing, helping you craft a more engaging and coherent narrative. These interactions foster a dynamic learning environment where feedback becomes a tool for continuous improvement.

Exploring different art styles broadens your creative horizons, allowing you to experiment and discover new facets of your artistic identity. ChatGPT encourages this exploration by generating prompts that challenge your stylistic boundaries. If you're intrigued by Impressionism, a prompt like "Generate prompts for creating art in the style of Impressionism" can guide you to capture fleeting moments with loose brushwork and vibrant colors. This exploration might involve painting en plein air or focusing on how light interacts with your subject. For those drawn to abstract art, ChatGPT can suggest exercises that push you beyond representational forms. Imagine experimenting with shapes, textures, and colors that convey emotions or concepts without depicting recognizable subjects. These exercises encourage you to think beyond traditional constraints, opening doors to new artistic possibilities and personal expression.

5.4 CHATGPT FOR MUSIC AND SOUND CREATION

Imagine the thrill of crafting a new song, the lyrics capturing emotions that words alone struggle to convey. ChatGPT steps in as a lyrical collaborator, ready to spark inspiration and refine your ideas. Suppose you're dreaming of a vibrant and catchy love song in the pop genre. By prompting ChatGPT to "Generate lyrics for a love song in the style of pop music," you receive verses that weave emotion with rhythm, capturing the essence of love's joys and complexities. Each line suggests imagery and feelings, offering a starting point for your creative process. Alternatively, you might seek a powerful chorus for a motivational anthem. Here, ChatGPT can craft a refrain that resonates with determination and hope. Imagine lines that uplift, urging listeners to persevere and chase their dreams. This collaborative effort with ChatGPT transforms songwriting into a dynamic and engaging experience, one where creativity flows freely and ideas come to life with each verse.

Creating music goes beyond lyrics; the composition itself sets the tone and mood of each piece. ChatGPT can provide valuable prompts that inspire the musical structure of your work. For instance, when composing a jazz piece, you might ask, "Suggest a chord progression for a jazz piece." With ChatGPT's guidance, you explore harmonies that evoke the complexity and improvisation jazz is known for, encouraging experimentation with sounds and rhythms. If classical music is your focus, imagine requesting, "Create a prompt for composing a classical piano sonata." ChatGPT might suggest a theme that intertwines elegance and sophistication, inviting you to explore variations and motifs that echo the great composers. These prompts serve as a catalyst, guiding you through the intricate process of music creation with clarity and inspiration, allowing your compositions to take shape with elegance and depth.

Sound design is an essential aspect of storytelling, whether in films, games, or multimedia projects. ChatGPT can assist in brainstorming sound design ideas, helping you craft immersive audio experiences. Consider the task of generating sound effects for a horror film. ChatGPT might suggest eerie whispers, chilling footsteps, or ambient creaks that build tension and suspense. These sounds create an atmosphere that heightens the audience's emotional response, drawing them deeper into the narrative. For a fantasy video game, you might seek ambient sounds that transport players to another world. ChatGPT can propose the gentle rustle of enchanted forests, the distant echoes of mystical creatures, or the soft hum of ancient magic. These auditory elements enhance immersion, allowing players to fully engage with the game environment. By collaborating with ChatGPT in sound design, you expand your creative toolkit, crafting audio landscapes that captivate and enthrall.

Music creation often thrives in collaborative settings, where diverse perspectives merge to create something extraordinary. ChatGPT can facilitate collaborative music projects by proposing themes and prompts that unify and inspire. Imagine embarking on a collaborative album with fellow musicians. ChatGPT might suggest a theme that explores the intersection of past and future, encouraging each artist to contribute their unique interpretation. This thematic cohesion fosters creativity, resulting in a cohesive and compelling collection of tracks. For a songwriting group, ChatGPT can generate prompts that spark new ideas and challenge each member's creativity. Consider a prompt that encourages writing from the perspective of a historical figure or exploring a specific emotion. These collaborative exercises build camaraderie and push creative boundaries, leading to innovative compositions that reflect the collective talent of the group.

Working with ChatGPT in collaborative settings enhances the creative process, fostering collaboration and innovation.

5.5 BRAINSTORMING CREATIVE IDEAS WITH AI

When you're embarking on a new creative project, the blank canvas or empty page can feel intimidating. That's where ChatGPT becomes an invaluable ally. Imagine you're conceptualizing a new graphic novel series. You might be searching for a unique angle, something that sets your work apart from the rest. By asking ChatGPT to brainstorm ideas, you'll be presented with a myriad of possibilities. It might suggest an intriguing setting like a dystopian future or a parallel universe where mythical creatures coexist with humans. It could propose a storyline involving a protagonist who grapples with their identity amidst societal upheaval. These sparks can ignite your creativity, providing a solid foundation upon which to build your narrative. Similarly, ChatGPT can help generate concepts that engage and captivate audiences if you're considering an interactive art installation. Picture an installation that responds to viewer movements, transforming shapes and colors in real time. This level of interactivity invites viewers to become part of the art, expanding the boundaries of traditional exhibition spaces.

Creative blocks are a common hurdle for artists and creators alike. When inspiration wanes, ChatGPT is there to rejuvenate your creativity. Suppose you're stuck on a project, feeling like you've exhausted every avenue. By requesting prompts to kickstart creativity, ChatGPT can introduce fresh perspectives. It might suggest exploring a different medium or incorporating an unexpected element into your work. For instance, if you're a painter, it could prompt you to integrate digital elements into your canvas, creating a hybrid piece that challenges conventional boundaries.

Alternatively, if you're a writer facing a stalled project, ChatGPT can generate alternative perspectives that breathe new life into your narrative. A shift in point of view or a change in setting might be just what you need to overcome creative inertia. These strategies not only help navigate creative blocks but also open up new pathways for exploration and discovery.

Collaborative brainstorming sessions are a dynamic way to refine ideas and foster innovation. Imagine organizing a virtual session for a film script, where participants from various backgrounds come together to share insights and suggestions. ChatGPT can facilitate this process by generating discussion topics that ignite conversation and encourage diverse viewpoints. It might propose exploring themes like resilience in the face of adversity or the impact of technology on human connection. These topics serve as a catalyst for dialogue, allowing participants to build on each other's ideas and craft a richer, more nuanced narrative. Similarly, in a creative writing workshop, ChatGPT can provide prompts that challenge attendees to think outside the box. It might suggest writing from the perspective of a seemingly inanimate object or crafting a story that unfolds in reverse chronological order. This collaborative environment fosters creativity, pushing participants to expand their creative horizons and produce work that is both innovative and engaging.

Once you've gathered your initial ideas, the process of refining and developing them begins. ChatGPT plays a crucial role in this phase, offering feedback and suggestions that elevate your concepts to new heights. Imagine you have a rough draft of a novel's plot. By asking ChatGPT to provide feedback, you gain insights into plot structure, character development, and pacing. It might suggest tightening certain chapters or expanding on subplots to enhance the narrative's depth and complexity. Similarly, if you're working on a visual art concept, ChatGPT can offer suggestions for expansion and enhancement. It might propose experimenting with scale, integrating multimedia elements, or exploring different color palettes. These insights help you refine your work, ensuring that your final product resonates with your audience and fulfills your creative vision. The collaboration with ChatGPT transforms the refinement process into an engaging and iterative journey, one where ideas are continually shaped and polished until they reach their full potential.

5.6 CHATGPT IN GAME DESIGN AND DEVELOPMENT

Creating immersive game worlds requires a blend of creativity and meticulous planning. Here, ChatGPT shines as a tool for generating captivating narratives and backstories that breathe life into virtual realms. Suppose you're developing a fantasy RPG set in a magical land. ChatGPT can assist by crafting a rich backstory that delves into the history of the land, its mystical creatures, and the ancient prophecies that drive the plot. This narrative foundation provides depth, inviting players to lose themselves in a world where every corner holds a new story. Character profiles are another essential element, and ChatGPT helps flesh out both main and supporting characters. Whether it's a valiant hero or a cunning villain, ChatGPT can outline their motivations, strengths, and flaws, ensuring they resonate with players and enhance the overall narrative.

Game mechanics and rules are the frameworks that guide player interactions and experiences. With ChatGPT, you can explore innovative mechanics that challenge and engage players. Imagine designing a strategy board game. ChatGPT might suggest mechanics like resource management, where players must balance short-term gains against long-term goals, or asymmetric gameplay, where each player has unique abilities and objectives. These mechanics add layers of strategy and replayability, keeping players invested. For a multiplayer card game, ChatGPT can generate rules that encourage cooperation and competition, such as drafting systems where players build their decks from a shared pool of cards. These elements create dynamic and evolving gameplay, fostering an environment where players must adapt and innovate to succeed.

Level design and layouts are crucial for maintaining player engagement and ensuring a cohesive gaming experience. ChatGPT can provide inspiration for designing game levels that challenge and intrigue players. When crafting a platformer level, you might explore the use of verticality and hidden paths to create a sense of exploration. ChatGPT can suggest including environmental hazards that test players' reflexes and timing, such as moving platforms and rotating obstacles. For puzzle games, ChatGPT can generate concepts that test players' logic and creativity, such as spatial puzzles that require manipulating objects to unlock new areas. These level designs challenge players and encourage them to think critically and experiment with different strategies.

Writing dialogue and scripts for games is an art form that captures the essence of storytelling and character development. ChatGPT can assist in crafting dialogue that enhances the game's narrative and immerses players in the story. Imagine a key interaction between characters where emotions run high. ChatGPT can help you write dialogue that conveys tension, betrayal, or camaraderie, adding depth to the characters and the story. For a game's cutscene, ChatGPT can generate a script that seamlessly integrates with the gameplay, using visual and audio cues to heighten the drama and convey critical plot points. This collaboration ensures that every word spoken and every scene played out contributes to the game's immersive experience, drawing players deeper into the narrative.

As we conclude this chapter, it's clear that ChatGPT offers versatile tools for game design and development. From crafting rich backstories and characters to designing engaging mechanics and levels, ChatGPT empowers creators to push the boundaries of interactive storytelling. It stands as a valuable ally in the creative process, enhancing each aspect of game development with fresh ideas and innovative solutions. As we transition to the next chapter, we'll explore how these creative applications extend beyond entertainment, shaping various industries and influencing everyday life.

CHAPTER 6
ADVANCED FEATURES AND CUSTOMIZATION

I magine opening the door to a bustling digital marketplace, where countless apps and tools chatter away in their own languages. In this vibrant ecosystem, APIs—or Application Programming Interfaces—act as translators, enabling these disparate systems to converse seamlessly. The API is your bridge to interconnectivity, and when it comes to ChatGPT, it transforms the way this AI can be woven into the fabric of your digital world. By integrating ChatGPT with other software, you unlock the potential to enhance applications with conversational intelligence, opening avenues for creativity and efficiency.

At its core, an API is a set of rules that allows different software applications to communicate with each other. Think of it as a universal language, enabling one program to request and send information to another effortlessly. In the context of ChatGPT, the API establishes a link between OpenAI's powerful language model and your chosen applications, facilitating smooth interactions that can enhance user experience. This communication is vital, allowing applications to leverage ChatGPT's capabilities, whether for generating content, answering queries, or automating responses. The benefits of using ChatGPT's API are manifold. It offers flexibility, enabling developers to tailor the AI's functionality to suit specific needs. Additionally, it provides scalability, accommodating growth as your application's demands increase. By tapping into ChatGPT's API, you gain a tool that adapts to your unique requirements, fostering innovation and efficiency.

Setting up API access might sound daunting, but breaking it down into manageable steps makes the process straightforward. To begin, you'll need to obtain an API key from OpenAI. This key serves as your access pass, granting permission to interact with ChatGPT's API. Once you have your key, configure your API settings to align with your project needs, ensuring compatibility and optimal performance. Authentication is a crucial step in verifying your identity and securing your connection to the API. This process typically involves adding your API key to your application's code, a step that safeguards your interactions and maintains system integrity. With these elements in place, you're ready to explore the possibilities that ChatGPT's API integration offers, setting the stage for dynamic interactions that elevate your application's capabilities.

Basic API operations form the backbone of your interactions with ChatGPT. At the simplest level, you send text to the API, a request that prompts ChatGPT to generate a response. This exchange is akin to sending a message and receiving a reply, a process that unfolds with remarkable speed and accuracy. Once you receive the AI's response, handling it becomes your next task. This involves parsing the data, extracting the needed information, and incorporating it into your application. Error handling and troubleshooting are essential components, ensuring that any hiccups in communication are swiftly resolved. By implementing robust error-handling mechanisms, you maintain a smooth flow of information, minimizing disruptions and optimizing performance.

Advanced API functionalities offer a deeper level of customization, enabling you to refine your interactions with ChatGPT. Running batch requests is one such feature, allowing you to send multiple queries simultaneously. This capability enhances efficiency, especially when dealing with large volumes of data or complex tasks. Effective use of rate limits is another consideration, as well as ensuring that your API interactions remain within acceptable parameters. Monitoring and logging API usage provide valuable insights, allowing you to track performance, identify trends, and make informed adjustments. These advanced functions empower you to tailor ChatGPT's capabilities to your specific needs, maximizing its potential and driving innovation.

Interactive Element: API Setup Checklist

- **Obtain API Key**: Secure your access by acquiring a key from OpenAI.
- **Configure Settings**: Align API configurations with project requirements.
- **Authenticate Requests**: Add your API key to ensure secure interactions.
- **Implement Error Handling**: Establish robust mechanisms for troubleshooting.
- **Utilize Advanced Functions**: Explore batch requests and monitor usage for efficiency.

By grasping the intricacies of ChatGPT's API integration, you open doors to enhanced functionality and creative possibilities. Each step, from understanding APIs to leveraging advanced features, equips you with the tools to transform your applications, enriching user experience and driving technological advancement.

6.1 CUSTOMIZING RESPONSES AND PERSONALIZATION

Imagine conversing with an old friend who knows exactly how you like your coffee, remembers your favorite movies, and uses just the right humor to make you laugh. That's the kind of tailored interaction you can create with ChatGPT when you customize its responses. Adjusting the tone and style is akin to fine-tuning a radio to your favorite station. Want a formal tone for business emails or a casual vibe for friendly chats? You can set these preferences, ensuring that ChatGPT speaks your language. It's about aligning the AI's voice with your expectations, creating a seamless dialogue that feels natural and intuitive. Setting response formats further refines this experience. Whether you need bullet points for clarity or a narrative style for storytelling, ChatGPT can adapt its responses to suit the context, making your interactions efficient and engaging. Including specific keywords or phrases tailors the content even more, guiding ChatGPT to focus on what's most relevant to you, ensuring the information it provides hits the mark every time.

Tokens and parameters are powerful tools that give you control over the nuances of ChatGPT's replies. Control tokens, for instance, allow you to regulate the length of responses. Whether you require a succinct answer or a detailed explanation, these tokens provide the flexibility to adjust the depth of information. Temperature settings introduce a creative twist, influencing how adventurous or conservative the responses are. A higher temperature invites more variability and creativity, which is perfect for brainstorming sessions. A lower setting yields more focused and predictable results, which is ideal when precision is paramount. The frequency penalty is another tool at your disposal, reducing repetition in outputs. This ensures that responses remain fresh and varied, enhancing the richness of interaction and keeping the conversation dynamic and engaging.

Creating user profiles adds a personalized touch, transforming ChatGPT from a generic tool into a bespoke assistant. By storing user preferences, you ensure that ChatGPT remembers your likes and dislikes, tailoring each interaction to reflect your unique personality. This might include your preferred topics, favorite authors, or specific interests, all of which help the AI craft responses that resonate with you. Utilizing context for personalized responses means ChatGPT doesn't just answer your questions —it understands the bigger picture. Whether you're planning a trip or exploring a new hobby, the AI draws on past interactions to provide insights that are contextually relevant and meaningful. Updating profiles based on user interactions keeps the AI attuned to your evolving preferences, ensuring that your experience remains fresh and aligned with your current interests.

Dynamic personalization brings a layer of sophistication to your interactions with ChatGPT, enabling real-time adjustments that enhance the user experience. Adapting responses based on conversation history allows the AI to weave past dialogues into current ones, creating a coherent and continuous narrative. This approach ensures continuity, making each interaction feel like an extension of the last. Real-time sentiment analysis takes this a step further, allowing ChatGPT to gauge your mood and adjust its tone accordingly. Whether you're seeking encouragement or a more analytical perspective, the AI can pivot its responses to match your emotional state, providing empathetic and responsive support. Contextual awareness in responses ensures that ChatGPT remains sensitive to the nuances of your queries, offering insights that are not only accurate but also aligned with the subtleties of your conversation. This level of personalization transforms ChatGPT into an intelligent companion capable of adapting to your needs with precision and empathy.

6.2 UTILIZING CHATGPT'S MEMORY CAPABILITIES

Imagine interacting with someone who remembers what you talked about yesterday, knows your preferences, and can recall details from previous conversations. This is the power of ChatGPT's memory capabilities. At its most basic, memory in AI can be divided into short-term and long-term categories. Short-term memory allows the AI to retain information from the current interaction, making it capable of maintaining context and coherence within a single session. Long-term memory, on the other hand, involves storing information across multiple interactions, enriching the AI's ability to provide personalized experiences over time. The benefits of memory in AI interactions are vast. They include tailoring responses to individual preferences, offering consistent user experiences, and anticipating needs based on past behaviors. However, limitations exist, such as the potential for outdated or irrelevant information to impact the quality of responses. Additionally, considerations around privacy and data security must be addressed to ensure users feel confident that their information is handled responsibly.

Incorporating memory into interactions with ChatGPT is like giving the AI a diary of your preferences and past exchanges. This capability allows the AI to store user preferences, enabling more personalized interactions. Imagine having a conversation about your favorite book genres, and the next time you chat, ChatGPT recalls this preference and suggests new book titles. This dynamic retrieval of stored information enhances the AI's ability to engage in meaningful dialogue, making it feel more like a conversation with a thoughtful friend rather than a machine. Customizing responses based on memory means that ChatGPT can adapt its replies to align with your interests and past interactions, creating a more engaging and relevant experience. For example, if you frequently ask about healthy recipes, the AI might prioritize nutritional content in its suggestions, tailoring its responses to your lifestyle.

Consider the practical applications of memory in various contexts. For customer support interactions, memory can transform how businesses engage with clients. By remembering a customer's past issues or preferences, ChatGPT can offer customized support, improving satisfaction and efficiency. In gaming applications, memory allows the AI to track a player's progress and preferences, delivering a more immersive and tailored experience. This could mean remembering a player's favorite strategies or the levels they've completed, adding depth to the gaming narrative. Education, too, benefits from memory capabilities. By tailoring educational content based on user progress, ChatGPT can offer personalized learning paths. Imagine a student using the AI to study math; the AI could retain information about the student's strengths and weaknesses, adjusting its explanations and exercises accordingly to provide targeted support.

Managing and resetting memory is crucial to maintaining the quality and relevance of interactions. Clearing memory for new interactions ensures that the previous context doesn't interfere with current conversations. This might involve resetting the AI's memory before starting a new session, allowing for fresh and unbiased interactions. Updating stored information is equally important, ensuring that the AI's memory remains accurate and reflects current preferences and needs. This might involve regularly reviewing and revising stored data to align with evolving interests or circumstances. Handling memory-related issues requires a thoughtful approach, as errors or inaccuracies in

memory can impact the user experience. Implementing mechanisms to address these issues, such as allowing users to edit or
delete stored information, enhances trust and ensures that the AI
continues to provide valuable and relevant interactions.

6.3 ADVANCED CONFIGURATION SETTINGS

As you explore ChatGPT, you'll find a wealth of configuration
options that can transform your interaction from basic to bespoke.
These settings are the levers and dials you use to tune the system
to your liking. At the heart of this customization lies the distinc-
tion between default and advanced settings. Default settings offer
a standard experience, providing a straightforward user interface
with basic functionality. It's like stepping into a familiar car, where
everything is set for a typical drive. However, advanced settings
allow you to dive deeper, giving you control over nuanced aspects
of the system. Navigating the settings menu is your first step in
this exploration. Here, you'll discover key configuration parameters that govern the behavior and performance of ChatGPT.
Whether you're adjusting the verbosity of responses or altering
interaction styles, these parameters provide a toolkit for tailoring
your experience to align with your specific goals and preferences.

Optimizing ChatGPT's performance is akin to fine-tuning an
engine for peak efficiency. It's about ensuring that the system runs
smoothly, delivering responses quickly and accurately. One of the
first adjustments you can make involves processing power and
resources. By allocating the appropriate resources, you can
enhance the system's ability to handle complex tasks without lag.
Configuring response time and latency is another crucial aspect.
By tweaking these settings, you can strike a balance between speed
and accuracy, ensuring that ChatGPT delivers timely responses
without sacrificing the quality of information. Balancing perfor-

mance and cost is a consideration, especially if you're working within budget constraints. It involves making strategic decisions about resource allocation to maximize efficiency while keeping expenses in check. This configuration aspect is crucial for individuals and businesses looking to leverage ChatGPT's capabilities without breaking the bank.

Security and privacy settings are paramount in today's digital landscape, where data integrity and user confidentiality are top priorities. Within ChatGPT, data encryption settings play a critical role in safeguarding information. Encrypting data ensures that sensitive information remains protected from unauthorized access. Access controls and permissions are another layer of security, allowing you to define who can interact with the system and what level of access they have. This feature is especially important in collaborative environments, where multiple users may engage with ChatGPT. Compliance with privacy regulations is an essential consideration, particularly for businesses operating in regions with stringent data protection laws. These settings ensure that your use of ChatGPT aligns with legal requirements, providing peace of mind that your interactions adhere to best practices in data privacy.

The user interface is your primary point of contact with ChatGPT, and customizing it enhances the overall user experience. Changing themes and layouts is a simple yet effective way to personalize your interface. Whether you prefer a minimalist design or a more vibrant aesthetic, these options allow you to create a comfortable and engaging environment. Configuring notification settings is another aspect of customization, enabling you to control the flow of information and alerts. By adjusting these settings, you can ensure that you receive timely updates without being overwhelmed by unnecessary notifications. Personalizing interaction options further refines the experience. This might involve choosing how ChatGPT presents information or selecting the types of interactions that align with your needs. These customizations make the system feel more intuitive and responsive, enhancing the sense of a personalized dialogue between you and the AI.

6.4 CREATING CUSTOM CHATBOT PERSONALITIES

In the ever-evolving landscape of artificial intelligence, creating a chatbot personality is akin to giving life to a digital companion. Imagine interacting with a chatbot that not only answers your questions but does so with a flair that mirrors a favorite character or embodies the professionalism of a seasoned customer service agent. The concept of chatbot personalities is essential for crafting experiences that resonate with users, imbuing interactions with warmth, humor, or authority as needed. Custom personalities offer significant benefits. They transform generic exchanges into engaging dialogues and create a sense of familiarity and trust. By defining personality traits, you guide the chatbot's behavior, ensuring consistency in tone and style. Whether it's a friendly, conversational bot for a youth-oriented app or a formal, precise assistant for corporate environments, the possibilities are vast. Examples abound, from a witty and sarcastic chatbot that delights users with clever banter to a nurturing and supportive one that offers gentle encouragement.

Developing a detailed personality profile is the cornerstone of crafting an authentic chatbot persona. Picture it as writing a character for a novel. Begin by defining the tone and style. Is the chatbot warm and friendly, or cool and analytical? This choice will influence every interaction, setting the mood for conversations. Next, establish behavioral rules and guidelines. Consider how the chatbot responds to common queries or how it handles complex questions. These rules ensure that its behavior aligns with the defined personality, maintaining consistency across interactions. Crafting a consistent character backstory can anchor the chatbot's identity, providing context that informs its responses. This back-story need not be elaborate but should offer a framework that guides the chatbot's interactions, helping it remain true to its personality under varying circumstances.

Once the personality profile is in place, the next step is to integrate these traits into chatbot responses seamlessly. This involves using consistent language and style, as the choice of words and sentence structure should reflect the defined personality. For instance, a playful chatbot might use informal language and emojis, while a formal one sticks to precise grammar and professional wording. Incorporating personality-specific phrases further enriches the interaction. These phrases can be catchphrases or signature expressions that reinforce the chatbot's identity. Imagine a chatbot that always starts with "Howdy, partner!" for a cowboy-themed persona or "Greetings, esteemed user" for a more formal vibe. Additionally, adapting responses based on personality ensures that the chatbot remains authentic. If a user asks a difficult question, the chatbot might respond with humor if it's light-hearted or offer a detailed explanation if it's more serious.

Testing and refining chatbot personalities is an ongoing process akin to rehearsing a play until the performance is just right. User feedback sessions are invaluable in this regard. By gathering insights from real interactions, you can understand how users perceive the chatbot's personality and make necessary adjust-ments. Analyzing interaction logs provides a wealth of data, revealing patterns and identifying areas for improvement. Perhaps the chatbot's humor doesn't land as intended, or its formal tone feels too stiff. These insights inform iterative improvements, allowing for fine-tuning that enhances the user experience.

Iterative improvement based on feedback is key. It involves making incremental changes, testing them, and refining them further. This cycle of improvement ensures that the chatbot's personality remains fresh and engaging, adapting to evolving user expectations while staying true to its core traits.

6.5 INTEGRATING CHATGPT WITH OTHER TOOLS AND PLATFORMS

In the digital age, the ability to integrate technologies across multiple platforms is a game changer. Identifying opportunities for integrating ChatGPT with other tools and platforms involves understanding common use cases and their benefits. For instance, integrating ChatGPT into a customer service platform can streamline responses, reduce wait times, and increase customer satisfaction. Similarly, incorporating ChatGPT into an e-learning platform can provide personalized tutoring, adapting to each student's learning pace and style. Successful integrations abound across industries. In e-commerce, ChatGPT can assist with user queries, provide product recommendations, and provide troubleshooting support. In healthcare, it can help patients schedule appointments or answer frequently asked questions, freeing up staff to focus on more complex tasks. The benefits of multi-platform integration extend beyond efficiency; they enhance user engagement, improve data flow, and create cohesive experiences that drive user satisfaction.

Using webhooks to connect ChatGPT with other applications opens up a world of possibilities. Webhooks are essentially automated messages sent from one app to another when something specific happens. Setting them up involves specifying a URL endpoint where events will be sent. This setup is your gateway to seamless communication between ChatGPT and other tools. Configuring webhook triggers and actions is the next step, allowing you to define what events will initiate the webhook and what actions will follow. For example, you might set a trigger for when a new customer inquiry comes in, prompting ChatGPT to generate a response. Testing and troubleshooting are crucial to ensure webhooks function as intended. This involves running tests to confirm that data is sent correctly and that the desired actions occur without errors. Mastering webhooks enables ChatGPT to interact dynamically with other systems, creating automated workflows that save time and enhance productivity.

Integrating ChatGPT with productivity tools can revolutionize how teams collaborate and manage tasks. Take Slack, for instance. By integrating ChatGPT into Slack, you can facilitate smoother communication between team members. ChatGPT can answer questions, provide updates, or even generate reports directly within a Slack channel, keeping everyone in the loop without switching applications. Trello, a popular project management tool, also benefits from ChatGPT integration. It can help prioritize tasks, suggest deadlines, and even automate routine updates, ensuring projects stay on track. When it comes to scheduling, integrating ChatGPT with Google Calendar can simplify the process of setting meetings and reminders. ChatGPT can suggest optimal times based on availability, send invites, and manage RSVPs, leaving you free to focus on the content of your meetings rather than the logistics. These integrations illustrate how ChatGPT can enhance productivity tools, turning them into more robust solutions that streamline workflows and improve efficiency.

Custom integration projects allow you to tailor ChatGPT to unique needs, creating innovative solutions that address specific challenges. Consider a customer service chatbot integrated with a CRM system. This setup allows ChatGPT to access customer data, providing personalized responses that enhance the customer experience. It can summarize email histories, analyze customer sentiment, and even suggest next steps for resolution, all while maintaining a human touch. In the realm of home automation, creating an AI-driven personal assistant with smart home integration can transform everyday living. Imagine ChatGPT managing your smart devices, adjusting lighting, controlling temperature, or even making coffee at your command. In education, developing a platform with ChatGPT-powered tutoring can offer students personalized learning experiences. The AI can adapt to each student's progress, providing tailored exercises and feedback that align with their learning pace. These custom projects showcase the versatility of ChatGPT, demonstrating how it can be molded to fit diverse applications, enhancing functionality and user engagement across sectors.

By integrating ChatGPT with other tools and platforms, you unlock its full potential, transforming it from a standalone application into a dynamic component of your digital ecosystem. This chapter has explored various integration strategies, highlighting how ChatGPT can enhance productivity, communication, and user experience. The seamless flow of information across platforms not only boosts efficiency but also enriches user interactions, paving the way for innovation and growth. As we look ahead, consider how these integrations can impact your work and personal life, opening new possibilities for collaboration and creativity.

CHAPTER 7
OVERCOMING CHALLENGES AND TROUBLESHOOTING

I magine driving a futuristic car, one that promises to take you anywhere with ease. Yet, beneath the sleek exterior, you know it's powered by a complex system that requires careful handling. Similarly, while ChatGPT offers remarkable capabilities, it also demands an understanding of its ethical and operational intricacies. As AI becomes more integrated into our daily lives, the ethical challenges it poses must not be overlooked. We are all navigating this digital landscape together, and it's crucial to address the profound implications of privacy, misinformation, and accountability.

Ethical concerns surrounding AI, including ChatGPT, are multifaceted and merit our attention. Privacy and data protection stands at the forefront, as AI systems often handle extensive volumes of personal information. This raises questions about how data is stored, used, and potentially compromised. The risk extends beyond mere data breaches; AI systems can inadvertently infer sensitive details about individuals, even from anonymized data, posing significant privacy threats (Capitol Technology University, n.d.). Another pressing issue is AI-generated misinformation. ChatGPT, while sophisticated, can occasionally produce inaccurate or misleading information, which can have real-world consequences. This underscores the importance of accountability in AI decision-making. As AI systems play larger roles in critical sectors like healthcare and finance, ensuring their accurate and responsible outputs is paramount (Simonite, 2023).

Bias in AI responses is another significant challenge, often stemming from the data used to train these systems. ChatGPT may inadvertently reflect societal biases present in its training data, leading to skewed or prejudiced outputs. For instance, if the training data overrepresents certain demographics or viewpoints, the AI might generate biased responses that perpetuate stereotypes or misinformation (Bhattacharyya, 2020). The implications are vast, affecting everything from hiring practices to content recommendations. Identifying bias requires vigilance and a deep understanding of the potential sources, such as sample bias or exclusion bias, which can skew results by underrepresenting certain groups or perspectives.

Diverse training data is crucial to mitigate bias. By ensuring datasets are representative of the real world, we can reduce skewed outcomes and foster more equitable AI interactions. Implementing fairness algorithms is another strategy designed to balance outputs and minimize prejudicial results. Regularly auditing AI outputs helps catch and correct biases, ensuring the system evolves with a fairer outlook. Involving diverse teams in AI development can further reduce bias, as varied perspectives contribute to a more comprehensive understanding of potential pitfalls (Bhattacharyya, 2020).

Promoting ethical AI usage involves several best practices. Transparent communication about AI capabilities and limitations is essential. Users must understand that while ChatGPT is a powerful tool, it is not infallible. Encouraging responsible usage means guiding users to verify AI outputs, especially concerning critical decisions. Continuous education on AI ethics is vital, preparing users to navigate the evolving landscape responsibly. As AI continues to advance, staying informed about its ethical implications ensures that technology serves human purposes without compromising our values (Simonite, 2023).

Interactive Element: Reflection Section

Consider your own interactions with AI. Reflect on moments where you encountered biased or unexpected responses. How did you address them? What steps can you take to foster more ethical AI usage in your personal and professional life? Write down your thoughts and explore ways to implement these strategies moving forward.

By understanding and addressing these ethical concerns, we can harness ChatGPT's capabilities while upholding our commitment to fairness and responsibility. The path forward requires collaboration, vigilance, and a shared dedication to using technology as a force for good.

7.1 HANDLING INACCURATE OR IRRELEVANT RESPONSES

Interacting with ChatGPT can sometimes feel like trying to have a conversation with someone who misunderstood your question. You've probably experienced this: a response that seems out of place or misses the mark entirely. This often happens when prompts are misunderstood, leading to answers that don't quite fit the bill. Misunderstandings can stem from unclear wording, lack of detail, or even when the AI doesn't interpret the context as intended. Out-of-context replies tend to occur when the AI needs help to grasp the complete picture of what you're asking, leading to responses that seem unrelated or off-target. These issues can be frustrating, but they are common hurdles in the realm of AI interactions.

Clarity in your prompts is pivotal for steering the AI in the right direction. Imagine giving directions without a map; vague prompts can leave ChatGPT wandering aimlessly. To improve the clarity of your prompts, start by providing clear and specific instructions. Rather than asking, "Tell me about apples," specify what you want to know, such as, "Explain the nutritional benefits of eating apples." This specificity narrows the AI's focus and helps it generate a response that aligns closely with your intentions. Including necessary context in your prompts is equally important. Just like a good story needs a setting, your prompts should set the scene for what you expect from the AI. For instance, if you're asking about a historical event, mentioning the time period or key figures involved can lead to a more accurate and relevant response.

Refining prompts is an iterative process, much like sculpting a piece of art. You start with a rough shape and gradually refine it until it matches your vision. Begin by evaluating the initial outputs you receive from ChatGPT. Ask yourself whether the response meets your expectations or if it seems to veer off course. If the answer is unsatisfactory, consider what might have confused the AI. Was the question too broad? Did it lack context? Once you identify these gaps, make incremental adjustments to your prompts. This might involve rephrasing the question, adding more detail, or simplifying complex language. Each tweak brings you closer to a prompt that extracts the ideal response, fostering a more productive interaction.

Feedback mechanisms embedded within ChatGPT serve as valuable tools for enhancing response quality. These tools allow you to rate responses, providing the AI with insights into what works and what doesn't. If you encounter inaccuracies, reporting them helps improve future interactions. By flagging errors, you contribute to refining the AI's understanding and performance. Additionally, suggesting corrections when you spot inaccuracies can aid in fine-tuning the system. This collaborative process not only benefits you but also enhances the AI's overall capability. Engaging with these feedback tools is akin to having a direct line of communication with the developers, enabling you to influence the evolution of ChatGPT in real time.

When you approach these challenges with patience and precision, you transform your interactions with ChatGPT from frustrating exchanges into rewarding dialogues. The key lies in understanding the nature of the tool and its potential limitations. By refining your prompts, utilizing feedback, and embracing an iterative mindset, you unlock a more intuitive and effective communication channel with the AI, paving the way for more accurate and relevant interactions.

7.2 ENSURING DATA PRIVACY AND SECURITY

Our digital world is immense and interconnected, with our personal data often strewn across multiple platforms. This makes safeguarding user information not just a priority but a necessity. Encrypting data is one of the most effective ways to protect it from unauthorized access. Encryption transforms your information into a coded format, decipherable only to those with the proper key. This ensures that even if data is intercepted, it remains unreadable to prying eyes. Another pillar of protection is the use of secure authentication methods. Think of it as a digital security guard verifying identities before granting access. This could involve multi-factor authentication, where you need more than just a password to log in, adding an extra layer of security to your accounts.

Configuring privacy settings in ChatGPT can significantly enhance your data protection. Start by adjusting data-sharing preferences. This means controlling what information you allow the service to access and share. For instance, you could limit data sharing to essential functions only, minimizing exposure. Anonymizing user inputs and outputs is another critical step. By ensuring your interactions with ChatGPT remain anonymous, you reduce the risk of personal information being linked back to you. This can be achieved by using pseudonyms or opting for settings that strip identifiable details from your inputs and responses.

Compliance with data protection regulations is crucial for maintaining trust and legal integrity. Regulations like the General Data Protection Regulation (GDPR) and the California Consumer Privacy Act (CCPA) set clear guidelines for how data should be handled. Understanding these regulations is the first step toward compliance. GDPR, for example, emphasizes user consent and the right to access personal data, while CCPA focuses on transparency and the right to opt out of data sales. Implementing necessary compliance measures involves aligning your data practices with these legal standards. This might include updating privacy policies, ensuring data portability, and providing mechanisms for users to exercise their rights.

Educating users on privacy is not just about informing them of risks but empowering them to take control of their data. Sharing best practices for data security can help users protect their information more effectively. For example, encourage using strong, unique passwords for different accounts and regularly updating these passwords. Discuss the importance of being cautious about the information shared online and recognizing phishing attempts. Encouraging regular reviews of privacy settings ensures that users remain aware of who has access to their data and can adjust permissions as necessary. This proactive approach fosters a culture of vigilance, where users are not passive participants but active defenders of their digital privacy.

Knowledge is power in navigating the complexities of digital privacy. Understanding these principles equips you to make informed decisions and safeguard your personal information in an increasingly interconnected world. It's about taking control and ensuring that your digital footprint remains secure and private. Active engagement with privacy settings and regulations, combined with a commitment to ongoing education, arms you with the tools needed to protect your data effectively.

7.3 MANAGING SYSTEM ERRORS AND GLITCHES

Navigating the digital world with ChatGPT can sometimes be like dealing with a moody appliance that works perfectly one day and acts up the next. Common system errors users might encounter include connection issues, API response errors, and unexpected system crashes. These glitches can disrupt your workflow, causing frustration and delays. Connection issues are often the culprits when the interface seems unresponsive or takes too long to load. This might be due to intermittent internet connectivity or server problems on OpenAI's end. API response errors, on the other hand, occur when the system struggles to process your requests, leading to incomplete or delayed outputs. You may find that responses are missing vital details or fail to load altogether. Unexpected system crashes are less common but can be disconcerting, often requiring a full restart of the application to restore functionality.

Following a step-by-step approach can be invaluable in tackling these issues head-on. First, check your internet connection. It might seem obvious, but often, a simple disconnect and reconnect can resolve many connectivity problems. Ensure your Wi-Fi signal is strong, or switch to a wired connection if possible. If you're dealing with API response errors, re-authenticating your API keys could help. This involves logging out of your account and logging back in or refreshing your API token if you're using ChatGPT in a developer setting. Should you experience a system crash, restarting the application is usually the first step. Close the app completely, wait a few moments, and then reopen it. This can clear temporary glitches and restore normal operations.

When faced with persistent issues, knowing where to seek support is crucial. OpenAI's support center is a treasure trove of resources designed to assist with troubleshooting and common queries. Here, you can find detailed guides and FAQs that cover a wide range of topics, from basic setup tips to advanced troubleshooting strategies. Additionally, user forums and community groups offer platforms for sharing experiences and solutions. Engaging with these communities can be incredibly helpful, as fellow users often provide insights or workarounds that aren't covered in official documentation. These forums act as collective brains, pooling knowledge to solve common problems. For on-the-go assistance, keep a list of troubleshooting guides handy. They can serve as quick references to address issues as they arise, minimizing down-time and ensuring a smoother experience.

Proactive measures can significantly reduce the frequency of these errors and glitches. Keeping your software up-to-date is a funda-mental step. Regular updates often include patches and improve-ments that address known bugs, enhancing overall stability. Make it a habit to check for updates regularly and install them promptly. Reviewing system logs can also provide insights into recurring issues. By examining these logs, you might identify patterns or specific triggers that lead to errors. Addressing these underlying causes can prevent future occurrences. Implementing robust error handling in API calls is another proactive strategy. This means designing your API requests to handle potential failures gracefully, ensuring that your application can recover quickly from disruptions. By incorporating these measures into your routine, you create a more resilient framework for using ChatGPT, minimizing interruptions, and maximizing productivity.

7.4 OPTIMIZING PERFORMANCE AND SPEED

Imagine you're in a bustling kitchen during dinner service. Every second counts and efficiency is key. Similarly, when using ChatGPT, understanding performance metrics is vital for smooth and speedy interactions. Response time is one of the most critical metrics. It measures the time taken for ChatGPT to process your input and deliver a response. The shorter the response time, the more efficient the interaction. Throughput, another important metric, refers to the number of tasks the system can handle simultaneously. High throughput means ChatGPT can manage multiple requests without bottlenecking, just like a chef who can juggle several dishes at once. Latency, often confused with response time, specifically denotes the delay before the system starts processing your request. Reducing latency ensures that ChatGPT begins working on your input without unnecessary delays, making interactions feel more fluid and immediate.

To optimize ChatGPT's performance, configuring settings thoughtfully can make a significant difference. Allocating sufficient resources is akin to ensuring your kitchen has enough cooks. Make sure your system has the necessary computational power to handle ChatGPT's demands. This might involve upgrading hardware or ensuring that background applications aren't hogging resources. Configuring response time and processing power settings can also help. By adjusting these parameters, you tailor the system's performance to match your specific needs, whether you require quick, concise answers or more detailed, thoughtful responses. This customization allows ChatGPT to operate at its full potential, efficiently meeting your expectations.

Caching strategies are another way to boost performance, much like pre-preparing ingredients in a kitchen to speed up meal prep. Response caching involves storing frequently used responses to common queries, allowing ChatGPT to retrieve them quickly without recalculating each time. This is particularly useful for repetitive tasks or inquiries that don't require unique, real-time processing. Implementing data caching for frequently requested information serves a similar purpose. By keeping often-used data readily accessible, ChatGPT reduces the time spent re-fetching details, speeding up the overall interaction process. This approach not only enhances performance but also ensures that resources are used efficiently, minimizing unnecessary computation.

Regular performance monitoring is crucial to maintaining ChatGPT's efficiency, similar to checking the kitchen's workflow during service. Setting up performance dashboards provides a real-time overview of key metrics, allowing you to spot potential issues before they become problems. These dashboards act as a control center, offering insights into system performance and identifying areas for improvement. Using automated monitoring tools can further streamline this process. These tools continuously assess performance metrics, alerting you to anomalies or trends that might require attention. Analyzing performance data regularly enables you to make informed decisions about adjustments, whether it's tweaking configurations or scaling resources.

Consistent monitoring ensures that ChatGPT remains responsive and efficient, ready to handle your queries with ease.

With these strategies in place, ChatGPT can operate seamlessly, transforming potential bottlenecks into free-flowing interactions. By understanding and optimizing performance metrics, you ensure that the system responds with the speed and accuracy you expect, enhancing the overall user experience. It's about creating an environment where ChatGPT can thrive, delivering reliable and efficient responses every time you engage with it.

7.5 STAYING UPDATED WITH CHATGPT DEVELOPMENTS

In a world where technology evolves at lightning speed, staying informed about the latest developments in ChatGPT is crucial. One effective way to stay in the loop is by subscribing to OpenAI newsletters. These newsletters are a direct line from the creators, offering insights into the latest updates, features, and even behind-the-scenes glimpses of what's coming next. They provide a curated source of information, ensuring you never miss out on crucial updates or enhancements that can impact how you use ChatGPT. Alongside newsletters, following OpenAI's official social media channels also keeps you connected. Platforms like Twitter and LinkedIn are often where OpenAI shares real-time announcements, tips, and community highlights. Engaging with these channels allows you to receive information as it happens, keeping you ahead of the curve.

Engaging with the community is not just about staying informed —it's about being part of a collective learning experience. Joining ChatGPT user groups can open doors to new perspectives and innovative ways to use the tool. These groups are often vibrant spaces where users share experiences, solutions, and creative applications of ChatGPT. Participating in discussions allows you to contribute your insights while learning from others, creating a dynamic exchange of knowledge. Whether you're troubleshooting an issue or exploring a new feature, community forums can offer invaluable support and inspiration. They are places where collective intelligence thrives, enabling users to learn from shared experiences and collaborate on finding solutions.

For those eager to deepen their understanding of ChatGPT and AI, accessing educational resources is a step in the right direction. Online courses and tutorials offer structured learning pathways, guiding you through both basic functionalities and advanced features. These courses are designed to cater to varying levels of expertise, ensuring that both beginners and more experienced users can find valuable content. Webinars and workshops provide interactive experiences, allowing you to engage with experts and ask questions in real time. They are opportunities to expand your knowledge and to hear firsthand from those at the forefront of AI development. Additionally, diving into research papers and publications can offer a more in-depth understanding of the theories and technologies that underpin ChatGPT. These resources are treasure troves of information, providing a deeper look into the innovations driving AI forward.

Testing new features is an exciting way to contribute to the development of ChatGPT. By signing up for beta testing programs, you gain early access to new functionalities and have the chance to shape their evolution. This involvement not only gives you a sneak peek into future updates but also allows you to provide constructive feedback directly to OpenAI. Your experiences and insights can influence how features are refined and implemented. Sharing these experiences with the community can further enhance the collective understanding of new tools and capabilities. It's a collaborative process where your input can lead to improvements that benefit all users.

As you navigate the evolving landscape of ChatGPT, these strategies can empower you to make the most of what this tool has to offer. Staying updated, engaging with the community, and continuously learning are keys to unlocking the full potential of ChatGPT. By embracing these practices, you position yourself to leverage the latest innovations and contribute to the ongoing dialogue around AI, ensuring that you remain at the forefront of technology's exciting developments.

CHAPTER 8
FUTURE TRENDS AND CONTINUOUS LEARNING

Picture a world where cars drive themselves, making traffic jams a relic of the past and freeing you to focus on more fulfilling pursuits during your commute. This isn't science fiction; it's an emerging reality, thanks to the rapid advancements in artificial intelligence. AI is revolutionizing industries at a pace that few could have imagined, and it's transforming how we interact with the world around us. As we stand on the cusp of this new era, understanding the potential trajectory of AI and its implications becomes crucial.

In the realm of autonomous vehicles, AI is poised to redefine transportation. Companies like Wayve are pioneering new approaches by integrating AI into vehicles, enabling them to navigate complex urban environments. These advancements promise increased efficiency and safety, reducing the need for human intervention in driving tasks. These systems learn from countless scenarios by utilizing generative AI and synthetic data, improving their decision-making capabilities. This evolution in autonomous driving not only holds the potential to reduce road accidents but also to reshape our urban landscapes by alleviating congestion and pollution.

Similarly, AI is making significant strides in healthcare diagnostics, promising early disease detection and personalized treatment plans. AI algorithms can analyze vast datasets to identify patterns and anomalies that might elude even the most skilled human practitioners. This capability enhances diagnostic accuracy, leading to more effective interventions and better patient outcomes. The integration of AI in healthcare does not replace the expertise of medical professionals but rather augments it, enabling a collaborative approach to patient care that leverages the strengths of both humans and machines.

In the education sector, AI is personalizing learning experiences and tailoring instruction to meet the unique needs of each student. By analyzing data on student performance, AI systems can identify areas where learners excel and those where they may need additional support. This individualized approach empowers educators to create more effective curricula and fosters an environment where students can thrive. As AI continues to evolve, its role in education is likely to expand, offering new opportunities for innovation and accessibility in learning.

The impact of AI extends beyond these sectors, promising to transform industries such as finance, retail, and manufacturing. In finance, AI-driven algorithms optimize trading strategies, manage risks, and detect fraudulent activities with unprecedented precision. Retailers utilize AI to enhance customer experiences, offering personalized recommendations and streamlining operations. Meanwhile, in manufacturing, AI improves supply chain management, predicting demand and optimizing production schedules to enhance efficiency and reduce waste.

As AI becomes more pervasive, ethical considerations take center stage. As automation takes over routine tasks, the potential for job displacement raises questions about the future workforce. It is crucial to develop strategies that mitigate these impacts, such as retraining programs and policies that support workers in transitioning to new roles. Additionally, ensuring unbiased AI systems is paramount. AI must reflect diverse perspectives and experiences to avoid perpetuating existing inequalities. Maintaining data privacy and security is another critical concern, as the vast amounts of information processed by AI systems must be protected against misuse.

AI also holds promise in addressing global challenges, such as climate change and disaster response. In climate change mitigation, AI analyzes environmental data to identify trends and develop sustainable solutions. This technology can optimize energy consumption, reduce emissions, and enhance resource management, contributing to a more sustainable future. During natural disasters, AI systems provide real-time data analysis, aiding in efficient resource allocation and improving emergency response efforts. In the realm of global health, AI supports initiatives by predicting disease outbreaks, optimizing vaccine distribution, and enhancing public health strategies.

Reflection Section: Imagining AI's Future in Your Life

Consider how AI advancements might shape your personal and professional life. Reflect on areas where AI could enhance your daily routines or solve challenges you face. How might these transformations impact your industry or community? What ethical considerations are most relevant to you, and how can you contribute to shaping a future where AI serves the greater good?

AI's potential to drive innovation and solve complex problems is immense as we look to the future. By understanding its capabilities and implications, we can harness its power responsibly and ethically, ensuring that its benefits are shared widely across society.

8.1 EMERGING TRENDS IN NATURAL LANGUAGE PROCESSING

Natural Language Processing (NLP) continues to evolve, driven by remarkable advances in technology and the increasing demand for machines that understand human language. At the forefront of these developments are transformer-based models, which have revolutionized how machines process language. Unlike their predecessors, these models excel at capturing long-range dependencies in text. This ability translates into a deeper understanding of context, resulting in more accurate and coherent responses. Transformers don't just stop there. They also introduce the concept of contextual embeddings, where the words around it influence the meaning of a word. This nuanced understanding allows for richer interpretations, enabling AI systems to grasp subtleties that were previously out of reach.

Zero-shot learning is another exciting advancement in NLP. This approach allows models to make predictions about tasks they have yet to be explicitly trained on. Imagine teaching a child to recognize apples and then asking them to identify oranges without prior exposure. Zero-shot learning empowers AI to make such leaps, broadening its applicability across various tasks with minimal additional training. This capability is particularly impactful in dynamic environments, where the ability to adapt quickly is crucial.

As the world becomes more interconnected, the importance of NLP in multilingual contexts grows. Translation systems are evolving, becoming more sophisticated in their ability to bridge language barriers. These systems don't just convert words; they capture the essence of meaning, ensuring that translations remain true to the original intent. Cross-lingual information retrieval is another area where NLP shines. It enables users to search for information in one language and receive results in another, opening up access to global knowledge. Multilingual chatbots are becoming common, allowing businesses to reach diverse audiences by providing seamless communication across languages. These advancements make the world smaller and more connected, fostering understanding and collaboration on a global scale.

Conversational AI is undergoing a transformation, driven by a desire for more natural and intuitive interactions. Context-aware chatbots are leading this charge, capable of remembering previous interactions and using that information to inform current conversations. This continuity creates a more personalized experience, akin to speaking with a friend who knows your history. Emotionally intelligent AI is also emerging, with systems that can detect and respond to human emotions. This capability adds a layer of empathy to interactions, allowing AI to tailor its responses based on the user's emotional state. Voice-activated assistants are becoming more sophisticated, offering hands-free convenience and accessibility. They are learning to understand not just words but the nuances of tone and intention, making interactions smoother and more effective.

NLP is also playing a crucial role in enhancing accessibility for diverse user groups. Text-to-speech technology transforms written content into spoken words, making information accessible to individuals with visual impairments. This technology also supports those who prefer auditory learning, offering an alternative way to consume information. Speech-to-text applications are equally transformative, converting spoken language into written text. This capability benefits individuals with hearing impairments and those who find typing challenging. Assistive AI is emerging as a powerful tool for individuals with disabilities, offering tailored support that enhances independence and participation in everyday activities. By addressing diverse needs, NLP-driven technologies are creating a more inclusive digital landscape where everyone can engage and thrive.

8.2 EXPLORING NEW FEATURES AND UPDATES

In recent times, ChatGPT has seen some exciting updates that enhance its functionality and user experience. One of the standout improvements is in response accuracy. The developers have fine-tuned the model, enabling it to understand the nuances of human language better, which results in more precise and relevant replies. This adjustment is particularly beneficial when you engage the AI for complex queries or when you need detailed information. Alongside this, the user interface has undergone a facelift, making it more intuitive and user-friendly. The streamlined design not only looks appealing but also facilitates smoother navigation, allowing you to focus on your tasks without unnecessary distractions. Moreover, new API capabilities have been introduced. These allow developers to integrate ChatGPT more seamlessly into various applications, broadening its usability across different platforms and enhancing the potential for personalized automation.

Looking ahead, several promising features are in the pipeline that promise to elevate ChatGPT's capabilities even further. One such feature is real-time collaboration tools. Imagine being able to work alongside ChatGPT while it assists you in drafting documents or brainstorming ideas, all in real time. This functionality will enable smoother and more interactive workflows, especially in team settings. AI-driven analytics is another exciting development. By leveraging data more effectively, ChatGPT will offer insights and analytics that can inform decision-making processes, providing users with actionable information. Additionally, advanced personalization options are set to redefine user interaction. These features will tailor responses based on user history and preferences, offering an experience that feels uniquely catered to each individual.

User feedback plays a crucial role in shaping these updates and future developments. OpenAI actively solicits feedback and analyzes it to identify common themes and areas for improvement. This feedback loop ensures that the features being developed align with user needs and expectations. By prioritizing feature requests, the developers can focus on enhancements that will have the most significant impact. Implementing user-suggested improvements not only refines the platform but also fosters a sense of community where users feel their voices are heard and valued. This collaborative approach is essential in maintaining a cutting-edge tool that evolves with its user base.

For those eager to explore these updates before they become widely available, beta testing and early access programs offer a unique opportunity. By signing up for these programs, you gain early access to the latest features, allowing you to test them in your environment. This can be particularly advantageous for power users or developers looking to integrate new functionalities into their projects. Providing feedback during this phase is invaluable, as it helps refine the features, ensuring they meet user expectations upon release. Early access not only gives you a competitive edge by staying ahead of the curve but also allows you to shape the development of the tools you rely on. Engaging with these programs is not just about getting a sneak peek; it's about being part of a collaborative effort to push the boundaries of what's possible with AI.

8.3 LEARNING FROM AI EXPERTS AND THOUGHT LEADERS

Engaging with AI thought leaders offers a unique window into the minds driving this transformative field. These individuals are not only at the forefront of technological advancements but are also shaping the conversation around the ethical and practical implications of AI. Andrew Ng, a pioneer in machine learning, co-founded Coursera and has played pivotal roles in projects like Google Brain. His insights into AI and education are invaluable for anyone eager to understand the intersection of these domains. Similarly, Demis Hassabis, the founder of DeepMind, has made groundbreaking contributions through projects like AlphaGo. His work exemplifies the potential of AI to tackle complex challenges. Fei-Fei Li's research in computer vision and AI in healthcare highlights the importance of human-centered AI, making her a key figure to follow for those interested in the societal impact of technology. These experts, along with others like Geoffrey Hinton and Yann LeCun, regularly share their findings and perspectives, offering a wealth of knowledge to those who seek to deepen their understanding of AI.

Attending AI conferences and seminars is another way to immerse yourself in the latest developments and network with professionals in the field. Events like the AI Summit and NeurIPS (Conference on Neural Information Processing Systems) attract thousands of attendees, including leading researchers and industry professionals. These gatherings provide opportunities to hear keynote presentations, participate in panel discussions, and engage in workshops that cover a wide range of topics. At the ICML (International Conference on Machine Learning), you can explore cutting-edge research and applications in machine learning, gaining insights into the methods and tools that are shaping the future of AI. These conferences are not just about learning; they're about connecting with a community of innovators who are passionate about advancing the field. The exchange of ideas and perspectives at these events fosters collaboration and inspires new approaches to solving complex problems.

For those who prefer a more flexible approach to learning, webinars and online courses offer a convenient way to stay informed about AI. Platforms like Coursera provide a range of AI courses, from introductory classes to advanced specializations. These courses, often led by top university professors and industry experts, allow you to learn at your own pace while gaining a solid foundation in AI principles. MIT also offers online programs that delve into the intricacies of AI, providing a rigorous academic perspective. OpenAI hosts webinars that cover various aspects of AI development and application, offering insights directly from the creators of some of the most advanced AI models. These resources are invaluable for anyone looking to expand their knowledge and skills, providing the tools needed to engage with AI more effectively.

AI research papers and journals are essential for keeping up with the latest findings and breakthroughs in the field. The Journal of Artificial Intelligence Research (JAIR) publishes high-quality articles that span the breadth of AI, from theoretical foundations to practical applications. Reading through these papers can deepen your understanding of the methodologies and technologies driving AI innovation. The Proceedings of the AAAI Conference on Artificial Intelligence is another critical resource, offering peer-reviewed papers showcasing recent research and trends. For those interested in the bleeding edge of AI, arXiv provides access to preprints of new research, allowing you to explore emerging ideas before they are formally published. Engaging with these publications challenges you to think critically about AI and its implications, equipping you with the knowledge to contribute to the ongoing conversation around its development and use.

8.4 COMMUNITY AND SUPPORT RESOURCES

Discovering and participating in online AI communities can significantly enhance your understanding and engagement with artificial intelligence. These digital spaces connect you with like-minded individuals who share a passion for AI and machine learning. For instance, the Reddit AI and Machine Learning communities offer platforms where enthusiasts and experts alike discuss the latest developments, share resources, and troubleshoot challenges. These forums are bustling with activity, where questions about AI algorithms, coding challenges, or ethical considerations are met with diverse insights. Similarly, LinkedIn hosts various AI discussion groups, providing a professional setting where industry leaders and newcomers exchange ideas, debate trends, and build valuable connections. These groups are excellent for networking and staying updated on industry news. AI forums and subreddits serve as informal hubs where you can dive into technical discussions or explore broader topics like the societal impact of AI, making them a valuable resource for both learning and interaction.

Support groups and forums are invaluable when you need advice or troubleshooting assistance. The OpenAI Community Forum is a dedicated space for users to seek help, share experiences, and collaborate on projects related to AI. It's a place where you can find answers to your questions, whether you're facing technical issues or seeking guidance on best practices. Stack Overflow, known for its vast repository of coding and tech-related queries, is a go-to for AI-related questions. Here, developers and AI practitioners share solutions to common programming challenges, making it a vital tool for overcoming obstacles in your AI projects. Discord also hosts numerous AI user groups, offering real-time communication with fellow AI enthusiasts. These groups facilitate direct interaction, allowing for quick exchanges of ideas and solutions, which can be particularly beneficial for those who prefer instant feedback and collaboration.

Mentorship and networking opportunities in the AI field can significantly accelerate your growth and understanding. AI mentorship programs pair you with experienced professionals who provide guidance, share their expertise, and help you navigate the complexities of the field. These relationships can open doors to insights and career opportunities that might otherwise remain out of reach. Networking events and meetups offer more informal settings to connect with peers and industry leaders. These gatherings provide a platform for discussing recent advancements, exchanging ideas, and forming collaborations. AI hackathons and competitions are exciting venues for applying your skills in real-world scenarios. They challenge you to solve complex problems, often under time constraints, promoting innovation and teamwork. These events hone your technical abilities and expand your professional network, making them an excellent opportunity for personal and career development.

Contributing to the AI community is not just about receiving knowledge but also sharing it. By engaging actively, you can help shape the future of AI. Sharing your knowledge and insights, whether through blog posts, tutorials, or discussions, enriches the community and fosters a culture of continuous learning. Participating in open-source AI projects is another impactful way to contribute. These projects welcome developers of all skill levels and provide a collaborative environment for building and refining

AI tools. Your contributions, no matter how small, can lead to significant advancements and innovations. Writing and publishing AI-related content, such as articles or research papers, is another way to leave your mark. It allows you to present your ideas and findings to a broader audience, sparking conversations and inspiring others in the field. Engaging with the AI community in these ways not only enhances your knowledge and skills but also strengthens the collective wisdom and progress of the field.

8.5 BUILDING A LIFELONG LEARNING PLAN FOR AI AND CHATGPT

Creating a lifelong learning plan for AI and ChatGPT starts with setting clear, realistic goals. Begin by identifying the AI topics that pique your interest. This could range from natural language processing to the ethical considerations of AI in society. Once you've pinpointed these areas, set both short-term and long-term objectives. Short-term goals might include completing an introductory course on AI or experimenting with ChatGPT to understand its capabilities. Long-term goals involve mastering a programming language commonly used in AI, such as Python, or contributing to open-source AI projects. Establishing a timeline for these goals can keep you on track. Allocate time each week or month to focus on these objectives, and adjust your schedule as needed to accommodate new interests or changes in your availability.

Curating your learning resources is another crucial step. The internet brims with courses and tutorials tailored to various learning styles and levels. Websites like Coursera and edX offer structured courses, while platforms like YouTube provide free, accessible tutorials. Selecting relevant books and research papers can deepen your understanding. Look for works by respected authors in the field or browse academic journals for the latest research findings. Following AI blogs and podcasts can keep you informed about trends and innovations. Blogs often provide insights from industry leaders, while podcasts allow you to absorb information during commutes or while multitasking. Tailor your resource list to align with your goals and interests, ensuring it evolves as your understanding deepens.

Keeping your knowledge up-to-date is vital in the fast-paced world of AI. Schedule regular study sessions to review the latest developments and explore new topics. This consistent engagement helps solidify your understanding and keeps you from falling behind. Attending AI webinars and workshops can provide fresh perspectives and practical insights. These events often feature experts sharing their experiences and offering advice on applying AI in real-world scenarios. Engaging with the latest AI research can also be enlightening. Reading research papers or attending conferences exposes you to cutting-edge innovations and encourages critical thinking. By staying informed, you position yourself to adapt to new challenges and opportunities in the AI landscape.

Evaluating your progress is essential in maintaining motivation and ensuring your learning plan remains effective. Set milestones to track your achievements and celebrate your successes. Whether it's completing a course or successfully implementing a new AI tool, acknowledging these accomplishments can boost your confidence. Reflect on your learning experiences to identify areas of strength and those requiring further attention. This reflection can guide you in adjusting your learning plans as needed. Perhaps a particular topic has sparked a new interest, or maybe you've encountered unexpected challenges that necessitate a shift in focus. Being open to adapting your plan keeps your learning journey dynamic and aligned with your evolving goals and interests.

In wrapping up this chapter, remember that lifelong learning in AI and ChatGPT is a continuous process. It requires curiosity, commitment, and a willingness to adapt. By setting goals, curating resources, staying updated, and evaluating progress, you lay a solid foundation for growth. This approach not only enhances your understanding of AI but also equips you to navigate an ever-changing technological landscape.

CONCLUSION

As we reach the end of this journey together, I want to reaffirm the vision and purpose that guided us from the very first page. This book was crafted with one goal in mind: to make ChatGPT accessible, understandable, and useful for beginners across various fields. Whether you're stepping into the world of technology for the first time or seeking to enhance your existing skills, my aim has been to provide you with a comprehensive yet approachable guide to harnessing the power of ChatGPT.

We began by exploring what ChatGPT is and how it can revolutionize everyday interactions. From setting up your account to navigating its interface, you were equipped with the foundational skills necessary to start using this tool effectively. We delved into the art of writing effective prompts and understanding how to communicate with ChatGPT to receive precise and relevant responses. This core skill is vital, as it forms the basis of all interactions with the AI.

In subsequent chapters, we explored practical applications across personal productivity, professional use, and creative endeavors. You learned how ChatGPT can assist in organizing tasks, drafting emails, and even creating art or music. Each example demonstrated the versatility of ChatGPT, showing how it can seamlessly integrate into various aspects of your life.

As we ventured into advanced features and customization, you discovered ways to tailor your ChatGPT experience to suit your personal preferences and professional needs. We discussed API integration, memory capabilities, and even how to create custom chatbot personalities. These tools empower you to extend ChatGPT's functionalities beyond the basics, opening new possibilities for innovation and efficiency.

We also addressed the challenges and ethical considerations associated with AI usage. You were encouraged to think critically about AI's ethical implications, including data privacy and bias. Understanding these concerns helps ensure that your use of ChatGPT is responsible and aligned with ethical standards.

Throughout this book, the key takeaway is that ChatGPT is a tool of immense potential. It is capable of transforming how you work, learn, and create. But like any tool, its effectiveness hinges on how you use it. By crafting clear prompts, experimenting with its features, and applying it thoughtfully across domains, you can unlock its full potential.

Now, I urge you to take what you've learned and apply it. Experiment with ChatGPT in new ways, push its boundaries and explore its capabilities. Whether you're using it to streamline work processes, create art, or learn something new, continue to engage with it actively. The world of AI is constantly evolving, and staying curious and open to learning will keep you at the forefront of these advancements.

Let this book be a stepping stone in your journey with AI. Use it as a reference and a source of inspiration. Remember that learning is an ongoing process, and your interaction with ChatGPT can evolve as you do. Embrace the possibilities and let your creativity guide you. The future with AI is bright and full of potential, and I am excited for the opportunities that lie ahead for you.

Thank you for allowing me to guide you through this journey. I hope it has been as enlightening for you as it has been fulfilling for me to share. Together, let us continue to explore, innovate, and make the most of what technology has to offer.

KEEPING THE JOURNEY GOING

Now that you have all the tools to master ChatGPT with ease, it's your turn to share what you've learned and guide others to the same help.

By leaving a review on Amazon, you'll help other curious minds find *Master ChatGPT Effortlessly* and discover how to make the most of this amazing tool. Your honest thoughts will guide them on their path to confidence and creativity with ChatGPT.

Thank you for your support. When we share what we've learned, we keep the excitement of discovery alive—and you're helping me do just that.

Scan and share what you've learned!

REFERENCES

CapTech University. (n.d.). *The ethical considerations of artificial intelligence.* https://www.captechu.edu/blog/ethical-considerations-of-artificial-intelligence

Canda, J. (2024, October 1). *5 common generative AI prompt writing mistakes (and how to fix them).* Forbes. https://www.forbes.com/sites/bernardmarr/2024/10/01/5-common-generative-ai-prompt-writing-mistakes-and-how-to-fix-them/

Cook, J. (2023, June 26). *How to write effective prompts for ChatGPT: 7 essential steps for best results.* Forbes. https://www.forbes.com/sites/jodiecook/2023/06/26/how-to-write-effective-prompts-for-chatgpt-7-essential-steps-for-best-results/

Copy.ai. (n.d.). *AI for content creation: How to get started (& scale).* https://www.copy.ai/blog/ai-content-creation

Day Optimizer. (n.d.). *How to use ChatGPT to organize your tasks.* https://dayoptimizer.com/task-management/how-to-use-chatgpt-to-organize-your-tasks/

Hootsuite. (n.d.). *How to use ChatGPT for social media: Expert tips + 75 examples.* https://blog.hootsuite.com/chatgpt-social-media/

Harvard Gazette. (2020, October). *Ethical concerns mount as AI takes bigger decision-making role.* https://news.harvard.edu/gazette/story/2020/10/ethical-concerns-mount-as-ai-takes-bigger-decision-making-role/

Innodata. (n.d.). *Best approaches to mitigate bias in AI models.* https://innodata.com/best-approaches-to-mitigate-bias-in-ai-models/

Marr, B. (2024, March 3). *ChatGPT: A game-changer in game development.* IFS Blog. https://blog.ifs.com/2024/03/chatgpt-a-game-changer-in-game-development/#:

Medium. (2024, October 1). *AI in music: Composition, production, and recommendation.* https://medium.com/@jam.canda/ai-in-music-composition-production-and-recommendation-4b5bbde1b10b

Microsoft. (n.d.). *How to write poetry using Copilot.* https://www.microsoft.com/en-us/bing/do-more-with-ai/write-poetry-with-bing-compose?form=MA13KP

OpenAI. (n.d.). *Quickstart tutorial - OpenAI API.* https://platform.openai.com/docs/quickstart

OpenAI. (n.d.). *Custom instructions for ChatGPT.* https://openai.com/index/custom-instructions-for-chatgpt/

Persona Talent. (n.d.). *19 ways to use ChatGPT to boost your productivity.* https://www.personatalent.com/productivity/ways-to-use-chatgpt-to-boost-your-productivity/

Salesforce. (n.d.). *Everything you need to know about AI in customer service.* https://www.salesforce.com/service/ai/customer-service-ai/

Scott, A. (2023, May 29). *The integration of ChatGPT in smart homes: Voice-activated home automation.* https://scottamyx.com/2023/05/29/the-integration-of-chatgpt-in-smart-homes-voice-activated-home-automation/

Search Engine Land. (n.d.). *ChatGPT fails: 13 common errors and mistakes you need to know.* https://searchengineland.com/chatgpt-fails-errors-mistakes-400153

Technology Review. (2023, March 3). *The inside story of how ChatGPT was built from the people who made it.* https://www.technologyreview.com/2023/03/03/1069311/inside-story-oral-history-how-chatgpt-built-openai/

Tipalti. (n.d.). *ChatGPT for finance: 12 powerful uses.* https://tipalti.com/blog/chatgpt-for-finance/

Towards Data Science. (2020, October 2). *Transformers in NLP: A beginner friendly explanation.* https://towardsdatascience.com/transformers-89034557de14

WikiHow. (n.d.). *How to create a ChatGPT account: 8 steps (with pictures).* https://www.wikihow.com/Create-a-ChatGPT-Account

WordStream. (2023, March 6). *6 ways to use ChatGPT for small business marketing (+6 more tips).* https://www.wordstream.com/blog/ws/2023/03/06/how-to-use-chatgpt-for-small-business-marketing

ZDNet. (n.d.). *7 advanced ChatGPT prompt-writing tips you need to know.* https://www.zdnet.com/article/7-advanced-chatgpt-prompt-writing-tips-you-need-to-know/

Anodot. (n.d.). *Top 10 thought leaders in AI/ML we're following.* https://www.anodot.com/blog/top-10-thought-leaders-in-aiml/

Forbes. (2023, February 20). *Top AI conferences 2023: Roundup of top AI conferences.* https://www.forbes.com/sites/qai/2023/02/20/top-ai-conferences-2023-roundup-of-top-ai-conferences/

Atlassian. (n.d.). *AI for project management: Tools and best practices.* https://www.atlassian.com/work-management/project-management/ai-project-management

CSIS. (n.d.). *Protecting data privacy as a baseline for responsible AI.* https://www.csis.org/analysis/protecting-data-privacy-baseline-responsible-ai

Medium. (2024, September 15). *Emerging trends in the future of natural language processing.* https://medium.com/@faaiz.ul.haq3333/emerging-trends-in-the-future-of-natural-language-processing-62aee94630ac

www.ingramcontent.com/pod-product-compliance
Lightning Source LLC
Chambersburg PA
CBHW070931050326
40689CB00014B/3165